MEET YOU IN ATLANTIC CITY

MEET YOU IN ATLANTIC CITY

TRAVELS IN SPRINGSTEEN'S NEW JERSEY

JAMES PETTIFER

Signal Books
Oxford

First published in 2018 by
Signal Books Limited
36 Minster Road
Oxford OX4 1LY
www.signalbooks.co.uk

A catalogue record for this book is available from the British Library

ISBN   978-1-909930-70-4 Paper
        978-1-909930-71-1 Cloth

Cover Design: Baseline Arts Ltd
Typesetting: Tora Kelly
Cover Image: ESB Professional/Shutterstock
Print in India by Imprint Press

In Memoriam

Christopher Hitchens (1949-2011)

'A writer who falls in love with a new and strange country will always find experience heightened in this way. The dawns are more noble, the crags loftier, the people more genuine...'
Arguably (2008)

CONTENTS

INTRODUCTION
A RIP CURRENT
ON THE JERSEY
SHORE

Concerning New Jersey, the Numbers, the music of Bruce Springsteen and the E Street Band, and the movement of the seas

September 2017, near Ocean Grove, NJ

The American Dream in New Jersey has been around for a long time, and music and numbers have been central to it, the control of a vast land through enumeration, a Hegelian impulse of number over the flux. Some illuminati like David Chase, the progenitor of *The Sopranos* TV series, have speculated that New Jersey is a state of mind as much as a state. Way back, seventeenth-century English colonist Richard Hartshorne wrote of his state of mind in 1676 in *A Further Account of New Jersie*:

> Now friend, I shall give thee something of an information concerning New Jersie, but time will not permit me to write at length. Thou desirest to know how I live, through the goodness of the Lord I live very well, keeping between 30 and 40 head of cows, and 7 or 8 Horses or Mares to Ride upon. There are 7 towns settled in this Province, Shrewsbury and Middletown, upon the Sea Side, and along the River side and up the Creeks there is Piscattaway, and Woodbridge, Elizobetown, New wake, and Bergane: most of these Towns having about 100 families: and the least 40. The country is very healthful.

Colonist Hartshorne wrote his American Dream out in numbers of livestock in his agrarian society; showing the state his affairs had then reached, he did the math. The Dream has been hard to find for many, but that has not stopped people looking. It has come and gone many times in New Jersey, so that reviving Asbury Park was a town of boarded up and derelict hotels when *Born to Run* was selling a million vinyls in 1976. People had come and gone and then returned again. Earlier, the nineteenth-century American author Mark Twain began the dialogue about whether travelling is the same as tourism. The poor had travelled to the Jersey Shore, the rich had toured. Travelling, questing is at the heart of what the American Dream has been about and for many people in the last forty years the figure of Bruce Springsteen has been central to their understanding of what has happened to America, seen through a New Jersey music prism.

South of Ocean Grove on the wide sandy beaches of the Atlantic shore of New Jersey is a place for this journey to begin, with the immensity of the Atlantic Ocean, churning, a kaleidoscope of blues in the sun. People lie finishing off their summer holiday novels and maybe kiss a girlfriend amongst the cotton grass tufts. The author of the whaling classic *Moby Dick* would have liked it here, the ocean as alpha and omega, a setting for drama. The first colonial wealth on the Jersey Shore came from the blood and pain of whales, and the men who harpooned them. Sometimes they won, sometimes the whale won. Either way, blood was spilt into the salty water.

The beauty and the pain can coexist here. The north-east New Jersey Shore is a dramatic, conflicted place, with the Atlantic winds stirring the broad ochre sand, the sea holly and grass swept by a gentle cooling breeze that draws New Yorkers by the thousand in the summer. In the winter you are never wearing enough clothes, while in high summer a swimsuit seems too much. The beach is very wide and has remained wide since the Vikings (possibly), the Basques (definitely) and Henry Hudson and the early European explorers and colonists and religious refugees landed in their wooden sailing ships. Inland in the northern part of the state is Monmouth County, where a singer and storyteller called Bruce Springsteen was born on 23 December 1949 and where he still lives, sixty-eight years old at the time of writing. He is a rock superstar, still working after the death of key members of his E Street Band, Clarence Clemons and Danny Federici. He was the star of the 2008 Obama inauguration and is known for his music in every country of the world. Yet standing in Asbury Park, where much of his early music was born, so many of the key landmarks have disappeared by 2017, and a new Asbury Park is developing.

Like many people of my age in the United Kingdom I first heard Bruce Springsteen in my youth and I immediately liked his music but I did not begin to understand it or see why it has such a hold over so many people until beginning to spend time in New Jersey after 2000. Songs like 'Born in the USA' were sometimes seen in Britain as too direct, too 'American'; there was a burden of intense sincerity, it seemed an in-your-face encounter with issues, and some of it was culturally and geographically distant. Place is important in American popular music. Where would country singers be without the spell of Nashville, jazz without New Orleans, blues without the Mississippi Delta, Charlie Parker without Kansas City, John Lee Hooker without Chicago? The places in this book matter to me as metaphors to help understand a great popular artist, but I am sure others will have their own sacred groves in this respect. Different harvesters can pick different fruit. In Britain, Bruce Springsteen was clearly a patriotic American, perhaps too much so, some people thought, and his America was rooted in New Jersey—Essex on steroids plus guns, as seen in some British eyes, a suburban and industrial wilderness with more than its fair share of criminals and a byword for corruption in the eyes of many Americans. He was also inaccurately seen as wholly Italian, or maybe with a bit of Jewish mixed in, and a 'greaser', half-way to having a dark skin and wearing that semi-criminal shirt, the muscle vest. There were many British prejudices around.

A rip current swirls and pushes its way to and for a little way out from the shore, stirring up dark vegetable matter from the Atlantic winter backwash left from huge storms washing out the coastal marshes into the sea, a tell-tale moment showing a rip current is around. There is a sign warning you about rip currents if you are swimming and another one saying there is no lifeguard on duty. The sea, like the land, has its bad guys. The rip current is one of them. It steals up on the swimmer silent and without warning, and suddenly takes you in a direction you are not planning to go, usually right out to sea. It is best to swim sideways along the shore to get out of one; swim against it and you get exhausted and drown. The current under the surface is fierce, and can rip off shorts or bikinis. So the sea makes you a naked person, Odysseus or Venus emerging from the waves, except you may not emerge. And if you are very, very unlucky you may meet a serious shark. Great White and other sharks have been coming in to hit the older dolphins along the shore recently. It may look pretty but the sea is tough out there. Great Whites are nothing like as common here as in the seas off South Africa and Australia but sometimes they do appear. The events that led to Peter Benchley's 1974 novel *Jaws* that in turn led to the hit film of the same name happened off this shore. The shark in the film is in direct line of descent to the whale in Melville's novel *Moby Dick* published in 1851, a symbol of menace to the civilized order of America. In the summer of 1916 a rogue Great White had regularly attacked swimmers all along the Jersey Shore, devoured several people and set off mass hysteria and the biggest shark hunt in history. Yet as E.O. Wilson has pointed out, people love their predators, real and mythical, sharks in the sea and gangsters and mobsters on land. We spin stories about them and we watch Tony Soprano in action to learn how to protect ourselves against what he represents. In New Jersey, as elsewhere, the Devil always has the best tunes, as Bruce and the Band illustrate in songs like 'Murder Incorporated' and 'Atlantic City'.

But a rip is the usual thing to worry swimmers, although very dangerous conditions can develop if the fag ends of hurricanes make the shore in late summer and early fall. The rip is the gangster of the Jersey beach. If you are wearing flippers the first thing to do is kick them off, quickly, or they will make things worse. If you do not panic and go with the flow, rips can be handled, ridden out; if you fight them they may drown you. So it's best to go with the flow, a useful metaphor for many things in life here. Rips have a deadly strategy, they often build up on calm sunny days when the sea looks idyllic and the innocent do not expect them. Some twenty-seven people have drowned off the Jersey Shore in rips in the last fifteen years. Broken surf is a useful sign, as there are often sandbars under it and you can stand on one and reorient yourself. Then you should survive. The sea, like the land, has its own laws and traditions and conventions: the Unwritten Laws of New Jersey Shore like the Unwritten Laws of the Northern Albanian Highlands.

Over these years getting deeper into the music was also getting deeper into a shore, a landscape, a musical ecology. Place as named and registered place is not actually as important in Springsteen's songs as in those of many other popular stars. Songs like 'Atlantic City' and 'Youngstown' are the exceptions rather than the rule in being narratives tied up with particular places. There is no grand Springsteen set piece like Sinatra's 'New York, New York' that seems to sum up the American Dream in a particular song. The great early album set deep in place, **Nebraska**, is mostly not in New Jersey at all. The ambiguity and poetry of middle and late Springsteen is the ambiguity of the New Jersey landscape in a much more undifferentiated way, tangible yet mysterious, straightforward American working-class suburbia on one level, a home territory of mystery and uncertainty on another. In the mythical landscape the poetry has room to move, stalking reality like a Native American moving along a forest trail watching the colonists arrive on the shore from Europe. Perceptions between the trees are fragmentary, glimpses, patterns of shifting light, a line in a song sketches them out and then moves on: shadows, ghosts, wraiths all looking for America.

Yet some New Jersey places illuminate the music of Springsteen and the E Street Band much more than others, and after a time, and spending different times in the state, it seemed to me a pattern was developing where the questions I was asking myself about what the songs meant to me were also questions about what it meant to be in New Jersey in contemporary America. Who is in charge of New Jersey and allowed some of the destruction of the heritage past to occur? Were they just Bosses, legal Sopranos among all the illegal ones? How could I find out? As Jennifer Gillan has written, New Jersey is a fitting setting for an exploration of American identity. So there is travel if not exactly tourism in this book, and I hope it will encourage people to go to Jersey and have fun and explore but also think about and play Springsteen's music with the E Street Band. I hope it will also encourage them to reflect on American history and why some of the traits in state life that many non-Jersey Americans find strange, funny or just plain weird do exist and have probably existed for a long time. It is a cool so cool place, but somewhere that has suffered period eclipses in its reputation, so that a late nineteenth-century British traveller in the US, the Anglican divine Dean Hole of Rochester, never mentions New Jersey at all in his extensive and misnamed tour memoir, *A Little Tour in America*, published in 1895. He does however describe a visit to Princeton University, a place where after meeting the students, 'I seemed suddenly to ignore the last half century of my life, and feel as boyish as the merriest of them all.' The condition and perception of Princeton matter more to New Jersey than either the state or the university is often keen to admit, for a variety of different reasons on both sides.

There are many ways of seeing Bruce Springsteen, just as there are many ways of seeing Elvis Presley or Bob Dylan. There are fewer ways of knowing his material world. He has evolved through a modern history of New Jersey where some of the most important monuments and structures mentioned in his songs have already been destroyed by rampant property development and lack of respect for music and other heritage buildings. Perhaps the songs are, in Mick Jagger's famous words, 'Only Rock and Roll', but they also tell a valuable story now for the social and economic historians.

An impetus to write was the privilege of seeing some of the buildings that inspired songs before the bulldozers moved in. There was much more of this world left in 2001 than there is now seventeen years later. Asbury Park, in particular, has suffered very badly in the 'gentrification' process and some Springsteen devotees refuse to go there any more, preferring their memories of the past. This is not my opinion but I understand how those people feel.

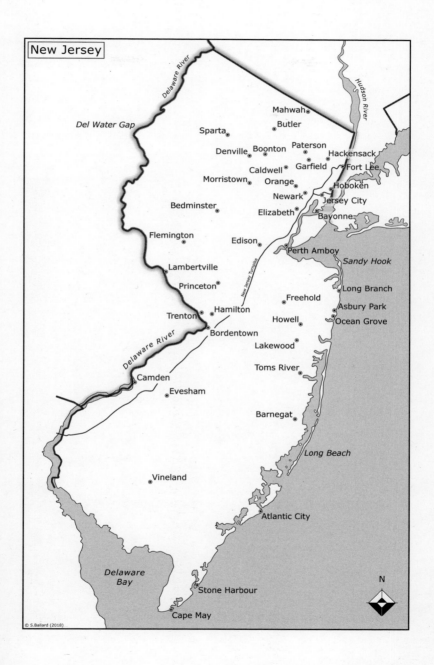

I
SOMEWHERE
IN THE
UNKNOWN
UNITED STATES

A Cave: In New Jersey?

Concerning a punctured tire, thoughts of Plato's philosophy, and S.G. Warburg a founder of modern merchant banking with Plato's Republic *often on his desk*

It was a quiet afternoon by the Ford garage at the side of Route 23, the way up from the Turnpike to the wilds of the first Appalachian hills and the nice town of Butler. Then you could go over the River Delaware to Pennsylvania, the Keystone State. But the car tire was flat with a screw sticking in it and wasn't going anywhere and the tire needed was not in inventory in the garage and there was a waiting period. A philosophical thought—New Jersey is not a bad place to break down; in this huge country there are many worse places, in the West, with thorns, tarantulas, rattlesnakes, no garage for a hundred miles, only cactus to eat and maybe a homicidal cultist living in a shed in the distance? It is wild over there. Are there any philosophers? Some of the most intelligent people in the world live around the shores of the United States. There are far fewer away from the sea in the interior. The Jersey suburbs have their good points, as New York City had its Five Points. Where better to look at the ancient philosopher who would bring measure and calm to the situation, and pass the time as the new tire sped nearer from the Wayne City depot?

The banker Sir Siegmund Warburg always kept a copy of *The Republic* in his desk, the only book. Plato wrote in the Republic of the Ideal State, so do bankers make an ideal state, and was New Jersey an Ideal State? Had it ever been one? Maybe in the times when no one had ever heard of Arizona and when California had not been invented, maybe there was a colonist's cowshed then where the Ford garage stands now. Or more aptly, a blacksmith's forge, to help after your horse had thrown a shoe. Many blacksmiths fought here in George Washington's army, sturdy men with big leather aprons and smelling of their own moonshine. The garage is now much more important than the forge was then. As Edward Luttwak has pointed out, four wheels and an engine might have been grafted onto *Homo Americanus*, in a world where few live within a walk of a useful food store, there is often no public transport, and the car gives *that reassuring sense of freedom*. Bruce Springsteen understood this, and no one else has ever written so many fine songs about driving. Bernie Sanders and Donald Trump may not have much in common but both realized there was something very wrong with Obama's legacy when maybe half of US households cannot afford a new car. Fordism was dying, even by this Ford garage. The state of NJ was no longer ideal. Why? Can Plato cast light?

Plato saw no use for artists but music was allowed. Music was important here in this stymied old Lincoln, Bon Jovi was on the radio. A retune might bring Bruce and the Band into the old Lincoln. It was a wager, a bet, Bon Jovi versus maybe Bruce. Bon Jovi won and then a limo swished by with a finely attired driver and a tiny man in the back. The lights changed and the traffic from Kinnelon crossed in front of them. The tiny man with gold rimmed glasses and a beautiful dark blue overcoat with a fur collar was reading a Merrill Lynch document and was presumably a banker. He could have been reading Plato but he was reading office work.

Bankers admire Plato; they often see themselves as Guardians. As the most influential and innovative banker of the twentieth century Warburg rarely travelled from London without a copy of *The Republic* in his luggage. As a young man he had grown up in Hamburg as a scion of a long established and very wealthy banking family and at school in the World War I period had excellent reports on his study of the ancient classics. Hitler had driven him from his homeland for being Jewish, and he adopted Britain and Switzerland, and they adopted him. Ancient philosophy was his standard reading on the liners he preferred for Atlantic crossings long after air travel had arrived on the scene. But was he a modern neo-Platonist, if such a category is possible? These were distant abstract thoughts, inspired by a limo. Then it drew smoothly away and a tire was arriving in the distance. Siggy Warburg's life was forged through turmoil, exile and the accumulation and then loss of great wealth, but the processes of the struggle for enlightenment and education never ceased for him. He was never thrown from his chosen path by the back wall images of the Platonic cave. What would he have made of the looming banking crisis in this year in America? The numbers were moving badly, moving from their zenith, the numbers that as the children's rhyme goes were fascinating and were once our friends and can help illuminate the world around us. The Jewish people began with the Numbers. The early Book of Numbers in the Bible sets out the command from God to Moses to enumerate all the men of military age among the Israelites. Christians have perhaps less to go on; the later Bible does not contain reflections on the nature of number, unlike Plato, although Augustine was to be interested in the symbolic properties of the figure 7, and Basil argued that the monad which is God is not numerable. Maybe the parable of the loaves and the fishes makes an exception. Many Old Testament numbers fade into myth, as in the immense and impossible ages of some prophets and dignitaries of the Israelites.

Warburg was not a religious man and hardly ever attended a synagogue, but the numbers never left him be and he died of two massive strokes in 1982 after a stressful visit to Europe to try to rescue one of his banks that was in serious trouble.* The numbers turned against him and made his final fate. Maybe in some ways he was closer to the Pythagoreans with their obsessions with number and ratio as the clue to reality?†But as in slots down the shore at Atlantic City, the numbers do not always go your way. That year, 2007, the last good year, the numbers were turning against the banks.

What does Plato actually say about the process of education and enlightenment that obsessed Warburg and which he sets out in his *mythos*?

Plato, *The Republic*, Book 7 (514a)

Socrates

Imagine human beings living in an underground, cave like dwelling, with an entrance a long way up that is open to the light and as wide as the cave itself. They have been there since childhood, with their necks and legs fettered, so that they are fixed in the same place, able to see only in front of them, because their fetter prevents them from

---

* See Niall Ferguson's fine biography *High Financier* (London, 2010) for general background.

† Plato is frequently seen by liberals as a philosopher of the Right. But he wrote (*The Republic* Book 8 (546) of 'inharmonious inequality, and these always breeds war and hostility whenever they arise'. And so on, another story.

turning their heads around. Light is provided by a fire burning for above and behind them. Between the prisoners and the fire, there is an elevated track. Imagine that along this track a low wall has been built—like the screen in front of the people that is provided by puppeteers, and above which they show their puppets.

Glaucon
I am imagining it.

Socrates
Also imagine, then, that there are people alongside the wall carrying artificial objects that project above it—statues of people and other animals, made of stone, wood, and other material. And as you would expect, some of the carriers are talking and some are silent.

Glaucon
It is a strange picture and they are strange sort of prisoners.

Socrates did not ask if these people trapped may have been rock fans. The car was a kind of cave, with the new tyre meeting the wheel and the spin of the wheel balancing machine. I would be back inside it soon, and in movement. The music fills this little cave. Is the fanatical Springsteen fan a prisoner of the E Street Band and the Boss? Plato was stillness, New Jersey was movement. In the library back at Princeton there was also stillness, purpose, the sense of a superbly designed and tuned intellectual machine quietly ticking over, purring contentedly like the engine of a Bentley, so generously funded and very self-confident. Yet there was a wider New Jersey which was few or none of those things, and the music of Bruce Springsteen was always there, a way into its contemporary history, as President Barack Obama said years later when awarding the Presidential Medal of Freedom in November 2016 to 'New Jersey's Greatest Ambassador... His songs capture the pain and the promise of the American experience.'

New Jersey does not simply have a history, it has histories. In the life of New Jersey, the year marking the height of the Bush administration was also the year of release of the *Magic* album from the Boss and the Band, and the last (triumphant) series of *The Sopranos* on television. The history of the presidency is the official history, the music is the secret history and its meaning is not always clear. It was one brief time in American history. The year 2007 was after the recovery from 9/11, but before the banking crises broke, although the first straw in the wind was the Société Générale bank bonds crisis in August. The 'Great Recession' officially started in December, at a time of huge storms in the Pacific north-west. Hillary Clinton's friend Jon Corzine was still Governor of New Jersey, although after his car crash in April ex-Governor Richard J. Codey returned to do the job for a while. General Petraeus was leading the administration's 'surge' to reach an acceptable end to the long Iraq War.

Times were difficult, as now. It was six years after the attack on the Twin Towers in Manhattan, which could be seen burning from some parts of New Jersey as far as twenty miles away. New Jersey and its inhabitants do not always have a good press, either in America or outside it. It is the state whose name is a metaphor for crime and corruption and the best television crime series ever made, *The Sopranos*, has not assisted. Yet it remains an ambiguous labyrinth, the most crowded state in the Union, a confused and unending urban sprawl in the eyes of its critics, a ferment of life and creativity seen by its friends, an incomprehensible wilderness of interlocking roads without signs, or the path of the clear and dominating Turnpike, an expression of American Cold War power and transport modernity.

The state has a long and complex story, from the time of the British royal colonial land designation to the Carteret family, the seventeenth-century barons of the island of Jersey in the English Channel who gave New Jersey its name. New Jersey was at the heart of the American Revolution with the battles at Trenton and Princeton and was a centre of the industrial revolution in the United States, and saw the birth of a powerful labour movement. Capitalism and innovation were led by men like Thomas Edison, and it produced countless late nineteenth-century

inventions like wire cable, modern dentistry, the phonograph, celluloid and the light bulb without which life now would be unimaginable. Until the end of the Cold War and the arrival of Silicon Valley the state was the main centre of scientific (particularly pharmaceutical) research in the United States. New Jersey then was modernity: now it does not seem modern in the same way since Silicon Valley has taken over. Yet Jersey had, as the song says, its Glory Days.

The music of Bruce Springsteen and the E Street Band springs from the state, and has also captured it, but it has also done more. As Ruth Padel has observed, most writing about rock music—or perhaps any music— always seems dull and often inconsequential compared to the excitement and passion of the music itself. Music is Beyond Words, like the deepest experiences of life, but that does not stop authors from using them. I have in general avoided the temptation to try to describe the unique experience of a concert performance.

2
THE
LANDSCAPE OF
DREAMS

Concerning the New Jersey landscape, its origins and qualities

Day and Nights in Primeval New Jersey

In distant days, before rock and roll, before the Ice Age, before New Jersey became the most densely populated state in the union, more so than Japan, inhabited, according to the non-Platonic myth, by suburbanites, gangsters and women with Very Big Hair, before the state legislators in Trenton put a six per cent tax on facelifts and botox jobs, before a leatherjack turtle weighing in at a record eight hundred pounds was rescued on a Jersey Shore beach by the US Coast Guard, there was no Jersey Shore, there was no Federal government

New Jersey now lies on the eastern slopes of the Appalachian region, but then it did not did not exist. There were no independent and flourishing underground record labels. The Turnpike was not laid, not a single oil refinery or container port spewed fumes, not a single new pharmaceutical product had been developed and no public official had taken a bribe. It must have been a long time ago. New Jersey is now a leader in those industries.

North America was then part of Africa and Europe, and the land that is now the 127 miles of beautiful wide sandy beaches on the Jersey Shore lay in fathomless depths. In its present form, Jersey is perhaps two hundred million years old, and the mountain range of inner New Jersey, the Appalachians, are in consequence among the oldest rocks in the world. (Thus beyond measureable Time, but existing in Space.) Appearances can be deceptive; the Jersey Shore is now a place of ever shifting transience, the mountains of the interior a place of permanence and solidity, the masculine stasis against the feminine mutability of the shore. This number (127) is the first to be mentioned in this text, though number and mathematical calculation are important in New Jersey. It is a State of Computation, but in strange ways. New Jersey has given us both Bruce Springsteen and much modern mathematics, physics and cosmology, so there can't be much wrong with the place, as Joel Garreau has pointed out.

The Ice Ages shaped the New Jersey landscape. About 50,000 (a tidier number) years ago the vast Laurentide Glacier covered most of the north-east of the American continent, and reached as far south as central New Jersey to make a boundary. Material was deposited scraped from the Canadian rocks and dumped as the glacier melted as it met milder air. When it melted, the land reared up like a horse from Colts Neck, freed from a million ton weight. The ice sheet was overwhelming to the north of the Passaic Valley, in the northern quarter of Jersey. There it was very cold, not merely cool. The ice was thick enough to cover all the mountains in northern New Jersey and most of those in New York State. The pressure at the base was stupendous, and the ice wall moved forward with grinding, irresistible force.

The ice stopped dead, right across central Jersey. About 10,000 years ago (the first number illustrating chronological linear time in this text when human beings existed), its last remnants disappeared and left a cruel and damaged landscape, with floods of melt water unhappy and alienated and trying to find a place to go. Critics of Jersey people maintain that damage has remained in the collective psyche ever since. Many Americans think there is something wrong with coming from New Jersey, like Muscovites think there is something wrong with coming from the Stans. Anyway, to return to primeval Jersey, some melt water ran into the sea, the rest stayed in swamps and lakes. The tag for New Jersey, 'the Garden State', is a schmaltzy invention, the 'Ice Age State' a more accurate guide to what actually formed the landscape. And with the melting of the ice, humans spread into the more hospitable land.

Much later, the Lenni-Lenape tribe of Native Americans came to live in New Jersey. Maybe some lived in what is now Freehold, Monmouth County, where Bruce Springsteen went to school, fifty miles west of the sea. In Lenape days Freehold was a forested swamp. You could not buy a guitar or a DVD or recharge your phone there. Mr Max Weinberg's formidable drum set was unknown. Things were different. But not entirely different. Tobacco cigars, that great pleasure, mild intoxicant and source of wisdom, were smoked, then as now. A Lenape warrior could have sat down with Mr T. Soprano (a warrior in his way in the waste disposal business) together on the shore and enjoyed a stogie. Smoke would have drifted over the swirling ocean waters as the sun set. Lenni-Lenape in the Algonquin language means 'the original people'. The European settlers later called them the Delaware Indians. The Lenape had not been willing immigrants to New Jersey either, like many later arrivals. They came in as fugitives when the expanding Iroquois and their Plains Indian allies had invaded Algonquin and Lenape territories from the west under pressure of drought and climate change. Things were not great for the Lenape before the European colonization, if much worse after it.

The pressure from the Mohawk members of the Iroquois war machine put particular pressure on the New Jersey and Hudson Valley Lenape. Conflict was endemic. Maybe 50,000 Lenape had survived the Mohawk assaults and hung on in New Jersey and in New York on the banks of the big rivers, but after 1610 waves of epidemics took them. Before this catastrophe, the shore had been a place of celebration. The chief banqueted in ceremonial splendour. The tribe used to leave their homes in their fortified villages in the forests and spend summertime by the ocean. In the snowy winter woods they lived on bear, deer and turkey. Summer was the time to eat fish and shellfish. Small mountains of oyster shells found at different Jersey Shore points are all that is left of these transhumance feasts. The Lenape had no tool capable of shucking an oyster, so they wrapped the molluscs in seaweed and roasted them in hot ashes until they opened. Then they ate them, by the thousand. At the end of the summer they returned to their villages, leaving the shell hoards that can still be seen in some places today. The Jersey Shore was a magical place. Magic, then and now, is the word.

Nowadays other inhabitants live in Monmouth County, the county adjoining the sea in north-east New Jersey, current residence of Bruce Springsteen. There is magic at night, as the songs say, with or without faith. And in the day you go to work. Transhumance takes place daily to New York City from the Jersey suburbs in sheet steel boxes with a rubber wheel in each corner. These boxes are called Fords, Pontiacs, Hondas, Toyotas. You do not have to belong to the Ford or Honda tribe to own and drive a Ford or Honda. The main conduit of this travel is the New Jersey Turnpike, running through Springsteen and Sopranoland and the most exciting road in the world. The Lenape walked their dirt trails through the forests. Nowadays people listen on the car radio to rap or the Boss and the E Street Band, or are brought nearer to God. They listen to 'Born to Run' although they are born to drive. The Lenape were born to walk, and had no option as the wheel was unknown to them. The Turnpike is what everybody knows, but the eighteen-lane-wide asphalt lies on layers of different history.

New Jersey is a more interesting place than people think. Bruce Springsteen's music is part of the tradition of millennial hope deep in the subconscious of the state that Barack Obama so skilfully exploited in the 2008 presidential race. As a foreign academic I watched some of the Kerry campaign in Jersey in 2004 and knew it was doomed to failure but I could not clearly understand why. Nowadays it is easier to do so. Whatever John Kerry's qualities were, he did not touch the heart of American life in that election. In the last few years Springsteen has become identified with the Democrats, a symbol of intelligent dissent in the last few years. With *Magic* in 2007, his music entered a glorious Indian summer, with the immediate shadow of 9/11 that lay over *The Rising* album lifted. 2007 was the year that mattered.

It has been possible for him to explore the American condition here in his lyrics and music without losing his integrity or falling into the many traps of rock stardom. At a time when many European liberals have written off the liberal American Dream, Springsteen can and does keep it alive. He was a star visitor at Obama's victory event, and inauguration, but has many Republican fans. This book crystallized into its present form while I was at Princeton University in the very centre of the state at different times and making journeys around the place in my spare time with what seemed the difficult task of trying to finally understand where I was, in a small college town where George Washington's army fighting nearby in 1776-77 helped forge the nation. Some of the people who have helped me are mentioned in the text. There are many others who are not. The many kindnesses and generous help that I have received from so many different Jersey citizens made this writing possible. They were and still are anything from astronomically rich to desperately poor, black, white, female, male, Muslim, Christian, young, old, sober, drunk, criminal, law-abiding, some quite astonishing intellects as well as the pretty damn stupid, those new to the United States, those who have been around a long time, the endless tapestry of Princeton and New Jersey life.

These last years have seen a flowering of new poetry and music from Bruce Springsteen and the musicians working with him in the E Street Band that many—perhaps all of us—quite inevitably have yet to fully assimilate. A large scholarly, cultural studies, music studies and fanzine literature is booming around Bruce and the Band. The drama of the sea and the New Jersey Shore have never been far away. The Band's members have been both the conscience of the state in these bad times as well as romantic, sometimes Dionysian celebrants of life. I doubt whether Bruce himself really knows what he has achieved. We can try to hang a laurel wreath on the statue, even if the statue moves with that unmistakable lilting walk and sings, with a guitar in hand, black jeans, boots and a truck driver's haircut.

3
MAGIC

Concerning the myth of the rock fan as a free person, the quest for a concert ticket (a real ticket, not the Platonic form) and politics and mathematics on the shore of paradise

Asbury Park New Jersey

24 September 2007, During the Bushkratia

Kratos in ancient Greek means Power, Rule, which is a fact. There is always Power. But 2007 in Springsteen's music is the year that matters. Nineteenth-century Neo-Platonist Walter Pater sat in Oxford and wrote that all art should aspire to the condition of music; but his best pupil did the words, Oscar Wilde. The Ice Age is long over. I am fifty-seven miles due south of Manhattan on the Atlantic shore by the Asbury Park Convention Hall, where Bruce Springsteen as a teenager saw Jim Morrison and the Doors in 1966 and was never the same person again, 'the first mansion in my rock and roll dreams', as he has written. Where is George W. Bush this day? Maybe he is a fettered one, chained to his desk in the White House in Washington DC. There are caves everywhere, millions are fettered. I am fettered by my Blackberry cell phone in some ways. George W. Bush has the technical capacity to locate me, through tracing the signal from my mobile phone in my pocket. I cannot locate him. Yet he does not control the sea. The ocean is a rising swell, deep and cold. It is about three o'clock. Numbers of seconds coalesce to make time, but time has only been a Federal government responsibility in the United States since 1833. If we were on this beach before that, in 1832, here in New Jersey we might well be in a different time zone from inhabitants of neighbouring states. There is in fact only one notion of time available here today, which is the moment when the first note will be struck on stage by Bruce Springsteen and the E Street Band. Some will say that is the first number, as number means number but also means rock song. Using CNN vocab, that is a factoid. It is perhaps cyclical, in that the Band has played here many times. Nobody cares what time zone the president is in, or whether he is in Washington or somewhere else; all that matters is that he is not at Asbury Park. The slogan hanging over the boardwalk states 'LIFE IS GOOD AT THE BEACH'.

It has been written that New Jersey on a map exactly resembles a desirable (if hard to handle) woman, with her head in the New York clouds, and the rest in perfect shape. Her absent legs are shrouded in

Atlantic fog somewhere over the southern state line in little Delaware. On the Delaware River a gently sloping rear pouts at ever righteous Pennsylvania. The shore point at Asbury Park is on the breast. It is very appropriate; new life is nurtured there, like the new music has flowed over the shore for the last thirty years like the Passaic River into the sea. Tonight, the first open rehearsal show for the Boss and the E Street Band's new tour is about to happen. The door of the cave, the cave mouth, is open, the cavernous, open jaws of a great old theatre building. Jersey always has its danger, dynamism and excitement along with its lyrical natural beauties, but this is as good as it gets.

The sign under the massive orientalist portico of the convention hall is very simple, the date and in modest letters a few inches high, 'ASBURY PARK WELCOMES BRUCE SPRINGSTEEN AND THE E STREET BAND ON 9 24 AND 9 AND 25'. The portico belongs in a provincial cathedral in Puglia, rich, jazzy, effortlessly self-confident. Robber baron-era jazzy orientalism—Bruce is sharing his new music with his relentlessly fanatical and committed fans, as much part of the event as the boardwalk or the ice cream stall or the man selling salt water taffy.* These are small numbers, just nine and twenty-four and twenty-five.

The venerable convention hall is nevertheless a strange place. It was built for the pleasure seekers and summer crowds who thronged Asbury Park when the Jersey Shore was a nineteenth-century playground for New York City and Philadelphia. Famous people have lived in Asbury Park apart from Bruce Springsteen. 1940s stars Abbott and Costello were Jersey Shore products. Stephen Crane (1871-1900), the realist author of *Maggie: A Girl of the Streets* and the Civil War classic *Red Badge of Courage* that made him an international literary celebrity in 1895, spent his childhood and youth in Asbury Park. He got his first journalism experience writing for the Asbury Park Press Bureau. Nowadays cash-strapped Asbury Park is struggling heroically to preserve his old house and has restored it as a Museum of Asbury Park. The novelist's great-great

---

* A strange confection allegedly invented in New Jersey.

grandfather was a prominent New Jersey leader in the Revolutionary War and New Jersey delegate to the first Congress in Philadelphia. Then, as so often since, northern New Jersey was at the heartland of US history in a way few outsiders appreciate.

Crane was not a lucky man. Involved in a scandalous court case after he befriended a prostitute, Dora Clark, he eventually fled the United States and lived in England for a while before he died from a massive tubercular haemorrhage in 1900. The Crane family house still stands, in a difficult road mostly inhabited by hard-up Afro-American and Hispanic people and the municipality is struggling to keep it in some sort of condition. But the city also accommodates business conventions. The train ran from Penn Station (and still does) straight south down into the Jersey state shore. The theatre hangs on stilts uncertainly over the beach, and looks as if a big storm or the remains of a late summer hurricane might sweep it away down into the ocean depths. This has happened elsewhere; most of the first Cape May seaside town on the Delaware was washed away in a great storm in 1878, and they rebuilt a late Victorian gem in its place. Asbury Park, like all the shore, is edge city, its meaning coming from risk and danger, both real, of the present, the Boss's home turf, but also a strange uncertain construction with no defined future. It is not an innocent building, it has had much history since Italian craftsmen put it up, and history in Jersey can often mean bad things. Yet it is a lovely, fine, innocent, sunny day. People in the mid-afternoon litter the beach, some mothers and children putting up sandcastles and trading school gossip. Others are younger and more purposeful and there are also the older and more purposeful as well. The theatre has wooden walls hung on a steel frame, with metal piles sunk deep into the sand.

The Italian and Irish and other immigrant hands who worked on this and other Asbury Park buildings were not very popular. As Asbury Park historian Daniel Wolff points out in his *4th of July, Asbury Park* study of the town's history, Italian and other immigration into New Jersey was widely resented, and after World War I, New Jersey was a stronghold of the racist and white supremacist Ku Klux Klan. In 1924 at the height of its post-World War I influence, there were more Klan members in New Jersey than in some southern states like Georgia, over 60,000. Some of the Methodists of Asbury Park were particularly strong Klan supporters, and students of Klan history generally believe that the strong support in Jersey was a reaction to growing Catholic and Jewish power on the east coast generally. Oddly named Wall, west of Asbury Park, became a massive 369-acre holiday resort built on the site of the old Marconi transatlantic radio station. It was open only to members of the New Jersey Realm of the Klan. A Klan university was established to spread white supremacist ideology, the Alma White College in Zarephath, north of Princeton, and cross burnings, random violence and lynchings of Afro-Americans were common. The college went through various transformations over the years, particularly after the second Ku Klux Klan was banned and disbanded in 1944, and its original racist mission has been given up and the multi-racial Pillar of Fire ultra-evangelical Christian College now flourishes there although in trouble for a time after a Biblical-scale flood almost destroyed the site in 1999.

The pre-war Klan in Jersey made the mistake of allying itself with the vehemently pro-Nazi German-American Bund as World War II broke out, and Grand Dragon of the New Jersey Klan Arthur Hornbui Bell had become national vice-president of the Bund. The Bund had a camp at Norlund near Andover, NJ, where there had been significant German settlement in the nineteenth century and where Dutch-origin Calvinist churches were also sometimes sympathetic to racialist ideas. It was an ill-judged decision by Bell and he should have remembered the vigour with which the Federal government in Washington had cracked down on pro-German agitation in places like Hoboken and Jersey City in 1914, expropriating private property and interning individual activists.

So under the surface, some things don't change much here. A TV show like *The Sopranos* is brilliantly contemporary, but its appeal to a mass and mainstream American audience draws on a deep tradition of distrust of Italian-Americans, other outsiders, who are seen as inherently criminal, or semi-criminal, possibly un-American, and many were full of prejudice against them. The laugh at a joke in *The Sopranos* is also a laugh at those in the past thought to have failed to become fully American (had they even tried?), with a second-rate religion (Roman Catholicism) and ingrained criminal habits. As celebrity chef Anthony Bourdain once said, 'When I grew up in Leonia, it was Sicily on the Hudson.'

Under the building a few dogs are asleep. Around it is the black-jeaned and black muscle-vested security detail, prowling like hungry dogs and endlessly talking into CB radios. They hold the line between the Band and the public. The music is being given to them, but it is not free and Mr Springsteen is a superstar. That means two things: that someone or other may have a problem with him and try to slot him like John Lennon, or they may want to try to get in without a ticket, without paying. Either way, on either item, they don't stand a chance with these guys. Bruce is playing for the community, but he is not a community artist, he is a very rich man with a splendid home in Colts Neck and there is a potent market on the sandy concrete outside the ticket kiosk as much as in Wall Street—and like Wall Street, what is traded is invisible, so far. There is not a ticket on sale. Not a note has been played. The tickets went on sale on the internet a few days ago, at 9 am. They were sold out by five past. The whole subject is fraught. *Rolling Stone* ran a long story a few months before about how the whole system would be fairer by using auctions, but it has not happened by 2007.

So what are we all doing here? In order to try to beat the power of the market and help his most dedicated fans, Bruce decreed that a few hundred tickets can also be held back and sold on the day of the show. Some of us will be lucky, some will not. It will not be on a first come, first served basis. There will be a gamble, a lottery. New Jersey was after all the state where the pinball machine, in this country better known as the silverball machine, took off in the nineteenth century, and in some senses the pinball machine is the ancestor of the modern slot machine, the single most profitable part of every casino. It will be based on the principles of mathematics, in a state which has contributed more to twentieth-century mathematics than anywhere else in the world. This is the Jersey Shore, after all, in the United States of America. Mathematics can be pure, as at Princeton, or applied, as elsewhere. Atlantic City is not far away, but there is the only Silverball Museum in the world just down the boardwalk here at Asbury Park, a walk back into the clanging, pinging, light flashing world of The Who song 'Pinball Wizard' and the 1950s and 1960s. Chance rules NJ. Down there mathematics works hard to enslave the gamblers in the casino caves. In terms of those blackboards in the Princeton physics department, it will be done on the basis of Werner Heisenberg's Uncertainty Principle, and nobody will know what is happening until the last minute. The slot payers at Atlantic City also do not know where the spinning wheels will stop until that last minute. Then maybe you would go and pawn your wedding ring to carry on playing.

Much of what happened in the next few hours would—without the Harley Davidsons lining the park—have been understood at some shrine in classical antiquity on a Greek or Roman hillside. No Harleys then but the rich ones would have nice chariots with brass studs. Chrome plate and Harleys from the great temple city of motorcycle manufacture in far away and little known Milwaukee had not been invented then. But then and now there was/is the cult leader, a sacred man of the music cult who has magical powers (as it happens, his new recordings are actually called *Magic*). The followers assemble when he is reputed to be going to appear. He will be the shaman, put them into a trance, alter their state of consciousness with his music, they will go wild. There is a problem: there are too many potential worshippers to attend the musical celebrations and take part in the sacred dances and punch the air with clenched fists. So the shrine bosses set up a lottery to see who can get in and who has to stay outside. But it is not a simple matter of rolling bones to see who has been lucky, who the gods have smiled on. Certain rituals have to be followed.

In following them, the atomized individual fan becomes part of a wider community, first of Springsteen fans on a big night down on the shore, then part of a place, Asbury Park, and then part of New Jersey, a state, and then part of the hundreds of millions of Americans, the particular and the universal, the reality and the dream. So in following the Band, the American Dream is still alive.

In Bushland, though, many are very disillusioned with that dream. As many people look down on the Band and its fans as admire them or want to join them. There is also a touch of the days of Ellis Island. We are all immigrants in Asbury Park, strangers, and we will have to compete to do what we want, form lines, wait, then compete again. This is a very American event. We will all become more American here tonight, whether we are US citizens or foreign aliens. An All will be made from the individual Ones of us, the American melting pot on the beach. Some come just to sleep on the beach and hear the music and become someone new, like others came to classical Epidaurus to sleep and become someone new.

America still has the magic to make people and things new. Mathematics also developed on shores in ancient Asia Minor, when Pythagoras started to codify the secret wisdom of the cults of mathematicians who picked up the numbers from the Miletus traders who in turn picked up numerical permutations from the caravan routes to the East. Then they were persecuted and fled to little Kroton, then in *Magna Grecia*, now modern Crotone in Calabria. There are no Phoenician olive merchants who could cut a nice deal on the abacus out on the sand tonight, but they are there with us in spirit.

None of this bothers the super tanker crew five miles out to sea on one of the two container ships going into the massive Jersey container port of Elizabeth or direct to New York itself. They are just visible in the distance on the pale blue sea horizon behind the theatre. The crew will be watching Filipino football beamed to them by satellite, then reading girlie mags, maybe stroking the dongle a little before they sleep. The shops along the shore are quiet, some closing early, as the summer season is not very long at Asbury Park. I ask a man what is happening about ticket sales. Behind us is the new spick and span Salt Water Beach Cafe, where the old HoJo's bar used to be, gloomy, half-lit and with broken looking boozers crunched over the bar stools and a whiskey in front of them. HoJo's was full of people who looked as if they had walked out of a Woody Guthrie song, a woman with strange plaits held together with fuse wire twists, like I remember in semi-bankrupt Plattsburgh in upstate New York. In Plattsburgh women wear strange improvised equipment. They can't afford anything else

We slugged ditch water coffee in the old watering hole. Then she stood outside Mystic Meg's fortune teller's shed, and I took a photograph of the ancient historian. The few other HoJo customers then seemed to be on the point of suicide, or worse. Whatever Mystic Meg had said to any of them, it could not have been very good. On the wall of the shed nearby is a fine wall painting of Bruce and a long-finned Ford Fairlaine, car vintage 1959, Bruce aged about fourteen. He discovered life here, in the time of Eisenhower, that is the myth. The history turned out to be slightly different. Since, HoJo's has died. The Salt Water place does mostly lattes, the yuppies have come now, there is new white working class brightening up along the shore and there is hardly a black face to be seen.

'Five. They sell at five. Watch out for the scalpers.'

The leather jacketed man retreats to his motorbike bag, more interesting for him than an Englishman. He is tough looking, heavy long hair, over thirty, a book about graphic design sticking out of the bag. What is a ticket scalper? Did the Lenape scalp many people? I don't have a history of Native America with me or a Jersey speech dictionary. In front of us, tekkies in tight black jeans and T-shirts are unloading from a vast multi-wheeled container truck. The atmosphere is quiet, expectant, someone says the Boss is already inside, the security heavies look more bad-tempered than ever, but a very sweet and little police buggy winds up the boardwalk. New Jersey Police Department has many guises and disguises, from this agreeable Hispanic man, a good community servant on his buggy, to the space age SWAT teams going into the Camden ghetto armed to the teeth. But there is something utterly straight and decent about them, most of them; it is a very tough job in the NJPD, they are not well paid, they are just doing a job as a cop. They are not trying to change society, just keep things in some sort of shape. In Jersey that is not always very easy.

Meet Number 19757: Philosophy and Number on the Jersey Shore

There is a queue, a line by the back door and a man with a clipboard hands out a green plastic wristband with a number on it. He snaps it on, as if you were about to go into a hospital operating theatre and have something serious done. It is number 19757. It is a relief to have a number, and so to be part of the United States. The United States is a numeracy. I have no idea whether 19757 is a prime number or not. It is a relief when someone says there are 500 tickets up for today, and they will be drawn on the last three numbers, those are the ones that matter, there is no invisible queue of 19,000 people in front of me. We are playing the numbers like on the street in Harlem in 1925, when the day's winner was the last three from the racetrack handle. Five hundred is an easy number to understand, but I am actually immigrant to Asbury Park Number 757. Let's hope it is a lucky number for the queue. But you don't queue in this country, you make a line. Line is an important word in the United States, as Tony Soprano's son observed in an episode when he was looking at a dead woman's body; the cocksucker got outta line, Tony said, so she will feed the fishes.

Number and music have always been closely connected. For those interested, Plato writes at considerable length on this relationship. Music was allowed in his Utopia. We call a rock song a number. Why? Before Plato there were the Pythagoreans, and the very early philosopher Philolaus of Kroton, seen as a follower of the Pythagorean School. He was interested in mathematics and music and his writing reflects the knowledge and background in early number mysticism of whole number ratios that govern the concordant intervals in music, and seems to have known of 'musical proportion'. He was a man of the numbers, and used mathematics to work on philosophical problems. Later Aristotle identified certain concepts such as justice with certain numbers, whereas the sage Philolaus did not believe all things are numbers but that all things are known through numbers, and the task of the philosopher was to search for the right numbers that give us knowledge of things. His sense of number is shared by the American government with its endless efforts to collect numerical data about the population, the mania for Big Data. Or maybe it is all just part of the reverence for numbers that many primitive peoples have in their efforts to find simple mathematical solutions to everyday problems. Even founding father and English ideologist of the American Revolution Tom Paine was fascinated by statistics. Maybe here on the shore we are the sophisticated, rational people who have escaped the cave and the prisoners are in the Federal world in Washington?

Those outside the line are beyond numbering, they are at risk and if they are unlucky they may die. Stay in line and Uncle Sam will look after you. Or he will make your life hell if you don't. Try Trenton gaol on a hot summer day during a lockdown with a man twice your size wanting to ride your arse. This is a vast county, it is not idling British Somerset or quietly wandering Hampshire, everyone high or low has to get used to being just a number sometimes, and stand in line. This prospect was to happen to George W. Bush on 21 January 2009. Barbara sent him shopping at the local supermarket and he stood there in good order, wallet in hand.

It is time to relax, play the Olympian slots for a while. You need a particular temperament to be a good slots player, whether they have it in Asbury Park or not. Events will reveal the truth. Modern Greeks do not make good slots players; you cannot have an argument with a fruit machine. Perhaps modern Greeks rebel against Pythagoras. I have a look at a local newspaper. The *Asbury Park Press* (since 1879), it is called. Bruce Springsteen is not the centre of things today, in their view. It is hard to be a prophet in your own country. There is another important visitor to the shore today apart from anyone to do with the Boss or the Band. On the front page the headline story is headed SPRINGSTEEN WARMS UP IN ASBURY, but there is a much bigger central splash on VIRGIN MARY, NINE FEET TALL VISITS CHURCH. This tall, willowy lady didn't need her Jimmy Choo's.

The newspaper explains:

Our Lady of America is as much a dream come true as is an apparitions request almost fulfilled. Standing nine feet high with contemplative eyes, a hesitant smile, bare feet and wearing a simply tailored white robe, Our Lady of America, the Immaculate Virgin, is the nation's first canonically approved ikon.

She sounds a decent sort of woman, if not quite dressed by Bergdorf Goodman or Prada. All this seems to beg some questions. Like, say, that she is a statue nine feet tall and not an ikon. Most people think an icon is something that hangs on a church wall. And most difficult, and maybe worst of all, she is not a Jersey Girl. She is based on the appearance of 25 September 1956 of the Virgin to a nun in Ohio, one Mildred Neuzil, who was a member of the Precious Blood Sisters of Ohio. This lady had been seeing visions and having mystical experiences since 1938, but 1956 was the big one. The statuesque lady is on her way to a permanent home in the Shrine of the Immaculate Conception in Washington DC, where the powerful ones will come to see her. She will have a clear message. Her current guardian, the Rev Angelo Geiger, has been travelling the country with her, and tells the paper that 'our Lady of America came to talk about the sanctification of the family'. Nine feet tall, she is being looked after by the Jackson fire company on an appliance, and the upstanding men of the Monsignor John F. Baldwin Knights of the Columbus. She is in good hands. There is no shortage of strong male Catholic hands near this sea. However Catholic the Jersey Shore always seems to be, it can always be more Catholic than you think.

And Howell has plenty of Catholic worthies. I heard in New York and then again in Princeton that this was going to be quite a Catholic album, with a song about Springsteen finding fragments of his Cross ... A man from Fordham University, the Jesuit fortress in the Bronx, knew all about it; they monitor Bruce like the DIA monitor Russian submarines. The Lady has come to the right place, and she couldn't have come down to the holy shore on a more beautiful, purple-touched evening. And being nine feet tall, she will have a good view out to the ocean, where two small yachts with white sails have appeared, passing north on an azure-blue patch of water. It will be a nice break for her before spending hundreds of years ahead staring into space in the nation's capital.

So go for it. This is the last look at the Atlantic waters you will ever get, no seaside holidays for the saints. There are a lot of people here who need your help. She has some local rivalry. Asbury Park is also the site of a Greek Orthodox shrine. They celebrate Orthodox Easter here by throwing a cross into the sea. Then everyone eats vast amounts of food. Evil is near, as well as good. At Jackson up shore, Corporal Luigi Marcinate is being mourned; he was blown up about fifty miles north-east of Baghdad at a place called Muqdadiyah. The Iraq War is hanging over everyone, and is said to hang over the new album *Magic*. The corporal was a 1999 graduate of Elizabeth High School. He will not be taking the long walk home, or see the cranes of the vast container port that was his home town again. The bomb was 'improvised', according to the Pentagon. That didn't make much difference to the outcome. The corporal is dead. His sister said he didn't want to go, or leave his family but he felt the army had done a lot for him and he had his duty there. The shadow of the Iraq War suddenly fall over the Asbury Park boardwalk, the sand a metre away here, the same infinite sands around Baghdad. The family would take a trip every year back to Italy. Luigi loved swimming and would spend most of his time on the beach. There would have been plenty of sand there. He died in a sandy place.

Suddenly camera, action. The drifting, waiting sunbathers and people lolling on benches smoking or reading about film stars are moving towards the theatre side door. A tall security man is standing on a box. Then Dije Perolli and two other women appear; she is an old friend, the daughter of one of the leaders of the Albanian community in the United States, and a deeply committed fan. She has seen Bruce more or less everywhere. She is relaxed about prospects: 'Don't worry. If we don't get in, we'll listen from the beach. You get a great sound. Bruce makes them leave the windows open so everyone can hear. The centre's a music box.'

That does not sound a bad idea in itself. Bruce seems a good shaman, with democratic instincts. It would separate the music from the gaze onto the Band, it would avoid looking like one of the older fans present, and it would be simple and there would still be the pure view of the sea. And it would be a cop out from the gamble, the lottery. This is a nation of gamblers, fate through numbers, gambling central to being an American, and it is part of the American competitive process to get a ticket and get the eyes to gaze onto the Boss, focus eyes tight on him, grip him in the gaze vice. It would be feeble not to try to do that, my ageing blue eyes on his ageing spruce hair. I was born in April 1949, he was born in September 1949. We are both 49ers. And now at 4.45 pm there are not many people waiting, maybe we will all get in. Maybe it isn't as bad being a suppliant at a Jersey shrine as you might think.

We are at a shrine on a remote beach, but could be on a much older shore. The war is far away in Troy (Iraq). Some of the most important speeches and events in classical literature take place on or near shores, from perhaps ten major spiels in Homer's *Odyssey* to the watchman speech at the beginning of Aeschylus's *Agamemnon*. Shores are a good place to study imperial societies at war. Pericles envisaged the heroes of war buried on some unknown shore, not needing a monument to their heroism. Most people here are oppositional, liberals or radicals. American soldiers are dying heroic deaths in Iraq, and sometimes their relatives and friends never know what has happened to them when they do not come back. The word is that in this new album, Bruce has found a way to say what he thinks about it all. So the new music is his, but it will soon also be ours. The Jersey Shore is a place of exchange, transition, pleasure, but also understanding. It was not only the only shore hereabout. In 1920s Newark, the downtown Coast district was the jazz and red light zone, where prostitutes found New Yorkers, and New Yorkers found prostitutes. Penises were put into women for a dollar-allotted short time. America was at peace then, not as now in Gore Vidal's view of American society as a society designed and run for endless war.

Then the Enemy appeared, although to begin with it was not clear that is actually what they were.

'Are we going to get lucky?'

A well-dressed Philadelphia type in chinos and sweatshirt was staring at his thin green wristband. His girlfriend stared at it too. She said nothing. Her silence indicated pessimism. Maybe as they came from the city whose only well-known contribution to rock and roll has been Chubby Checker and the Twist they don't expect much here.

'I don't know.'

But lucky ones are beginning to arrive, furtively or confidently showing each other the cherished tickets.

'I hit the phone at five seconds past nine. Got straight through.'

Long walls of female hair swing in admiration. She is very beautiful; it isn't too hard to get a beautiful lady to come with you for a night out on the shore if you have won trumps for a Bruce concert with Ticketmaster. She has the hair and the eyes and the bottom and the legs. He has only the ticket and the sweat slogan: YOU ARE IN NEW JERSEY – ONLY THE STRONG SURVIVE.

Not everyone survives the dangers of the Jersey Shore. At the very corner of this auditorium, 122 lives were lost in September 1934 when the steamer **Morro Castle** ran aground and caught fire. Souvenirs from the disaster were on sale in tourist shops for years afterwards. Seventy-four years later exactly to the month a trendy man with a soft voice stares at his ticket.

'The vinyl comes out tomorrow... that's a sweet ticket you've raised.'

'I got in right at nine o'clock and fifteen seconds. All sold out.'

'Something fishy there?'

This is New Jersey; it does not take long for a corruption allegation to surface about some situation. A face with thick glasses suddenly waves a ticket nearby

'Two fifty dollar's the price. That's it.'

'Jerk off, scalper.'

So the little man with thick glass is a scalper. I have learnt a new word today. He is what in England would be called a ticket tout. How did tout become scalper? The mysteries of American-English are everywhere here. With every word the tension is rising. People stare from ticket stub to the sky, running yearning eyes along the theatre roof.

Giant wood shells have been lined since 1904 along the length of it. As in so many other places in this state, the hand of the Italian craftsman who had decorated churches for centuries is not far away. Maybe the theatre will last a while yet, daring the fates between land and sea, well protected by a seawall or dark rough-hewn granite blocks. Or maybe it will crash into the sea as the Band pumps up the noise. The Rise and Fall of Asbury Park will be complete. Spars from the hall will be washed up in the Severn Estuary near Bristol. Birdwatchers will use them to prop their field glasses. Or maybe the huge granite seawall rocks will protect. They are rocks but they don't roll. Everyone and everything in Jersey needs protection except the Atlantic Ocean.

There is a seagull poking around on them, but no interesting birds like Cape May. Why were the birds down there so tame? Because they normally live in the Arctic and just migrate for Cape May vacations and feathery romance and to peck clams and horseshoe crab for lunch and never normally meet anyone much except other birds and bird fans in brown anoraks. Here there are thousands. There is no book of bird etiquette which assists in this kind of situation. The best plan is to look for lunch on a faraway rock, focus your penetrating beaky gaze down onto a barnacle and give him your spikey yellow beak to think about, just rub him out, slot that barnacle and keep out of the rockers' strange ways. Then Dije reappears and makes a perceptive observation: 'It's a community here. We don't have so many communities in the US these days. Following Bruce concerts, that makes you a member of a community. That's it.'

She could have said we were the Boss's tribe, his Lenape warriors, but she didn't. She has her father Gani's deep moving eyes, hawks from his birth on a northern Albanian mountain near the Kosova border. They had a stone *kulla*, the Perolli fortress. One of eleven, he arrived as a refugee child from the Yugoslavist terror against the Albanians in 1948, and stood on the concrete in New York port. Gani made good in Midwest and Carolina business and had six children. Dije went to Rutgers and is a real Jersey girl, cheerful, generous, resourceful, but she is not the only interesting woman nearby. Across from us teetering on high heels on the edge of the boardwalk is a tall pinnacle with a very good shape, a bottom and legs to die for and a very short skirt. On her howling orange T-shirt there are the momentous words and mathematical symbols:

PRINCETON UNIVERISTY
E=MC2

It is the theory of relativity, briefly stated. A representative from the college of Woodrow Wilson and endless Nobel Prize winners is present, from forty-five miles away. It must be an important event. Does she need the *Magic* album if she is at Princeton and displaying on her front Albert Einstein's key equation that expressed the nature of Time and Space in the Universe? She must be the freest person on the sand even if she is also a fettered fan. She has magic already by attending Princeton, after Oxford the best research university there is; she is drenched in it. And Einstein's key equation is on her T-shirt. The lady is a Pythagorean, asserting the magic of number, also, or at least in the symbolic form of an equation. Mathematics is queen of the sciences on this beach and she has to gamble like the rest of us for a ticket, however privileged. She lights a Marlboro and weighing in at a hundred pounds draws on it like a two hundred-pound Balkan truck driver. Even the gilded youth of the most elegant and ruthless of the Ivy League schools can get ticket stress. She has a long wristband stare, needs more Marlboro nicotine, she has no ticket. When Bruce is playing, it's an illness, we all have it, there is no cure except a piece of soft cardboard about three inches long and an inch wide. It might as well have a door code for the gates of heaven, or beyond that, and better for her, a Princeton PhD certificate. Echoing in my head, the TV show forecast: 'This is going to be tough ticket, this show, a tough ticket.'

Someone is going to judge us, some will be saved and get tickets and enter the hall of Utopia, eternal happiness, others will go down, just be swimming in the sea, then a giant whale might come down from Nantucket and swallow the losers up, that will be that. In mathematical terms, they will be Zero. Zero was a most important insight, perhaps invented by the early Hindu mathematicians, some believe, or was maybe bought into Ionian Greece as an import from China. It permitted an entirely different range of calculation. As many of us will be Zeroes if we don't get a ticket, this topic from the history of science is a matter of immediate interest. Does the whale know Zero? Maybe the whale will take plenty of Republicans. Or maybe he doesn't like Obama's people. Others may stay in limbo, and only hear the music, not go down to the dark ocean depths or see the stars. They will have no gaze at Bruce, or Max Weinberg, or any musician. They will hear the music. Just ears, not eyes.

'Time to make a line, guys. We are drawing only last three digits, eight hundred and below.'

Amongst it all, hardly anyone has noticed the decent college boy-looking security man on an orange box. At the time I did not know it, but they were using the old system of the illegal numbers game in the streets, the last three numbers of the racing track attendance. But within a minute, hundreds of people with the right numbers are crammed around him in a crowd below the end roof and a wood carved shell high up on the theatre wall that looks as if it might fall off and brain us. The Puritans' protective wood shingle has become a massive useless ornate shell bolted to decorate. The line is calm, decent, people are civil and polite in that American way, and there is no queue jumping. It is two hours until the Band is due to play. A schoolteacher in cheap worn clothes tells me through her misted glasses, 'This ticket system doesn't help the working person. I got lucky, my work stopped, I came down.'

She looks apathetic almost, hardly caring if there is a chance of a ticket, coming down the shore was the thing. Her faded T-shirt from the 2004 campaign says 'JOHN KERRY – VOTE FOR CHANGE'. It was Righteous to back Kerry, it was Righteous to come down to the shore. But many things in the US are not organized with the working person in mind. It is all there on her buttonhole badge.

A gasp from the past. 2004 seems a long while ago, the time of the Rockin' Rebels cover of *Rolling Stone*, Bruce in a neat blue shirt alongside Dave Matthews, Pearl Jam and others holding up the metaphorical flag for political rock against the first stage of the Bush administration. At the time it seemed too idealistic and optimistic and cynics said it was a total failure, but in fact the tour raised a lot of money for things like voter registration that started to lay some of the mass participation foundations for the Obama victory four years later. Speaking then, in that issue of the magazine, the Boss said: 'Sitting on the sidelines would be a betrayal of the ideas I'd written about for a long time ... I don't want to see the country devolve into an oligarchy, watch the division of wealth increase and see another million people below the poverty line this year.'

But it was a lost cause for John Kerry then. The Vote for Change campaign did not cut the mustard, and the blue collar constituency Kerry was trying to hold onto for the Democrats was leaking towards the Republicans every day. The Springsteen-led tour did get publicity for the Democrats but mostly just preached to the converted. Bush and Cheney fought a tough and effective campaign, if sometimes dirty, and they had enough of the American public still held by the spectre of 9/11 for it to work. Rockin' Rebels was something of an experiment and was feeling its way in some areas. And the start of the tour had been compromised by the news of Johnny Ramone's death after a long battle with cancer; the founder of punk guitar playing had gone to his grave. My work in the US in that year of 2004 was mostly connected with Washington DC and it was a difficult year with friends from the wartime period in gaol in Kosovo, pointless, interminable delays in the independence agenda, and in music the near-indifference of so many people to the wonderful solo album *23rd Street Lullaby* released by Bruce's much-loved wife and E Street Band stalwart Patti Scialfa. As *Rolling Stone* observed, it was a deeply personal album with some exquisite songs but it seemed to me an album that also got rather lost in what she later described as the situation where 'if you are married to someone really famous, people aren't really seeing you'. But she had been used to pressure, after a lashing from the tabloids as the Other Woman who broke up Bruce's first marriage in the 1980s.

This lady here on the sandy beach, like most of the American left, is at least used to losing. Like Orthodoxy, Bruce's entourage has its Old Believers. She will be the calmest and most philosophical person on the shore when she doesn't get a ticket, she can give therapy to the rest of us. We can sit on the sand and have a beer and pour out our hearts about the ticketless experience. We will be Tony Soprano; she will be Jennifer Melfi, even if she is a teacher from New Brunswick. But that time has not come yet. Everyone is unrolling a hundred dollar bill. The cash will be needed fast, this is not a world of credit, down on the shore, no sir. Money is transference to buy a set of blackjack cards, political favours, a handgun (known locally as a piece), that is how it is. But the money hardly matters, it just makes me feel a little better that the Moment of Judgement will be Coming, on this near Latter Day. Most of us will get the chop. A few will join the gods.

'First drawn... 19803!' a black security guard shouts out. Like a branded cow, a fat little man hands over his hundred bucks, waves his ticket and jolts out of the line with a triumphantly raised wristband.

'I'm in...'

He runs like a groundhog onto the beach and throws himself flat on the sand. The gods have smiled on him. The numbers are being drawn down, down from 803 not up. That is the decision the organizers have made. Numbers must rise, or must fall. Hegel the German philosopher wrote about the power of number over the flux. Kojeve misinterpreted Hegel for us, then others conceptualized the Gaze. My Gaze is on this small fat man. Here there is Number One, the small fat Ego, in the flux, which may achieve meaning and identity, or simply has got recognition through a ticket. He will not only hear the Band but gaze on it and Bruce will be a mirror of what he might become, a living ikon, Byzantium come to the shore.

Seeing the Band is a mystical experience for the cult members, mystical reverie is the condition of the initiate, and mysticism is a word derived from an ancient Greek word that means it is better to close the eyes so that you may better perceive the divine invisible. In other words it denies the gaze onto the world famous Band—so it may after all be better if I am unlucky and do not get a ticket. Bruce fans tend to be believers, if in very different and diverse things. A man lovingly locking his motorcycle with a mighty chain had a leather jacket on, advertising

SOLDIER OF CHRIST MOTORCYCLE MINISTRY INC
AND
SOLDIER OF CHRIST FELLOWSHIP

I can just hear the music, even without a massive purple Harley Davidson, almost crippled by the weight of chrome. There is also the philosophical issue of mortality. Springsteen's music is in a real sense immortal; or simply, thanks to technology, people will listen to it after the Boss is dead as long as people listen to popular music. Yet he is happily with us and can be seen, admittedly at a distance, on a stage or on a DVD recording of a particular concert. There is also the question of knowledge. Will seeing the Boss perform actually increase knowledge of his music? Perhaps all us fans should remember the famous ancient Greek paradox, that it is impossible to be taught what one does not know already. The Pythagoreans thought that what we call learning is actually reminiscence. All of us on the beach will have heard the songs hundreds or more times. Socrates later on showed how it is possible to find out what you do or do not know, in full use of the dialogue. So perhaps there will be a dialogue in the concert, with Bruce on stage yet again exploring what his fans know of him and his music, and the fans interrogating him and their own sub-conscious minds. So we are all Pythagoreans, geeks of the number mysticism, as the fact that we are here proves that with music, above all, you cannot be taught what those ancient philosophers said, what you are entirely ignorant of—but our Walkmans and car radio players will have done a good job, since we know the music before we come to hear it again. Apollo is our patron god, as Apollo was the god of the mathematicians.

Tiger orange T-shirt Princeton lady still has Einstein's equation for the theory of relativity on show over her breasts. You can learn a good deal about the philosophy of mathematics on this beach. Her breasts move braless under the orange cotton. Breasts are the antithesis of Euclidian geometry. They are binary, dual. There are many dead ends in the history of mathematics, like that followed by the Reformation-period Catholic theologian Peter Bungus who wrote a book of 700 pages seeking to prove that the number of 666 of the Beast in the Book of Revelation was a cryptogram for Protestant leader Martin Luther. Numbers can be random. So someone else nearby is lucky, a middle-aged woman with blue shirt with these words on it: 'MEMPHIS THE BLUES CITY'.

Memphis seems unimaginably far away. Memphis does cotton and blues, not equations let along cryptograms. It has revived recently with its wonderful Cotton Museum, its strange pyramid and the ever prescient story of Elvis at Graceland, a much more tasteful and interesting shrine than its publicists might lead you to think. Her Memphis shirt has no mathematical content at all. New York City and even Princeton also seem far. This is a vast and hard to know country. Few people really know what is happening or going on in America, least of all many in the Federal government. But Washington uses number magic to confuse the people and pretend that it does. Number was important in making sense of it, as it was to the first Federal governments which counted and enumerated endlessly. Mathematics reigns in the United States and the dream is an equation. $E=MC2$ is the perfect equation. Princeton can seem the perfect university. Mathematics has seemed to bring results to develop American world power. Einstein's calculations led to the atomic bomb and American global supremacy. His fellow Princeton mathematician John von Neumann became the direct father of Hiroshima and Nagasaki, even taking part in choosing those Japanese cities as the first targets. The world is contracting around little Asbury Park. On the beach here by the pounding sea

Princeton is an empty mathematical abstraction, even if those equations were written there. Einstein thought working in Princeton's mathematics department was Paradise, a City of Light. Memphis is a dark dream on a huge river I had not then seen, full of uncounted and uncountable billions of gallons of south-flowing water. It is time for a toilet stop, even at risk of losing a ticket. It takes place in a builder's facility, provided by Mr John, The Complete Source of Temporary Restrooms. This is the United States, a civilized, advanced country. Often there is a fly printed on the porcelain for you to aim your nice line of pee. Men are thought to need a target in Bush's America. The process of imposing order through enumeration has gone a long way.

Someone behind me was talking of the Hadrosaurus. They had visited Haddonfield, New Jersey, according to this learned monologue the site of the first ever discovery of a complete dinosaur skeleton. It was the Ground Zero of dinosaur palaeontology. The Jersey Shore is a place of pleasure but also a place of learning, it seems, unexpected learning. The bones were found in a ravine just before the Civil War broke out. Where was Haddonfield? I had no idea.

'You get a ticket, it makes you an inmate. That's how it is.'

Back to the Cave. Does the United States have citizens, or inmates? Woody Guthrie was an inmate in the asylum at Marlboro, a place not very far from here inland. It was a notorious old Jersey institution that is now closed down. Bruce visited Woody Guthrie there once, in an act of ancient Roman *pietas* to the great folk singer of the previous generations, confined there with Huntingdon's Chorea. Numbers play a part in the memory mechanism for the asylum; the old cemetery has many numbered graves without any name on them, and the numbers and names are only matched on a circular monument in the centre, so a number like twenty-one or forty-seven is all you get on your actual tombstone. The man in charge of the tickets is originally from Cheltenham, UK. I am told this awkwardly and ostentatiously by a cool, distant young man. Why I am being told? This is a sense of agenda. The warning systems are switched on. Customers from Pennsylvania in my cigar shop are the last people who seem to think

Republicans and Bush are wonderful. Maybe it is something in the water supply in Philadelphia. The rest of us would like to recycle him, as soon as possible, like now. Perhaps he can soon be taken to Pennsylvania for that purpose, as they say they know so much about recycling. There is a definite feel of a spin operation somewhere. People keep coming up to me and wanting to talk about Pennsylvania. The party line is coming from Pennsylvania. A few minutes ago yet another man was telling me how wonderful recycling is in that state. He spoke at length. I think I now know more than I ever need to know about recycling in Pennsylvania. A Pennsylvanian cuckoo is sitting in our neat little Jersey nest; hopefully it will fly back over the Delaware River soon, to Pennsylvania, where only recyclers survive. Then there is another liberal T-shirt:

UNTIL THE COLOR OF A MAN'S SKIN IS OF NO MORE SIGNIFICANCE THAN THE COLOR OF HIS EYES, THERE WILL BE WAR AND RUMORS OF WAR.

That is his prophesy for the night. This shore has a long prophetic tradition. It is time to join the line for the last three hundred tickets. Channel 5 have appeared and are starting to interview people about why on earth they go through all this. We could after all be watching the ball game or buying a dog or reading about late antiquity or the Balkans or doing something else intelligent. Someone discusses the motion of the line (the line is of course part of the myth of the cave).

'Is the line moving yet?'

'No.'

'It'll go fast once it starts.'

Does the line move at all? It doesn't seem like it. A line belongs to the world of geometry, of Euclid, and lacks interest for me. It must have been like this in Ellis Island. No one roots for Euclid there. But this is the United States, there are true believers around for more or less any system of belief, including the omnipotence of this hero, our hero, Bruce the Boss, the reason we are here. Some people believe the Antichrist runs the

European Union, and thus the end of the world is this near. Actually the European Union is in terminal decline, and this issue is irrelevant. How the Antichrist is running the line is not apparent. What matters is that the saint will assist salvation. Bruce is the appointed, if not anointed, saint.

'Bruce is good to the fans. Everybody with a wristband will get in.'

The Saint, the shaman Saint, the Boss, the Bruce. The Boss doesn't like scalping and profiteering on his tickets, that is true, and unlike many rock superstars, he is a good citizen of his state and nation. But unless he can make 500 tickets feed 5,000 people, there will be a lot of disappointed people. In that parable, Jesus broke the spell of number magic, showed himself to be above the limits, showed the power of God. Number may have power over the flux but he, even the scalper, does not have power over number. That power belongs only to God. Teachers in the line are disagreeing.

'They are dropping single tickets.'

'You get up there, you'll get in.'

'I won't.'

'You got no positive attitude. If you were in my class you wouldn't get a sticker. Never.'

It is much easier to look out over the sea than think about tickets or second grade school life in summer. I think I should get a star from the teacher for standing on this shore and going through it all. A crowd of gulls suddenly drop into the water and dive and fight.

'There's a shoal of bluefish in. Worth fighting over. They are working hard.'

Bluefish are not nice guys, and it is best to be on the side of the gulls. In their authoritative work, *American Food and Game Fishes* (1903) Jordan and Evermann assert that the bluefish is

> a carnivorous animal of the most pronounced type... it has been
> likened to an animated chopping-machine the business of which
> is to cut to pieces and otherwise destroy as many fish as possible
> in a given space of time. Going in large schools, in pursuit of fish

not much inferior to themselves in size, they move along like a pack of hungry wolves, destroying everything before them. Their trail is marked by fragments of fish and by the stain of blood in the sea.

They are at home on the Jersey Shore, they clearly have attitude. Maybe bluefish in the past have been elected as state governor, sheriffs? Are the bluefish a Mob? Or the Mob? A man next to me asks the number of my wristband. I tell him. He is forty numbers away. This was a serious error on my part, in retrospect. Then he is on his cell phone. I like being the sucker, you see how some people in the country operate. They think Brits are as green as cabbage, and also in this case deaf, as he passes on my number, 19757, to someone on his phone. I heard that as clear as a bell. We are working hard. To follow Springsteen means Work, Effort and, above all, Commitment, but in Bush's America, years of dealing with Balkan police apparats is also useful. This is a political event for many people, Governor Corzine's effort to get Bruce honorary New Jersey citizenship was blocked by the Bushistas. Some Republicans really seriously dislike Bruce Springsteen. I had been told at Princeton that the most powerful and richest ultra-rightist in the country was a man called Richard Mellon Scaife in Pennsylvania. Perhaps these are his people? A black propaganda expert tells me that the concert won't even happen, the drummer Max Weinberg is leaving the Band. I ask cell phone stooge's lady a bit about her job, as he has been asking about mine. She says she is a manager at the Eaton Corporation. I ask her if she works for the Yale local part. She doesn't seem to know they make good locks everyone uses. This ignorance does not strengthen her already thin credibility. She is growing, a plant in our queue on the concrete, in fact, she is one. I resist asking her what she thinks of the Pennsylvania tribe and their nasty extremist Senator Spector. Thank heavens for the burly black haired New York firemen, they really are the salt of the earth with none of the trendy missionary agendas of the NYPD.

'With a wing and a prayer we'll be OK. And we couldn't be in a better place in the world than on this mound of concrete with a view of the sea like that.'

That is true. A Bronx firehouse officer who protects society from its blazing nightmares has good values and knows what matters in life. He says Channel 12 have also appeared, a blond women, they will only interview people who are from New Jersey. So I am a Zero again, only a resident alien, even if I am temporarily Number 19757. Is this patriotism or bigotry? Or maybe they are aware of the problem of the Pennsylvania influx, just a few too many Lacoste shirts and neatly pressed chinos. The sound man has an anti-Bush T-shirt, the first direct feel of the coming presidential election. It shows the Texan walking towards Hell's opening, flaming gates, wearing a T-shirt saying, 'BUSH-CHENEY-SATAN 2008'.

The sound man thinks it is not good for a country to have a bad-tempered ranch manager as leader. You get on the wrong side of the ranch manager, you know it.

A fat man scowls at him, he is clearly a supporter of the administration, and disappears into the crowd by salt water taffy corner. This is a very deeply divided country. The administration to judge from the mainstream papers was losing interest in the Iraq War now, but that was not the case on this beach; it hung like a curtain over everybody and, as it would turn out, also over the new album *Magic*. George W. Bush himself wrote little about Iraq in the 2007 section of his memoir *Decision Points* he later published. A huge gold-disk harvest moon is dropping into the sea, and it is getting dark. You forget when you have been overseas for a while how beautiful the United States can be, as old BBC hand Alistair Cooke always used to be saying on the radio, this county is always new, always renewing itself. The mauve skydust has gone, there is just moonlight over the sea. The moon shines over a bitterly divided country, the beach divides the sea from the land, the Iraq War divides the people.

More numbers are called, at an increasing rate, and the line thins and shortens. There cannot be many tickets left. Numbers, the lifeblood of society here, they are running out, like blood from a wound. It feels as though I am not going to be lucky and the man calling his friend was worrying. It is like shooting craps, the bets that matter always go wrong. Dije has got lucky and got in, she runs fast past the security man.

'Bruce is up.'

He is no longer, zero, but the One, the Man, as Ms Padel explains. The teacher knows, somehow, by extrasensory perception, what our ears are about to tell us. On the shore we had been playing the numbers and 'Newsboy' Moriarty, the Numbers mobster, would have been proud of us all. His ghost had walked on the sands. Or his skeleton a walking zombie, the white bones rattling together a little, the wind blowing sand into the joints and ligaments.

Pause for a Plato Ad

It's what happens here (commercials screw up key moments).

Some numbers.[†] Numbers in New Jersey:

Population: 8,685,920 (about)
Per year: 380 murders (about)
                 1,050 rapes
                 12,549 robberies
                 14,622 aggravated assaults
                 37,482 burglaries
                 21,953 vehicle thefts
                 Average median household income: $69,669 (not bad)

There is a single drum roll, and then the old theatre becomes a giant stranded music box on the Jersey sand. The E Street Band is alive again, the Jersey Orpheus has returned to where he was born to draw strength from his native soil. The walls seem to pucker and shake and a couple of beautiful girls in bike leathers start to dance on the sand as the previewed number 'Magic' booms out. They make long, elegant, waving, shape-making arms, weaving the air in the dying light. The sound is powerful, coherent, rolling like a great wave towards the north Jersey Shore. There are no birth pangs. The

---

† Number preceded Plato; the Shore mathematics preceded him in ancient Ionia; number can get you in the Cave and out again (even Number 19757). 'Pythagoras was the first to draw triangles and polygons—and to teach men to abstain from eating living things' Fragment19160-62, Pfeiffer.

new album is alive, the E Street Band after so many thousands of concerts and times on the road is still there, still as good as it ever was. Rebirth zings death. The tribe, the *ethnos*, the Springsteen Nation, mythical descendants of the Lenape, has reassembled in Jersey, on the fabled shore, the tribe is very happy. They are free, outside the Cave of the Theatre. The last few tickets are drawn, my 757 is not one. My wristband feels like a handcuff. I am in Cell 757, about to be charged with unPennsylvanian activity, and being just a ticketless displaced person. The doors are shut, like the screen doors hiding the Orthodox priest in the liturgy.

The road to salvation through rock and roll is closed, as if by a great boulder blocking a tunnel. There is only sound not vision. The gaze man has been castrated and blood is running down his legs. This felt inevitable. This is a nation founded on the principles of ruthless competition. I am a loser. Others are winners, they have the sound and the gaze. I only have the sound, but the sound is intoxicating. Then a security man looms. He is a black muscle vest, Mob-style, biceps fed on protein enhancers, smells of cheap cigars, sweat. A small rather girlie Virgin, in her case a mere three inches tall, is living tattooed on his forearm. I have the gaze on her Holy Image. Her nine foot spiritual sister has long vanished into yesterday's newspaper. But maybe she is still on my side somewhere out there.

'You the British Prof?'

'Yes.'

'Hang out.'

He nods at the leaping man clearing the fence onto the shore near the salt water taffy stall. Behind him is the lady who didn't know who made Yale locks. He nods at her.

'Lines of Penn shite. They work with the scalpers.'

How all this relates is not clear to me, even if the shrine guardians knew. Why should the Pennsylvania Republicans who don't like Bruce work with the scalpers? I was missing what William S. Burroughs calls the frozen moment when you see what is on the end of your fork. I clearly didn't know the math, not the quantum theory or the construction of number sets between the sad dipstick Penns or the recondite mathematics of stacks and the agents of the capitalist market, boozed and pee-sodden on derivatives like a wino on cheap plonk. Maybe I need to read more science fiction or attend some kind of introductory course in the Princeton maths faculty building to cope with daily life in Bush's America. An ill-equipped immigrant in this strange but beautiful landscape and ruthless Jersey society, a stranger to the number magic; it mystifies me. Or maybe I'm too old to cope with Republican America? But I had a protector. Protection in this state is very useful, more than useful, vital. Protection can help you fight back against the mobsters' market mechanisms and the scalper mafia and Scaife's mini-Mob controlling Pure Gaze onto the Band.

In the nineteenth-century lemon groves around Palermo, where the Mob's founding fathers came from, a protector would see that your lemons were not stolen. Who were these fence leaping arseholes, clearing off fast? They were from the Pennsylvania group. Why is everyone from there such a problem? W.C. Fields went to Philadelphia and reported that it was closed' maybe other things in that state should follow. Perhaps the whole state should be closed altogether, and partitioned. Historians would study the Partition of Pennsylvania like Poland in the eighteenth century between its neighbours. Jersey could do with a bit more land and room. That great writer and chronicler of the modern American condition Hunter S. Thompson had a bad time in Pennsylvania, living at a place called, ironically enough, Jersey Shore. It was a bleak, hideous place with coal dust in the air, and no women in the town who were worth looking at, and the author of *Fear and Loathing in Las Vegas* fled when a disastrous date with his editor's daughter ended with the boss's car being destroyed by a tractor. So much for that Pennsylvanian Jersey Shore, it is a lot better here in the genuine Ice Age state breathing glorious Atlantic ozone.

The old theatre is becoming a prison for our hopes, but we willing convicts are outside, just like the prisoners in Plato, chained, living a half-life outside on the sand, ghosts, our shadows on the convention hall wall. The doors stay closed, the music washes over us. I can make out some words. 'A long road home'. There must be a song called that in the new collection. The long road home is what every grunt takes—that has been said since Atlanta, since Gettysburg. That would be an Iraq song. Then the side door opens, a friendly pull on the arm. You get treated appallingly by the system, then someone really nice helps you.

'You'll make the last few songs.'

The protector has protected. Who was he really? He is my secret agent, my Continental Op., but chained in New Jersey. He has dark eyes, long sideburns, hair gel, he looks very Italian. Why was he helpful? I think of Burroughs again, perhaps he was really the Exterminator, but escaped from New York and is hiding in Jersey. I need the music, I do not need these paranoid people stopping me getting a ticket. It is time to get nearer the Band and the singer and perhaps the meaning of the songs. Do Springsteen's songs have meaning? Or are they ways to open doors to understand this strange fertile endlessly alive state of NJ?

A couple of hay bales sit incongruously across the theatre lobby floor, an Appalachian touch. There is even a spaced out fat woman in a lumberjack shirt sitting on them, out of central casting for a Woody Guthrie film. She wears men's braces; it would be exhausting to be with a woman of that size. And there are more and more of them in NJ, wobbling and navigating the streets like overloaded barges. (Except barges don't eat crisps.) It has all been too much for her, she cannot take the gaze onto the Boss. The Boss cannot help her with her obesity crisis.

In a haze, the last three or four songs are rushed, there is only the real magic gaze onto the Band, so reassuringly familiar, so dynamic, and indeed Mighty Max Weinberg is there on his drums driving the night forward towards the light of day. It is a sound of unbelievable polish and solidity, more fitted to the last concert of a tour than the first. I hardly seem to be there before the hundreds stream out, before there is just the driving sound, Bruce at his most remote and most approachable almost simultaneously, a strangely improvised and half empty stage, poised above the sea, between time and space, earth and sea, relatively, E=MC squared, Bruce = Music, round and squared. That's how it was when the tour was born, 2007 September now years gone, when it was humid at Hightstown, the Canada geese hung out pecking grass near the Plasma Physics laboratory, the MS-13 boss got lifted, the cocaine lay hidden under the woodpile, and we watched the dolphins come up near the beach at Cape May. Like Mr Scott Fitzgerald returning to Princeton to recapture a lost part of himself, so Mr Springsteen does the same at Asbury Park, a little of his youth perhaps, but also the hope, the innocence. It was always like this; as he writes in his autobiography, when he returned to Jersey after his first band had made a small mark in California, it was returning home:

> How sweet it is. We trucked back into New Jersey as conquering heroes... we'd put Jersey, the butt of so many hack comedians one-liners, onto the rock and roll map.

It was a small, focussed world, that of the Springsteen childhood and adolescence, hardly leaving Central New Jersey. Exile from Jersey meant a journey but always a return.

It is time to come back to the Princeton apartment. I am booked in for gin and tonic with the sweet man who is one of the greatest living historians and likes his Gordons in Aristotelian moderation. That will mean back to the Turnpike, across fair and fertile Monmouth County with its space age headquarters buildings of Big Pharma looking like one headquarters of the CIA after another. There in 1774 the British redcoats were defeated and afterwards George Washington began to unite the new nation. The Turnpike is not far away from Asbury Park, just an hour. Or less. And nobody else has ever written as many songs about driving as Bruce Springsteen. But first there is the City of Ruins, we have to cross the City, back from the shore.

City of Ruins: A Utopia a Long Time Ago

The Boss observed at this time (1 November 2007, three weeks before, to be exact) in *Rolling Stone* magazine (and if it is written in *Rolling Stone,* it must be true):

> It was part of what I was imagining from the very beginning, just because I got a tremendous inspiration and a sense of place from

the performers who had imagined it before me. It was something I wanted to take a swing at, what thrilled and excited me. For me, I started with what I had. I walked down to the boardwalk about a hundred yards from here, and I looked into a little knickknack shop. There was a rack of postcards, and I pulled one out that said GREETINGS FROM ASBURY PARK. I said 'That's my album cover. This is my place'.

What is the history of this place? Does a boardwalk have history? Bruce Springsteen as a subject of history clearly has an identity that is very closely linked to Asbury Park, but what does that really mean?

What happened here anyway? Why was Asbury Park ruined? There are many opinions. As Dan Wolff writes, Asbury Park, too, was Paradise once, compared to the grimy places in New York most of its visitors came from. In acts of collective vandalism, some buildings mentioned in classic Springsteen lyrics, like the Palace amusement hall in the line 'Beyond the Palace' in 'Born to Run' have already been destroyed or torn down, as people say here. Torn down. I don't like the idiom. Can the history help?

New Jersey has had so many temporary Paradises. The first was of virtuous and Christian labour. A traveller in 1765 near the end of the colonial era described this part of Monmouth County thus, an image of lowland Scotland many of the inhabitants had only recently left.

It contains the villages of Shrewsbury, Middletown, Freehold and Allen-town: the courts are for county business and they are held at Freehold. The lands in Shrewsbury, Middletown, and part of Freehold, are mostly remarkably good; they raise grain, beef, sheep, butter, cheese and other produce for the New York market... the houses for worship in this county are, Presbyteries six, Episcopalians four, Quakers three, Baptists four.

But the values of the big city to the north began to intrude, and still do, so that it is a common view of Jersey people that half their difficulties are caused by the export of modern problems from New York City. There are certain facts that are beyond dispute. The northern New Jersey Shore boomed, in the modern sense, as a result of railway construction, but Asbury Park, unlike Atlantic City, did not depend on the railroad for its origins. In neighbouring Long Branch, now a single suburban sprawl conurbation on the shore, a few boarding houses began to be constructed in the late eighteenth century, after 1788, and guests arrived by stagecoach or pony and trap. It was a summer retreat for Philadelphians who brought with them the repressive Blue Laws that forbade drinking and dancing and insisted on daily religious meetings for holidaymakers. Thirty years later, ocean bathing was beginning to become popular but it was strictly segregated by sex, with a white flag run up when ladies might bathe, and a red flag at the men's time. The phallus was seen as dangerous.

Later in the nineteenth century the beach laws changed yet again, so that a woman could not go into the sea without a male escort. As a 1930s book pointed out, gigolos first appeared on the shore then, not only as potential dancing or sexual partners, but as bathing escorts. The Blue Laws had collapsed by about 1840, mainly under the influence of an influx of ever-hedonistic and more tolerant New Yorkers reducing Philadelphia's puritanical and moralistic cultural influence, and dancing halls, gambling dens and brothels were soon flourishing. By the 1850s, Long Branch was a rival of Saratoga Springs. A race track opened in 1870, and the railway came in 1874, bringing a long boom with it.

Asbury Park during all these early times was more or less an uncounted, unnumbered marsh and sand dune wilderness, and nature was uncorrupted by the rampant pleasure seeking of nearby Long Branch. In image, Long Branch has always been cool, cool, very cool, life in a stylish refrigerator. Now it is an open and slightly strange but charming shore settlement with some rundown areas of long straight streets with rather too many Empty Store to Let signs and a Portuguese working-class flavour. The Iberians came for the fishing, as they have done all along the north-east coast of the United States and Canada; there is even a Portuguese language bookstore and you can buy the

Lisbon papers. The wit Dorothy Parker was born here, like Bruce Springsteen. Long Branch was where the baby with That Voice first breathed.

In the 1880s and 1890s boom years, Long Branch was the capital of the fast living rich, with Lillie Langtry keeping her car here for the summer, and the Guggenheims built a vast, sprawling neo-Gothic mansion in the high Pullman style. Worthies liked to have their vehicles illuminated on the inside, so the poor could enjoy watching their wealth and style. The poor were permitted the gaze, while the rich enjoyed a guiltless celebratory ride through them. Fashionable authors like Robert Louis Stevenson lived there, as he was preparing his last journey to the South Seas to escape the ravages of tuberculosis.

Long Branch also achieved notoriety when President James Garfield died there in 1881 after his attempted assassination. The ailing president with a bullet lodged in him was brought by special train from Washington DC to die in his grand summer house on the shore. He duly did. Nearby, at little (but rich) Deal, is the Church of the Presidents, a strange little building a quarter of a mile from the sea in the style of a Scandinavian rural fort. A humpty dumpty tower sticks up from walls with decorations that look like something from a William Morris wallpaper. It has survived because it is far enough back from what can be a cruel and violent sea. At last there is some money from a Federal programme to restore it to its early fine state, and it is well worth a detour to see it.

The seaside Ocean Drive is the third road in Long Branch with that name, the first two having been destroyed in storms, and in its early days the resort stretched more than a mile further into the sea, land which is now covered in water. No fewer than seven presidents worshipped there in the town's heyday, including Ulysses S. Grant and Woodrow Wilson himself, so it is a numerate church, one of the Seven Wonders of New Jersey. Young bloods indulged in viciously dangerous driving races along the hard sand, the beginning of motor racing in the United States. It is worth lingering a while in and near the suburb of Deal as some of the great summer houses of the late nineteenth- and early twentieth-century rich remain, with vast neo-classical porticos and endless wide lawns, supremely self-confident, redolent of the robber baron stage of American capitalism.

Architecturally, as an old guide to the area points out, they vary from the 'merely gaudy to the noisily hideous'. Many stand near Whale Creek, a silly little river that trundles gently into the sea, but the name reminds the visitor of the eighteenth-century boom in that bloody industry that flourished then along the Jersey coastline. The only concession of the rich in the early days was that although the Deal beach was theoretically private, it was cheap for the white skinned public to get a ticket to sit on it, unlike many neighbouring shore resorts in those days. This world does not find its way directly into Springsteen's songs very much; it had largely disappeared as a result of the Depression by the time he was born there. There is a lot of Jersey and American history in Springsteen's lyrics, but it is not always upfront or obvious. The 'ruins' that come into many songs, directly and indirectly, are the ruins of popular life, shut factories, grass between rail-lines where no trains run, burnt out old automobiles, boarded up shops. The time when the very rich made the shore their summer home and playground had by 1940 passed into history. The sea anywhere near Newark Estuary was grossly polluted by polychlorinated biphenyls (PCBs) left from wartime industries. The Boss was a 1950s child.

The 1930s guide that comments critically on the architecture also notes the number of For Sale and To Let signs in the vicinity then, a very contemporary echo of the sub-prime crisis. Other 1950s children who came like the Greek-American writer Nicholas Gage evoked the last of the old days in his memoir *A Place for Us*: 'In 1958 before the days of race riots, drugs, and protest movements, Ocean City was the perfect American family resort. Liquor was prohibited on the island, and there was a strong Christian emphasis, bolstered by many churches.' It was the world Bruce Springsteen saw as a little boy when he was being taken to the seaside.

Asbury Park: The Dialectic of Virtue and Vice

Nobody has bothered much about Virtue on the shore here recently; money and power is all. But in little Asbury Park, Springsteen's mythical home, Virtue was at first doing the driving. The first urban developer was the temperance activist and New York business magnate James A. Bradley, who set up the resort on a strictly moral basis. Like all previous and numerous successive attempts to bring rigid morality to the Jersey Shore (or anywhere else in the state), it did not last long, and its heyday as a holiday place for the virtuous was short-lived. Ocean Grove next down the coast was more successful for Virtue. Founded in 1869 as a Methodist summer camp, it remained a closed and gated community until World War II, banning bathing and secular business on the Sabbath. Holidaymakers were expected to attend open air church services at 6pm on Sundays throughout the summer season. The lake there is still called Wesley Lake. In the last week in August vast conversion meetings were held, with penitent sinners and converts to Methodism hearing lengthy calls to repentance and a new life, and then tens of thousands of believers took part in the 'Jerusalem march' around the district, singing hymns and waving banners.

At one level, this would not be that many people's idea of a holiday these days, but cultural traditions often do not die but go underground for a while, and emerge transformed. Springsteen's lyrics have inherited some of this evangelical enthusiasm, for social awareness and the possibility of new life, of beginning again and belief in the power of music to bring about social and personal change. 'Is there anyone alive out there?' is his fervent call, but this is also to look into the heart of the nineteenth-century Shore evangelists, or, as in the E Street Band's New York concert at Madison Square Garden in 1995, a call to revive rock and roll as such, and rescue that musical faith from its detractors. Those puzzled by the fanaticism of many Springsteen fans should reflect on this past inheritance. The notion of reunion on the Shore was central to the nineteenth- and twentieth-century revivalists, often the reunion of scattered families, and so every opening of a tour is a revival of the mythic extended family of the Band and its fans—and the ruins certainly need revivalists and revival.

The ever excellent *Trentonian* newspaper recorded our struggles dryly on the following day: 'Several generations of fans gathered in warm sunshine on the boardwalk outside the hall hours before the show. Those without tickets hoped to be included in the group traditionally given last minute admission.' Perceptively, the paper went on to say, "the hall isn't far from the clubs—many now closed—where Springsteen and his band rose to fame in the 1970s.'

Some parts of Asbury Park still look as if they have been through a war. Our war was against the scalpers, Scaife's people and the Penn lines of shite, but others have fought there before. At the south end of the long beach, the collapsed roof of the old 1920s boomtown Casino dominates the landscape and seascape, while on the west side there are wrecked skeletons of buildings that would not have looked out of place in Sarajevo in the Bosnian conflict and half-built hulks and steel building skeletons. In the centre was an apartment block tower, unfinished since the developer went bust several years ago, but now under construction again. The Palace amusement complex was partly demolished in 2004, the palace of the Beyond the Palace line in 'Born to Run'. Only the picture of Tillie the Clown on the wall was saved. This town has a unique capacity to devour itself and its history. Is this what the song 'Born to Run' is really about?

> *Oh baby, this town rips the bones from your back*
> *It's a death trap, it's a suicide rap*
> *We gotta get out while we're young*
> *'Cause tramps like us baby, we were born to run*

A lot happens in this song or it would not have had the hold on millions of imaginations that it has had. On one level, it was immediately trivialized and commodified, just like 'Born in the USA' was taken up, absurdly, as a political anthem in the Reagan period. 'Born to Run' was seen at first by many people as the hymn to the jogging age, or as a hymn to driving.

This is understandable in a society based on commodity, but obscures the truth. The final verse says it all but in terms of a hidden tradition:

> *The highway's jammed with broken heroes*
> *On a last chance power drive*
> *Everybody's out on the run tonight*
> *But there's no place to hide*
> *Together, Wendy, we can live with the sadness,*
> *I'll love you with all the madness in my soul*
> *Oh, someday, girl, I don't know when,*
> *We're gonna get to that place where we*
> *Really wanna go, and we'll walk in the sun.*
> *But till then, tramps like us, baby we were born to run*

Why does all this seem familiar?

Remember the cave. The Platonic prisoners are out on the run, they have a lot do to get to the sun, and enlightenment.

Behind 'Born to Run' there is the anguish and hope of so many pioneers who faced every known and many unknown hazards to build America, and find human love and affirmation in that process. In some ways, you still have to be a pioneer in New Jersey or New York, however urbanized, however comfortable the lifestyle. Nothing more illustrates the trivialization of the original media response to this song than that some people made it a hymn to jogging. Who were Springsteen's forebears with this lyric? Exactly seventy-five years before the Boss was born, the Western novelist Zane Grey was born in Zanesville, Ohio, in 1872. His cowboy novels helped form the very image of the Old West, along with the novels of Jersey-born James Fenimore Cooper. In the most famous Zane Grey book (and President Eisenhower's favourite) *Riders of the Purple Sage,* his hero Lassiter also needs to leave town and find love, while his heroine Jane Withersteen is trying to work out how to relate to and capture the man she loves, and come to terms with the harsh masculine values of his society. In the finale, Grey writes

All of life, of use in the world, of hope in heaven cantered in Lassiter's ride with little Fay to safety. She would have tried to turn the iron-jawed brute she rode; she would have given herself to that relentless, dark-browed Tull. But she knew Lassiter would turn on her, so she rode on and on.

Whether that run was of moments or hours Jane Withersteen could not tell. Lassiter's horse covered her with froth that blew back in white streams. Both horses ran their limit, were allowed to slow down in time to save them, and went on dripping, heaving, staggering.

'Oh Lassiter, we must run-we must run!'

He looked back, saying nothing.

Descended from Jane Lassiter in the twentieth century stand many Springsteen heroines, from Mary in **Thunder Road**, who has to make the fateful decision about whether to get in the waiting car, to Wendy in 'Born to Run', who will have to accept a life of continual pursuit and escape as she goes along. Jane has to run with an iron-jawed brute of a horse, Wendy has to wrap her legs and strap her hands around a scared and lonely rider, as Lassiter undoubtedly was in backwoods Utah. Although Springsteen's songs are deeply grounded in New Jersey, they have, at their best, an epic simplicity and reference, but this is not only because of his genius but also because he stands in the direct line of popular American fiction, where the songs about driving are descended from the massive literature of the Old West about riding. The sense of danger and uncertainty in urban Jersey is an echo of the dangers of the journeys of the Frontier. Springsteen's songs are full of frontiers that have to be crossed, or dangers met, as he writes in 'The Promised Land', and overcome with faith and fortitude:

There's a dark cloud rising from the desert floor
I packed my bags and I'm heading straight into the storm
Gonna be a twister to blow everything down
That ain't got the faith to stand its ground

Standing your ground is an important motif in Springsteen's writing and occurs again and again. Tony Soprano stands his ground against the Feds every time he drives his black SUV into the Turnpike toll and heads home down Route 1, cigar firmly locked in his mouth. We admire his strength and integrity, thug though he is, for standing up to the oppressive state. The ordinary man often finds it difficult to cope with America, the demands America can make on its citizens, the tough decisions that often have to be made. To live a moral life, it is important not to be browbeaten by the authorities, never to lose your sense of your rights and dignities as an individual citizen. But the United States is a vast and sometimes unforgiving country, and even the most socially integrated often have to take these decisions and face the consequences in circumstances as lonely as the old cowpunchers in vast empty Wild West landscapes.

Dark stories are told about the Asbury Park developers. There was a vigil outside the Palace to try to prevent its demolition, but the citizens had not got the $2.5 million needed to buy the 1888 vintage building. It was torn down, it fell. This is New Jersey, where money and power are more or less the same thing most of the time; only the strong buildings may survive, but there is no guarantee that they will do so. Mysterious fires have swept through old buildings in the middle of the night. The word on the street at one time was that the Mob in Atlantic City did not wish to see a revival of Asbury Park, particularly its old casinos. On the establishment side of the tracks, *The Wall Street Journal* reported with its usual accuracy in 2004 that

> Asbury Park has taken a long slide from its glory days. A 1970 race riot produced heavy property damage and led many white residents to flee. In subsequent years, while day trippers flocked to the city's honky-tonk amusements and clubs, individuals discharged from mental health institutions moved into some of its aging housing stock.

In fact what happened was maybe slightly simpler, and less to do with race or the mentally ill. A 1980s development scheme just hit the buffers when the company ran out of cash and all local revenue sources from the property development stopped. There was no money for the City Council to pay teachers and nurses, mow grass or mend the holes in the roads. The plans of developer Hugh Lamle had shown some results, but there is a way to go, and it remains to be seen what the effects of plummeting property prices and sub-prime and banking crises will be. There is now life among the ruins, and some of the worst eyesores have gone, but many of the ruins are still there, like the Casino's poetic orientalist carousel pavilion, a fantasy of eastern promise of world power for the 1920s masses, a poem in wrought iron and glass and mild decadence. The years since 2004 and the beginning of the new development phase have been ones of continual bitter struggle between local people and the developers, so that in 2007, long and ultimately unsuccessful campaigns were waged by Asbury Park Historical Society to save the gloriously ornate Metropolitan Hotel and the equally distinguished Elks Lodge. Most Asbury Park developers have little vision and no sense of history, and see the future only in terms of mass market housing. There is every chance that the early optimism of the boom years will vanish as

ASBURY PARK ELKS' LODGE   B. P. O. E. NO. 128, ASBURY PARK, N.J.

SAVE THE ELKS' LODGE

recession looms and the sea pounds the new boardwalk, perhaps the most sincere and genuine achievement so far of the revival process.

Yet in the music the magic still remains. The Stone Pony is the most famous club, a strange single-storey white building that looks as though it may have come in pieces on a truck to be assembled on the spot. It is warm, welcoming, with ever changing bands and a place where the famous, including the Boss himself, can mingle and mix and sometimes jam to do a good turn to raise money for a local hospital or school.

But to understand more it is necessary to take the road. The road in the United States is unforgiving, but generous with its knowledge. To find a Utopia, a local Paradise, there is no alternative to taking it. Whether the Paradise is likely to be temporary or long lasting is difficult to evaluate. Or perhaps they are mirages, images from a lost and foundering American Dream, like unfortunate President James Garfield wandering lonely on the shore but in good health in hearty old age without a fatal bullet plugged into him. The Jersey road leads to some different places, some known, some little known. Turn on the car radio to a good rock station and think about them, sit, relax at the wheel. Some of the places will hardly seem worth visiting, but they have interesting history and may illuminate the music of Bruce Springsteen and the E Street Band. Some may not. Some songs have places mentioned in them, some don't, but they all have history, real history in a tangible place, probably of no interest to the Pharisees and Sadducees thinking of a global history where small places and geographical realities are unimportant. Hang in there, reader, you have protection, you have a Boss, that's what matters. In terms of ontology, the theory of knowledge, the Boss is there, his music is there, even if it is a wild and stormy night and the sea is beating against the seawall, and these words, they will spin and talk with the tyres on a great throbbing Turnpike rig with thirty-two wheels, EZ Pass in place and all fully tarped, ready to cross many state lines. Nearby is Newark. Newark is a music city and tells its stories to the visitor.

4
ARE THERE
OTHER CAVES
IN NEW JERSEY?

*Concerning Freehold, New Jersey, a town for a rock
star youth and little Porkopolis*

The Spine in the Seat

In New Jersey, in all central states, is the motorcar interior a cave? A place of imprisoned people? The fire is in the engine, but does it cast light? Is the driver a slave?

Little Fort Lee is the last place where you can leave the Turnpike on the way from Newark into New York City across the Hudson River on George Washington Bridge. The great city is behind you, or perhaps it is not. Newark waits on the shore to the south. Fort Lee has not found its way into any Springsteen song. Maybe the Boss visited it as a little boy, his head full of seeing Elvis on the *Ed Sullivan Show*, aged seven. Or maybe he didn't. There is a good Barnes & Noble nearby and some old warehouses now transformed into trendy condos for those who like the other side of the Hudson with a stunning view of Manhattan. It is a thoroughly decent place, Barnes & Noble do good book launches but nobody much seems to come to them. Fort Lee citizens seem to buy only books about cigar smoking and trotting racing. That's how it is near the spine. The Turnpike is there, grey, indifferent, dangerous and elusive; like the groundhog it lives near the runway at the airport and keeps away from the jet wheels.

The Turnpike is the spine. The spine has vertebrae, the exit points where sweeping coils of access roads feed onto the motorway. Other less important bones are attached to the spine. The tale of the Turnpike is also a tale of two cities. At one end is New York City, the capital of business and commerce, and the south track leads down to Washington DC, the capital of politics. It runs north to south through the state and at the top end of it is New York City; the southern terminus lies by the bridge into the little state of Delaware and then dipping further south to Maryland and the capital in Washington DC.

The New Jersey Turnpike is a road that can only be understood as an obsession. Road building in the United States in the twentieth century became an obsession intimately linked to world power and war. The main interstate highways were originally constructed as a response to the crises in World War I transport when the mass of munitions and stores to keep over a million men in Europe could not be moved on existing nineteenth-century roads. The roads out of New York all have their symbolisms. Pulaski Skyway is the road or rather bridge of the New Deal, looping as a bending arch in the sky and finding a way first to cross the marshes that blocked the way south from New York. Under the still breath-taking view it takes Route 1 south over stinking mud, the ghosts of thousands of eighteenth century pigs and fictional cadavers of people who got on the wrong side of Tony Soprano and his crew. Just away from the highway is little Secaucus, no myth of the Pork Store here, but real Pork.

Porkopolis

Modern Secaucus was once pig town, Porkopolis. This working-class Hudson County town south of Fort Lee was Pig City, where New York made its pork, the herds of nineteenth-century swine wallowing in the Jersey salt marshes. River valleys small and large that dissect the Jersey Shore sighted by the early Basque cod fishermen made safe havens from the Atlantic storms. In their deep mud banks, the first pigs to live in New Amsterdam rooted, dug and messed and just over the state line Porkopolis was made; this was in the middle settlement time, when real farming to feed a city began. There was a certainty of pork arriving in Manhattan. It was a predominantly Irish immigrant occupation, and little villages grew up on the higher dry hummocks in the Secausus marshes, like Kearny, all with more or less Irish names. Kearny is now a solid little working town and famous as a location in *The Sopranos*. But even in the television show, pork is present in Kearny. The fictional Sopranoland porcine joint of Satriale's Pork Store was in Kearny, before actor James Gandolfini drove his SUV into its doors for the last time. Later there were other Porkopoles in the United States until the last and biggest, Cincinnati Ohio, the smelliest city in the world, according to one nineteenth-century traveller, where tallow was made from pork fat. Millions of pigs a year walked into Cincinnati one side and rode out as dead bacon the other, travelling east and west, hung on a comfortable meat hook.

It is a commonplace for non-Jersey folk not to ask where you live, but at which exit of the road you take to get there. For many of them, it is all New Jersey is. It was built mostly by the same Corps of US Army Engineers that had dammed, bulldozed and steel podded hundreds of roads and buildings across the world during World War II, and in some ways it has the same spirit, of limitless ambition, superb technical capacity and unlimited belief in progress and technology. The Turnpike is the ultimate positivist highway. It is also a monument to the arrival of the automobile as the central symbol of the US manufacturing economy, and car as the means of transport, based on the opening up of the oilfields of Saudi Arabia under US control through ARAMCO, the Arabian-American Oil Company. The Turnpike is a hard power road.

It is not for nothing that *The Sopranos* TV show always opens with Tony chomping on his cigar as he hits the Turnpike driving south out of the big city as the viewer sees those unmistakable signs to the Turnpike and always feels the same sense of excitement. Tony is a man, so he is man. Soprano is riding home, on the corridor of world power, to his family in safe New Jersey, out of the anarchy, violence and ruthless competition in the Lower West Side garbage protection business. In reality New Jersey is not safe for him, for as hundreds of episodes demonstrate, he can never escape the conflicts from New York City or from his past, any more than the most honest and conventional suburban commuter can find purity down among the trees and well brought up children of Teaneck or the other places where Philip Roth sets his novels. But they try. When Bruce Springsteen was a little boy in Freehold in Monmouth County, thirty or so miles east of the new road, it was under construction, and all that concerned the citizens of Freehold about it was that it had been decided that it was not going to Freehold and to be extended to the coast. The Turnpike marooned Freehold.

What sort of a world did the little Bruce Springsteen see? Monmouth County was rich farmland, had one of the highest farm incomes in the whole United States and had grown crops to feed New York ever since Freehold was established in the early eighteenth century by religious

dissident Scots. Potatoes were then the prize crop, the Freehold White Giant spud. Freehold became a minor manufacturing town after industrialism began, and the local carpet and rug factory and the Nestle plant were the main employers. Tourists came to visit the famous racetrack, which was opened in 1873, and to watch the trotting races in splendid loud bookmakers check suits. But Freehold remained small, and Springsteen was and remains in some ways a small town boy. The 1930s population of about 7,000 people had swelled to maybe 11,000 by the early 1950s. The economy was strong and car ownership was booming, opening new horizons for all.

Civic pride was also strong. There was a fine late eighteenth-century core of public buildings, dominated by the enormous neo-classical county archive, the Hall of Records, still there today. As the county seat, at a time when counties still mattered, there was a small government office, and

Freehold was known for its uniform prosperity. It was also conservative, in the widest sense, with a very settled and mildly prosperous merchant elite and prosperous doctors, lawyers and land surveyors who were the Good Ol' Boys, back-scratching, often provincial and inward looking and very sure, after the triumphs of World War II, of the American place in the world and within that New Jersey's place in America. The richest lived on their estates around the outskirts, where there was room to swing a horse. The substantial black population that had arrived in the inter-war period and after were cramped into a segregated area near the railway, while white Middle America dominated the rest of Freehold. Their rows of white clapboard houses contained rooms full of late Victorian china and knickknacks, and books about Herbert Hoover and Calvin Coolidge, an awful lot of golf was played and freemasonry boomed. The Freehold elite was very pleased with itself, and the Official Record of worthies of the area is an endless catalogue of Illustrious Citizens, Skilled Managers, Leaders of Vision, Remarkable Entrepreneurs, Progressive Owners, Excellent Judges of Men who were Enterprising, Fair, Successful, Admired and Universally Popular. It was indeed the Promised Land (for Good Ol' Boys). The poor working-class area nicknamed 'Texas' off South Street where the Springsteen family lived was a place of newcomers, often, like Bruce's father, refugees from the Depression in the Appalachians and the collapse of the old mining- and timber-based economy. It was not a bad place to live but in the rigid and stratified society of little Freehold, there was no way up. The house was all there was, as he sings in 'My Father's House':

> *My father's house shines hard and bright*
> *It stands like a beacon calling me in the night*
> *Calling and calling, so cold and alone*
> *Shining 'cross the dark highway where our sins lie unatoned*

The Springsteen family might have lived in a prosperous and generous and supportive community, but they were blue collar newcomers, nobodies, outsiders, compared to the Freehold Good Ol' Boys, some of whom could trace their ancestors back to the eighteenth-century years of New Jersey as a British colony. Father Douglas Springsteen was a tough mountain man from the Appalachians who had served loyally in World War II but found it hard to settle afterwards and was often unemployed. Mother Adele, with her Neapolitan coast roots in Italy was often the main breadwinner and she bought Bruce his first guitar for eighteen dollars. Isolation was the script of Springsteen's youth. The Springsteens lived in several different houses, starting off at 87 Randolph Street, just off South Street, where he was a baby. The move to South Street itself came later. Douglas Springsteen never fitted in, and when he departed to California he thought at least Freehold would not have him to kick around anymore. Religion was a background factor. Most of the old town establishment were Protestants of one sort or another, along with a very few Jews. Hardly anybody mentioned as prominent citizens of Freehold or the Shore nearby in the late 1940s was a Roman Catholic, whereas Bruce had been an altar boy. Religion is important in the United States. Roman Catholicism can be a recipe for alienation and dissidence if you live outside the working-class Catholic big city areas founded by Irish, Italian and Polish families. Yet the days of effortless Good Ol' Boy supremacy were soon to be over, and their town that seemed so prosperous and successful when the Boss was a little boy was soon to change. The grinding poverty of his childhood come out forcibly in his autobiography, the world where the dentist cannot be afforded and treatment is a piece of string tied to a door knob. As he grew up, jobs became harder and harder to come by, traditional US manufacturing was under siege, and the Shore economy was in decline as automobile ownership made holiday rail travel to the Shore unfashionable. Florida was brought nearer by mass air travel. Ominously, race relations deteriorated, as blacks who had moved into Jersey twenty years before found themselves with nothing to do, and the future suddenly looked insecure. In 1984, looking back, Bruce sang in 'My Hometown' of a vicious race riot:

In '65 tensions was running high at my high school
There were lots of fights between black and white, there was
nothing you could do
Two cards at a light, on a Saturday night; in the back seat
there was a gun
Words were passed in a shotgun blast, troubled times had
come...

The ideal small town harmony of the 1950s in Freehold had been broken apart, the 1960s had arrived. The young teenage Springsteen was solitary, mostly interested in girls and playing his guitar. The struggle for his identity, guitar in hand, had begun. The school building at Freehold High School which Bruce attended still stands, a tidy respectable neo-Georgian brick structure with an impressive frontage and big playing fields and good facilities on the outskirts. Nowadays the newcomers are not from the Appalachians, but speak in the husky guttural Spanish of south Mexico and Guatemala far away. I stop and ask a couple of girls in impossibly tight jeans and much bling what they think of going to the same school as Bruce Springsteen. They giggle nervously and turn away. A boy comes in: 'Bruce? Yeah. He's made a lotta money. He lives in Colts Neck these days. Or Rumson. That's a gated town.'

In fact it is not, and Rumson is a friendly, open, if extraordinarily wealthy place, but it does not seem that way on the Freehold street, the world of 'Stultifying politeness and routine that covered corruption and decay'. There is not much hero worship; he might as well have been talking about the local plastic bucket millionaire. They are young, and Bruce is their fathers' age, and it is a long while since he played his first public performance in a trailer park off Route 34. They think Dad and his friends are interested in Bruce, the elderly Vietnam generation who knew that the eighteen-year-old Boss went to enlist and failed his physical and did not serve. Watching his sixty plus stage performances nowadays that seems hard to believe.

The Freehold school population has changed a good deal and now only thinks of rap and hip hop. There are not so many black people here as there were. With the end of the good economy in the 1960s they migrated down to find jobs nearer the shore. Some have even returned to jobs in the prosperous parts of the new South. The Mexicans have bought up their houses and live crammed in, as many as twenty people sometimes. So the school is full of Mexican kids. Freehold Conservatives see this Hispanic influx as the beginning of the Balkanization of the United States. How true could this be in Freehold? A mile or so away is the headquarters of the local Republican Party, there has just been a minor local poll, and there is a large photograph of the winner in the office window. There are also photographs of various cheerful and successful looking ladies who seem to run Freehold Republican things, all with broad smiles and many with Very Big Hair. This is at least a change from the days of the almanac of Jersey worthies, many of whom had almost no hair at all. Good Ol' Boys were often Bald Old Boys.

A walk to the pretty town hall, a replacement for one that burnt down in a great Freehold fire in 1873, certainly confirms that real progress has been made in many directions. There are the usual helpful leaflets telling citizens how to cope with the threat of foreclosure and the sub-prime mortgage crisis, as if 500 words could fix that for you, and information about what to do if somebody dies. But this is Freehold, and progressive Freehold and the surrounding county has one of the finest trash recycling operations in the entire United States. People from Pennsylvania could learn a lot here. Anyone with any doubt about this can consult a copy of the free sheet *Monmouth County Recycling Directory*, a real compendium of useful knowledge on the subject. It is printed on 100 per cent recycled newsprint produced at a New Jersey mill using 'post-consumer' newspapers and biodegradable soy-based inks. In it you can learn about the Municipal Leaf Composting Locations, the fact that County waste is 47 per cent paper and 15 per cent plastic, and many other things, such as the fact that tree stumps of greater than three inches diameter are banned from the landfill site.

Anyone with any doubt that the United States is and always was a Missionary country with an agenda to change the world for the better should read this humble publication. In it you can see how to build your indoor food composting facility (if you live in a condo) complete with devouring redworms (NOT earthworms), who are great guys and girls to have as tenants as they eat half their weight in food daily, have no fewer than five hearts and multiply quickly, each worm making 96 worms in six months. And the worms are classy. You order them from the Cape Cod worm farm … so it is not merely Two Hearts are Better than One, but Five Hearts are Better than One.

The revival of Freehold began fifteen or so years ago, when young professional couples with jobs in Newark or New York were attracted by the pretty and cheap houses and the quiet tree-lined streets. It is a complex place.

Seeking Springsteen in the cigar store is as unrewarding as at the school. A customer grumpily tells me that, 'He lived down South Street, that is where it was' before launching into a lengthy spiel on how he can't understand why Springsteen still lives in Jersey and not in California. In mainstream white working-class psychology here, New Jersey is a place you start, it is not a place you stay when you are a Big Success. I tell him that Bruce tried living for a time in California but it didn't work. Leaving it and bringing the E Street Band together again brought a magical revival in his music. The enigma of the story grows. Nobody is a prophet in their own country, of course, and in the mythical home of Asbury Park it is much easier to be a fan. On the seashore there is ambiguity and hope and transformation, while in Freehold there is the reality of low wages, a shortage of decent jobs and the yawning gulf between the prosperous college-educated and the rest. And most of all, there is the immigration problem. In the days when the fathers and mothers and grandfathers and grandmothers of the white working class arrived in America, everyone knew you had to speak and write good English to get a job, respect the flag, work hard, save and generally fit in. Nowadays there are as many signs in Spanish in some parts of Freehold as in English. Were the Past Days better days, if not Glory Days? I didn't get an answer and somebody asked me what people in England thought of Hillary Clinton. I didn't get a chance to answer either before a little old man in the corner cleaning out pipe dottle piped up: 'If Hillary got elected president, we'd go to Hell with the Jews driving.'

That was a clear enough viewpoint, if in politically incorrect language. It doesn't seem quite a harmonious Utopia, this Freehold, whatever the song says ... or perhaps not ... or perhaps the other side of Paradise ... ..

In town I pass Sal's grocery
The barbershop on South Street
I looked into their faces
They were all rank strangers to me
The veterans' hall high up on the hill
Stood silent and alone
The diner was shuttered and boarded
With a sign that just said 'Gone'

In this part of 'Long Walk Home', the masterly, heart rending and nostalgic keynote song of the *Magic* album, Springsteen captures the alienation of his youth, while later on he pictures his father's traditionalist patriotism:

My father said 'Son, we're
Lucky in this town
It's a beautiful place to be born
It just wraps its arms around you
Nobody crowds you, nobody goes it alone
You know that flag
Flying over the courthouse
Means certain things are set in stone
What we are, what we'll do
And what we won't'

The condition of Bush's America was that these simple certainties no longer existed in the era of the war on terrorism. People in Freehold and elsewhere were and remain disoriented, uncertain and worried about the future of their country, and Springsteen's writing and singing have embodied this mood and moved the original personal alienation and distance of his youth into a wider political and social critique.

It is particularly ironic that he grew up in Monmouth County, two centuries after the American Revolution, when in 1778 Freehold was fought over as part of the Battle of Monmouth, and British redcoat commanders lived along Main Street. The church was made into their military hospital and echoed with the screams of amputees. The colonial army was attacked by Colonel Butler's detachment of revolutionary militia, and dispersed the Queen's Rangers, a force of Tory troops. French General Lafayette then established his military hospital in Freehold after local residents had driven the retreating British from the town. There are non-political historic monuments of real quality, like the elegant St Peter's Episcopal Church in Throckmorton Street, which is one of the oldest churches in continuous use in New Jersey, dating from a building nearby constructed in 1783 by a Quaker group. In the Revolutionary War it was used by both sides, as a hospital by the British and an ammunition store by the Yankees. Although the Springsteen family lived in a place that in most contemporary eyes was nowhere much in status terms, in geography the little house off South Street was actually within two minutes' walk of one of the main thoroughfares of early American history. A Springsteen song is often an exploration of the American civic religion and what it means to believe in it. He is interested in the inner life of the American, what it means to believe in that flag. He is an outsider who has drifted into superstardom, and part of his integrity and charm is that he could drift right back again and sometimes, as on albums like *Nebraska* and songs like 'Tom Joad', seems to have done so already, singing back to us, his audience, from some remote place far from New Jersey that we do not know or see.

However conventionally non-academic Bruce Springsteen was, he soaked this up in his bones and spirit and it gave him his currently unique ability to speak for average Americans in his lyrics. Those who have done well since the Reagan years are antipathetic; they do not like being reminded of the world that has changed little on their doorstep, and above all, that most of their ancestors were thousands of miles away when the key events of the American Revolution were taking place. They have not heard of any Utopias let alone this one. It is time to turn on that car engine again. The political philosopher writes that freedom is the recognition of necessity. In New Jersey that means the car keys. They are limp little fellows, they hang from a key ring, but they are needed to start the time and number engine. It does start. Fuel, gasoline, is burning. It is a car engine on the end of an imperial chain stretching from South Street to the sands of Saudi Arabia, Kuwait, Iraq, so far away. *Kinesis* in Greek, *kinesis* means Motion. Bruce and the Band are kinetic.

5

ORPHEUS FROM HOBOKEN, THE PRODROMOS FROM NEWARK, HIS ESCAPE AND OTHER MATTERS

Concerning the world Frank Sinatra grew up in, his traditions, and the complexity of Newark, NJ

Newark is down across the Hudson River and was on edge. A headline on a recent piece by the fine NJ journalist Jessica Mazzola said Newark straddles the thin line between hope and homicide, and the mayor was calling for a peaceful twenty-four hours. That was this year; in fact six people died in various violent incidents in that period and the next two days. The Hudson River marks the boundary of New Jersey. The space of the other states in the Union opens out southwards. At Princeton, New Jersey, Albert Einstein abandoned Absolute Space and Time in 1929. The river is disinterested, indifferent to his calculations, his numbers beyond number. Broad and swirling and brown, it looks as though it ought sometimes to burst its banks but it does not. Over it the George Washington Bridge towers with a view that however many times someone has driven across it, they catch their breath with the buzz and excitement of being in America. It is always surprising, always new, always with gripping drama in the daily life of New York City.

Leaving New York, up the Hudson Parkway, it is less dramatic; the bridge suddenly arrives just before Harlem does with a difficult steep turn up from the Parkway. There is a choice of driving the lower level or the top level. The lower level is a brutalist dream, the poetry of iron and metal; the roar of the traffic and rush of the great rigs are like joining a vast mechanized army on the march, where the visitor is a simple auxiliary foot soldier. There is a little fear. There is always fear on the great highway as well as the excitement and anticipation. What would it be like to have a flat tyre or an engine breakdown? Would a big tarped rig on its way to Charleston or Atlanta, Georgia, veer towards you and run you down? The question seems dangerous to ask. The narcotic appeal of driving in the United States is as anywhere else but perhaps there without the intensity is the sense of possible imminent death; there is real danger on the big Jersey roads in anything but good dry weather. The car is the means of escaping New York City but can also be a way of leaving this world altogether.

On the right the road climbs towards Englewood, not so long ago very upmarket Jersey and very Italian, birthplace and home ground of singer Tony Bennett, jazz trumpeter Dizzy Gillespie and actor John Travolta, but now generally full of Korean-Americans and their banks, shops and restaurants. On the left before the Turnpike actually properly begins, there is a sign to Jersey City, and next to Jersey City is Hoboken. The Turnpike itself marches south, straight and utterly functional with the cranes of Elizabeth on the left, the huge IKEA and its beaten tarmac pathway. When it was built in a rush at the beginning of the Cold War the Turnpike was criticized as too straight, ugly, too functional and, above all, necessitating a drive through Jersey's landscape of industrial mess and some tough wastelands. It is an in-your-face road.

The 1930s Keynesian parkways of FDR had often been designed to skirt bad urban centres, and a drive on a parkway is a discreet and layered experience compared to the mighty Turnpike, which does not try to make Jersey better than it is, it tells the story how it is and costs the community several thousand road accidents a year, a toll sometimes like a small war. Environmentalists believe it is the road to perdition, a state global warming machine. In his autobiography Bruce writes eloquently about the guilt he feels about spending so much time in his youth driving cars. As Angus Gillespie and Michael Rockland, the historians of the Turnpike, observe, it was perhaps a pity that landscape architects were not included in the design team, but if they had been, the Turnpike would not be the Turnpike. But it is an old story. The French politician and political philosopher de Tocqueville observed in the nineteenth century that Americans usually 'prefer the useful to the beautiful', going back to the Puritans' dislike of arts and decoration, and without the Turnpike New Jersey would quickly grind to a gridlocked halt. The driver on the Turnpike is like a prisoner, a man or woman in a maze, part of the wider maze of New Jersey, a state with more roads per inhabitant than any other state in the Union. But visiting Hoboken is allowed and possible. A first tiny turn leads there.

Hoboken. It is a strange little name and like so many in and around the Hudson, comes from that of an original Dutch village. Hoboken has always been a vantage point, the place to make The Gaze at New York City. As a character in Jack Kerouac's *The Subterraneans* observes,

> Slim said it wasn't New York yet, jess the HOBOKEN SKYWAY he said, and pointed up ahead to show me New York. Well I jess could barely see a whole heap of walls and lanky steeples way, way off yonder and all cloudy inside the smoke... Well, how I told you how fearsome and grand New York was when I first seed it, and that aint all.

Hoboken is also a music heritage stop, in the awkward phrase of the New Jersey tourist promoters, for Frank Sinatra stemmed from here, born at 415 Monroe Street, and Sinatra is in his way one of the father figures of Springsteen in New Jersey, in Greek a *prodromos*, a forerunner, although the two hardly ever met. It was not particularly personal. Sinatra had his carefully nurtured dislike of most rock and roll starting with Elvis and the two at most levels had little in common. Sinatra was vehement in his dislike of the new rock scene, calling the new bands and performers of the late 1950s and early 1960s 'cretinous goons' and 'sideburn delinquents' on one occasion, and Elvis Presley a 'rancid smelling aphrodisiac'. Music where he grew up was the Italian tradition, lyric and affirmative and popular, and in some senses he stayed with it throughout his long musical life.

Hoboken was for most of its twentieth-century life after the later industrial revolution a chaotic, crowded and often insanitary mess of brownstones that became rat-infested, teeming and festering tenements after the original middle classes left for the suburbs. It had been very different in the mid-nineteenth century, when John Jacob Astor had built an enormous house in peaceful rural Hoboken, and the author Washington Irvine and other prominent New York City people had holiday homes there. But the glory days did not last long. The industrial revolution in the United States was born in many aspects in Jersey and the area soon became dominated by factories and workshops. Black people moved in after Reconstruction, a guarantee that many whites would soon move out. Social conditions were dire, and crime offered, like music, a quick way out for the successful. Sometimes, as with the Sinatra family, they went together. The authoritative but relentlessly positivist Federal Writers Project's *New Jersey, A Guide to its Present and Past*, produced in the 1930s, was tactful and euphemistic when it observed that Hoboken was the most crowded town in the United States, and that 'few of the stores show signs of rehabilitation'. In some ways Hoboken had never recovered its image since the terrible days when World War I began, when, as the most 'German' of all American cities apart from Cincinnati, the entire place was put under direct Federal control and secret service agents made mass arrests of suspected agents of the Kaiser.

Frank Sinatra was born in 1915, when the shore at River Road in Hoboken was still a wild, easy street of bars, brothels and, soon, speakeasies. It was always a troublesome area for the US Navy, and some scholars think the Shore Patrol in its modern form was invented to deal with runs onshore in Newark—ordinary service members who were temporarily turned into law enforcement and armed with a long stick baton. The patrols were meant to stop the sailors 'on liberty' from getting into trouble. That was, in the Jersey phrase, a tough sandwich. Frank Sinatra's later manicured image belies his origins in this rough world. His father Antonio was a bruiser from the mountains behind Palermo in the heart of Mob-dominated western Sicily. He made his living as a prize-fighter and seaman. Sinatra's mother Dolly Garaventa was from near Genoa, and her parents were bitterly opposed to her marriage to the Sicilian tough and boycotted the wedding. She was an illegal abortionist, and was arrested several times and convicted twice. A political radical and women's rights activist, Dolly Sinatra was a Democratic Party ward official in Hoboken. Young Frank as a spoilt only child soon fell foul of the law, with a conviction in 1938 for 'seduction and adultery'. He was magnetic for women, singing with jazz pianists as the silk-voiced Orpheus of the waterfront bars, and his mother's illegal earnings bought him natty gear and shoes and many female conquests.

The Sinatras had protection. Close links with the Gambino Mafia family, with its roots in Sicily's Palermo region, remained throughout Frank Sinatra's life and his recently released FBI files run to no fewer than 2403 pages, detailing endless Mob socializing, broads, boozing and communist sympathies (for a period after 1945). As one FBI stoolpigeon observes, he 'was not a true American'. But his songs and career were at odds with that. Although he lived the Mob life, his music tells us little or nothing about them, or Hoboken or New Jersey in any shape or form. Sinatra was, like many others in his profession, a great singer but not the best American citizen, and he cast a long shadow over the next generation. He had little or no sentimental attachment to New Jersey in later life; the slums were colourful but not a place to stick around. Modern gentrifying Hoboken has a quietly guarded admiration for him; there is a very small public park, the often windswept and lonely Sinatra Memorial by the Hudson River and a quiet inscribed slab. Hoboken now is a long way from the Godfatherland hill country of western Sicily. There are gentrified brownstones and mud-covered old teak beans sticking out of the Hudson foreshore mud at low tide. The sound of Tommy Dorsey and the big bands Sinatra fronted are distant dreams.

In contrast to Sinatra, Bruce Springsteen has always sought—after the usual indiscretions of a rock star youth with women—to be both a good citizen and singer, and had no links with the secret or not so secret criminal underworld where he grew up in and around bourgeois Freehold. In terms of American stereotyping, he had the advantage of his mixed parentage, a dominant Italian mother (as Sinatra had) who loved music counterpoised against his classic loser father from a mixed (Czech and Dutch) but non-Italian background in the poverty stricken Appalachians. In mathematical terms Springsteen Pater was a Zero.

Hoboken was not majority Italian originally: like many other places in New Jersey before 1914 there was a large and prosperous German community and all the other usual immigrant groups, but the events of World War I caused mass property expropriation of much of the

German-owned waterfront by the Federal government and an end to German-language use. It was the same everywhere in the US. Some little towns in Jersey like modern Denville were then primarily German-speaking. When the war broke out in 1914, Cincinnati, as the greatest 'German' city in the States, had about twenty local newspapers and magazines, of which eighteen were in the German language. By 1918, only two of them printing in German were left.

Italians in the slum world of Hoboken, Jersey City and many other places in the state fared better since they were nearly all working-class recent immigrants and owned little or nothing more than a shop or a market stall. The Italians had avoided the opprobrium of enemy culture although they felt like outsiders and not accepted; music was a sure way out of the darkness of the cave, the gloom of the lower depths, as much as it was for the black jazz musicians like Count Basie, born in nearby Newark. The rise of Sinatra almost exactly coincided, chronologically, with the rise of the second generation Mafia, exemplified by the booming gambling and sin city of Las Vegas controlled by Lucky Luciano, the so-called Father of Organized Crime, and his associates. Sinatra spent much of his time in some post-1950 periods as a celebrity in Vegas, with a long succession of different women in and out of his bed, as his sometime *inamorata* the actress Lauren Bacall sets out so graphically in her autobiography. Some of the most prominent and effective law enforcement officers working against the Mafia have also been Italian-Americans. In the recent period New Jersey-born Louis J. Freeh rose through the ranks of the FBI to become director for a period under the Bush administration. A feisty, amusing man with a lethal wit and stinging one-liners, he could have walked straight in or out of any *Sopranos* episode, but also deeply religious with members of Opus Dei in his immediate family and fiercely loyal to his nation of origin. He took Italian citizenship after retirement. He believed, as he sets out in his autobiography *My FBI*, that doing law enforcement is doing God's work, as no doubt Frank Sinatra believed his life and work was similarly blessed.

Bruce Springsteen has had no equivalent trajectory in his life, yet ironically the Mob influence is very current on some songs, much more than with Sinatra, and some of his greatest classics are in essence crime, Mob or murder stories, like 'Atlantic City', 'Nebraska' and 'Murder Incorporated'. The latter is a hymn to the inexorable power of the gangsters in the New York City and New Jersey underworld. A man like Luciano started in Jersey and NYC crime as a child shoplifter and then minor gambler. So later did 'Joey', the top Mob contract killer who was the model for Martin Scorsese's Donny Brasco in the film. His autobiography, *Joey the Hitman*, is an encyclopaedia of Jersey and New York criminal life. Although in 2014 over 10,000 packets of heroin were sold in Monmouth County every day, according to official data, there were still many on the streets a generation or two before. But the big payoffs were in booze during Prohibition and, above all, cocaine. The size of the winnings was worth the risk. In the darkness the heroin trade also flourished. It is not hard to find the metaphorical darkness at the edge of town in New Jersey, although the defenders of the state's reputation feel that much the same sub-cultures exist in the less attractive parts of every big American city. The darkness, the abyss, the cave with no escape path is found by driving from the pretty manicured suburbs into the night city to buy drugs.

The illusory escape path is a needle into a vein in the arm and temporary bliss. But in Plato, the cave always has an escape path. That is how it is. The mathematician sits near the cave entrance. He has a nice car nearby and can drive away. Or, like Joey and the US government in DC, you can play the numbers. Mob hitman Joey said,

> If there is one business that most Mob men cherish above all others, it is the numbers. The numbers is easily one of the most beautiful things ever invented. It is simple to set up, simple to run, almost risk-free, and incredibly profitable. Like me, most Mob men look on the numbers with nostalgia, because it is the first thing they did in crime.

Or maybe not. Stealing a car to be able to drive is pretty good competition. Numbers is in decline these days. Before 1939 in entire districts of New York City, Harlem particularly, minor criminal street culture was dominated by numbers gambling, the usually poor white boys starting up the Mob ladder and swindling (mostly) black people out of their money. How does it work? What are the odds? How do you know if you have won?

The Motel Room as a Cave

Nobody else has ever written as many songs about driving as Bruce Springsteen. Something like 'Cadillac Ranch' is only the best known. South of Newark it was a dark autumn night near Thanksgiving on Route 1. It was a mistake to take the hire heap anywhere much that night. The wheels wanted to stay in the city of Philip Roth's birth, in Newark's Weequahic neighbourhood, where way back in 1933 a baby boy born to a refugee family from ex-Habsburg Galicia who would go on to create Nathan Zuckermann first breathed and began what a critic has called 'the drama of American self-invention, a drama in which every American is his or her own Columbus, discovering America as she or he invents it'.

I was headed to Kinnelon after a good meal with Albanian friends in Summit, with its million-dollar Colonial and Tudor houses, the birthplace of actress Meryl Streep in 1949, the same year as Bruce Springsteen's birth. 'Thunder Road' was playing, a Bruce classic that everybody knows but endlessly renews itself as much as a Wagner or Mozart melody.

The screen door slams
Mary's dress waves
Like a vision she dances across the porch

Maybe he took more in songs like this from Sinatra and the Italian lyric tradition than I had thought. The perceptive academic commentator on his lyrics, Elizabeth Wurtzel, has written that there are many *leitmotifs* in Bruceiania and redemption through loving relationships is always one of them. The light in the fall evening was fading in the trees and dark bramble-clumps as the sign read to Butler on Route 23, and then there was the seminal moment when 23 crossed 287 South, the beautiful road cut through rock from the Alpine border on the wilds of New York State to the south where the road leads on the 206 South towards Princeton and gentle Flemington. Nobody has ever heard of Kinnelon. It is a speck on the northern New Jersey map near Pompton Lakes. A few miles south of Kinnelon is Morristown, where Washington garrisoned the remains of his army in the winter of 1776-77 and reformed the shattered men after their great advances against the British at Trenton and Princeton.

Newark airport was gloomy and confusing and concrete expressways leapt out of the swampland to take you to somewhere you maybe wanted to go, or maybe to somewhere you didn't. In the eighteenth century Kinnelon was famous as a charcoal making and iron founding centre. Then it went under and re-emerged in the 1920s as a summer holiday cabin settlement for Croatian immigrants hoofing away from the royalist Yugoslavs. Now it is small, wooded and very pretty with secure gated communities carved out of an old tobacco baron's estate but largely unknown, its Wordsworthian lakes feeders for Newark's water supply and home to a rich birdlife. In contrast, Newark was darkness and confusion; thousands of people were passing every hour through the airport and all of them indifferent to one another.

New Ark was what was once called a seventeenth-century theocratic fiefdom, one of the oldest settlements in the United States. South of New York, later, after the godly pioneers had moved away the town had always been at the front line of the US industrial revolution and had grown exponentially after the mid-nineteenth century and Reconstruction. When it was growing as a town in the eighteenth century the Atlantic shore line was different and the main centre of activity was at the British fortress town of Perth Amboy, but the wide lanes of Newark Bay and its wide, deep rivers were much more practical for large ships than shallow Perth Amboy. With industrial society, Newark boomed as all roads and rail routes had to go through it to avoid the treacherous swampland of the shifting Hackensack marshes, famous for disposal of New York cadavers long before the days of the Sopranos. The population exploded after 1820, with an index the building of the first Roman Catholic church for Irish immigrants in 1826 to be followed by a cathedral in 1848 and no fewer than thirty-two more churches constructed between 1850 and 1870.

It is still a very Catholic city and the Church plays a positive social role in helping the Newark poor, more or less the only welfare state they have, and trying to keep young people away from drugs and crime. Mass is said in over thirty languages on Sundays. Theology and clerical practice are firmly conservative, with an intense emphasis on holding family life together. All Souls Day is a good time to see the public strength of Newark Catholicism, with crowds of relatives of the dead praying in cemeteries throughout the city, particularly from communities like the numerous Haitian and other Caribbean Catholics where pre-Christian cults involving discourse with the dead are still fresh in many subconscious minds.

An important festival for Italian-Americans is the Feast of St
Gerard Majella in October at St Lucy's Church. Most of the inhabitants
of Little Italy, the old First Ward, left town, *Nevarca*, as they called
it, after the neighbourhood was bulldozed for urban development in
1953. A large proportion had come from the same few towns in the
Roman *campania* in Avellino and Salerno provinces. In 1870 there
had only been twenty-nine Italian families in Newark, but by 1920 the
number had risen to over 27,000, many dirt-poor and earning a living
as rag and bone pickers, prostitutes and street hustlers. They gambled
through illegal games of *ziginette* and were looked down on by the old
Newark establishment, who thought, according to one observer, 'they
are clannish because they do not know how to conform to American
customs', a view which is often applied to the Soprano family on TV
nowadays.

Ziginette (*zecchinetta* in Sicily) is a very simple game, descended
from one of the oldest card games in Europe, *landsknecht*, invented by
German medieval mercenaries, a vicious gambling game of pure chance
and still banned today in public places in Italy. In Jersey and Philadelphia
it became a near-religion in the closed and secret clubs located in the old
Italian Benefit Societies where non-members were strictly excluded as
possible cops' informers and membership often involved oath taking.
The wagers against the bank are straight, confrontational and blind, and
even a poor man can lose hundreds of dollars in a few minutes. The
banker is the enemy of all the other players, just as the banks became the
enemy of top number mobsters like Joe Moriarty. The Gambino 'family'
in New York City were prominent devotees and it became the ultimate
Mob card game in various forms, and a preface to many discussions
(real and cinematic) about dealing with enemies around blue check
tablecloths after plates of *ziti*. Film director Martin Scorsese is said to
be a mean player.

The nineteenth-century city attracted investors and Newark, like all
Jersey industrial centres, soon had its own pet invention, patent leather
in this case. The infant electrical industry was important later, with the

laboratories of Edward Weston, the inventor of celluloid and so founder of the movie industry. It was not an easy place to live. Always crowded, the vast surrounding marshes and mudflats were never very healthy, with a strong presence of the so-called 'Jersey Bird', the mosquito. The nineteenth-century town barons spent as little as possible of their massive profits on infrastructure and the only water supply for most people was the polluted Passaic River. This led to recurrent epidemics, including cholera and yellow fever, and extraordinarily high infant mortality rates. Social and political tension was high, with serious rioting in 1854 between the nativist 'Yankee' establishment and Roman Catholic newcomers, mostly Irish famine refugees. Many immigrant groups lived in close huddles for self-preservation reasons, like the large Jewish community around Prince Street. It was perhaps the first American city to experience serious decline in the nineteenth century, and was eclipsed as a manufacturing centre by the new Midwest boom towns like Chicago and Cleveland, Ohio, after the Erie Canal to the Great Lakes was opened.

Finance capital from New York brought respite in the twentieth century, in different forms. A main sewer was built, improving the dismal health situation rapidly, although polluting the beaches as far away as Sandy Hook. World War I led to a boom in military orders for New Jersey factories, and more immigrants moved in from the South and Puerto Rico to do manual jobs. A landmark was the beginning of Newark airport in the 1920s which transformed the economy, and it was soon the nation's busiest airport. In the 1950s things went on a dive again, with many factory closures and rigid control of City Hall by Mob-linked Mayor Hugh Addonizio. In 1967 race riots broke out and accelerated the white flight from the city, and authors writing on its history usually see those riots as the defining moment in the modern history of Newark.

Newark continues to bump along, but with maybe a third of the population living below the poverty line. Bruce Springsteen was a teenager when there was, as the lyric of 'Badlands' say, 'trouble in the heartland', but there was still the dream that these 'badlands start treating us good ' instead of

> *Workin' in the fields, 'til you get your back burned*
> *Workin' 'neath the wheels 'til you get your facts learned*
> *Baby I got my facts learned real good right now*
> *(You better get it straight darlin')*
> *Poor man want to be rich, rich man wanna be king*
> *And a king ain't satisfied, 'til he rules everything*

Large modern businesses like the Prudential Insurance Company have their American headquarters here, but the city centre is surrounded by gloomy parking lots, trailer yards and an unlit wilderness of streets that seem to lead nowhere much. In the days before satellite navigation devices, Newark was as certain a labyrinth as any in the United States. Most of the streets are communities of

black and Hispanic people. White people go there in the daytime but don't linger much at night. If you take any wrong turn off Route 1, you get lost. If you do not have a Sat Nav, you feel afraid. If you have a Sat Nav, you may still feel afraid. If you get lost you are in a world of uncertainty and anxiety. If Paradise is the American Dream, you are a frightened stranger in Paradise.

If you want to drive out of Newark it is difficult to find the way, as there are very few road signs of any kind, and very few people who might be asked the way on the sidewalks. You do not do that anyway. Unemployment is high, the crime rate is high, guns are everywhere, gang membership is high and poverty is very high, elderly black people shamble along pushing bag trucks laden with random shopping from cashing the week's food stamps. According to Drug Enforcement Agency sources, the most powerful gangs in Newark are Las Moicas and the Beltran-Leyva Organization, both effectively sub-contractors to the Mexican Sinaloa drug cartel. Less than an hour's drive from Manhattan, most of the city is not a good advertisement for the United States. It is not a good advertisement for New Jersey either, and typifies most of the things that make up one facet of the New Jersey stereotype. Hoboken, in contrast, has started to become gentrified, enterprising young couples taking over the old brownstones and some big corporations settling there to be near New York City without the exorbitant office rents of Manhattan.

Yet it was not always like this. And not all Newark is on the skids. The (partly) rebuilt city centre has its Gap and H&M and some jazzy office buildings, Newark Amtrak station is a 1930s masterpiece of old fashioned trusted station with beautiful time capsule woodwork that seems only to need W.C. Fields telling a joke to make it complete. In the early days of jazz, Newark was very important, with its bars and speakeasies attracting New Yorkers seeking a rough trade night out and the dynamic new music. It was at the forefront of music development, piano playing in particular, with ragtime arts bringing the name 'the ticklers town' (tickling was a metaphor both for fucking and piano playing), and a massive demi-monde district developed, the Coast or the Shore, where as in New York's 'Hell's Kitchen' and Atlantic City's 'Line' district, more or less anything could happen and often did. Pianists kept a gun in the piano stool. An important industry in the Coast were the brothels and much jazz piano playing developed from the artists whose job it was to entertain the women and their clients. Willie 'The Lion' Smith was the most famous of these pianists but there were many others.

It was, as the Newark Historical Society publication says, 'a Jazz City' with music pulsating out into the street from the little venues like the Kinney Club, the Piccadilly Club, Club Downbeat, and Sparky J's. Every club was a cave of mystery and new music, as much as the Cavern in Liverpool was a cave for the Beatles. New music starts in caves and underground. Those without fetters, in the Platonic sense, and with money journeyed out from their world of progress and enlightenment to take the steps down to the black (in many senses) Underworld, and step into the cave with its mystery and creativity and excitement.... and to listen to the unpredictable and disorderly new music of the fettered ones, now only economically fettered but not so long ago—if they rebelled—actually fettered in the cotton field chain gangs of the Old South. Then the punters went back to their suburban places in Teaneck, or wherever, or to New York City. This world wound down in the 1950s and most clubs closed. In the long Newark battle between the swamps, the badlands and the city, the badlands were winning at that time. People wanted blues and rock, as now rock is being eclipsed with the young by rap and hip hop, although WBGO radio station still carries the banner for jazz, as does the mighty Institute of Jazz Studies down Route 1 at Rutgers University. The John Cotton Dana Library there has the largest jazz collection in the world.

The refuge from the car is the motel. In Springsteen's song 'Reno', from a middle period album, there is a lonely john in a room with a hooker somewhere out west of Jersey. It is a powerful song and Bruce's wife Patti Scialfa registered mild disapproval of it in one interview. But it happens. Men wind up in motels with women they do not know. They are insecure places where more or less anything can happen, and sometimes does. Ordinary tired travellers can be next to very strange people. My car is parked in the lot, as near as possible to the front door of the rented room. The room is cavernous, with a smell of very old carpets. It is America, it is clean in a sense, it is not a fleabag motel of the old type, but so many bodies have passed through it, all unknown. The management does not waste money on the overheads. After a visit to the Polish liquor store earlier on, with fifty-one different vodkas to choose from, there is a small bottle on my table for company and a too large TV screen. The TV is pushing porn on Pay TV, attractive girls with no pubic hair; in the awful phrase of the pornographers, 'furry meat does not sell'.

Real sex is not far away. The walls are thin and a Deep South male voice in the next room is opening a transaction with a very Jersey lady. Her voice sounds like that of a black person. It is an interracial hook-up, on traditional lines. I can see the end of his pickup truck, big chrome bull bars, through a crack in my curtains. Somewhere in it there is bound to be a gun rack. It is an impressive vehicle. His fine stallion is tied up next to my nondescript Pontiac horse. And he is about to be a stallion in the next room to mine.

'You sure you got the money? Small bills?

'Yup,'

'I wanna see it.'

'There.'

'My guy knows where I am you know. He doesn't take shit from anybody. You don't putz around?'

'You're peachy with me, peachy. There's two hundred.'

'Then schvitz. We're in business.'

A pause. And a rush of water from the shower. Taking a shower is an important classless ritual. In ancient Greek, **Ariston men Udor**, water is the best of all. Better than gold that gleams in the night. That is what Pindar wrote.

I am a voyager, a voyeur, but not a voyeur. A voyeur in sound but not in sight.* There is nothing to see but everything to hear. Erica Jong discussed the zipless fuck, this is a gazeless fuck. So it's a legal situation, and I am not a criminal voyeur.

'Well you are well set there down, well set. A woody you got on. I can see down there.'

'He's been having a quiet time.'

'He's an eyeful. And you got me here, waiting. Your beanie'll spin … come on …'

'Yeah?'

'I don't take to waiting. Galosh?'

Then silence, then they fuck, she fakes a noisy orgasm, almost impossibly fast.

They bounce the bed so hard; maybe it will collapse under them, mine in this room doesn't seem too new. Then silence. Then Joisey vowels: 'You're good, good, good. You were great.'

'Yes?

'Quite a guy. As good as it gets.'

She is liturgical; she is speaking a very familiar script. She is very professional. Time is money in her business like any other. Then more running water. In what seems like no time there is a car starting. Out of the window I can see for a second a dark head, a big girl, bling on a pink dress, a trendy small Mazda sports car, she accelerates smoothly off into the night. Roadside life in the Jersey night is just glimpses; there is no steady reflective

---

* There is an extensive literature on voyeurism in and around motels, from Alfred Hitchcock's film *Psycho* set in the Bates Motel, Michael Powell's film *Peeping Tom* and Jersey-born author Gay Talese's 1981 hit novel and film *Thy Neighbour's Wife* and his recent book *The Voyeur's Motel*. Some states ban room rental by the hour in motels.

gaze. The motel is deadly quiet, as if she had never set foot there. And in half an hour very steady loud snoring. A deep southern white male snore. Is she the victim, the cave dweller, the chained one, selling her body to strangers? Or is he the victim, paying for something that is not what it seems to be? Are they following set rules for exploitation? Or just improvising, so it does not seem to be exploitation. Jazz is improvisation. Jazz is Newark music. And everybody exploits and screws Newark—that is how it is.

Where is Plato? He has been dead a long time. How would he see things, this hiding of the sausage? In ancient Athens a man had women available at any time day or night, it went without saying. Who is exploiting whom? Who is chained, who is free? In Britain, she would call him a john to her girlfriends, the client, and the customer. I wonder what he is really called. Maybe he is actually called John? The side of his pickup truck says something about the construction services industry in Georgia. They both offer services, He constructs; she deconstructs him on her back, for a short time. Then she is gone forever unless he comes this way again.

What is the motel? It is part of the road, as much as the tarmac, the white lines, the street lights; it is the box with the bed and wide empty spaces where nothing happens between the furniture and where an old copy of *USA Today* blocks out the draught around the crack in the bathroom window. It might seem to be a warm and useful refuge but it has all the dangers of the road, the car blown into the next lane of the Turnpike to be lacerated by a giant rig in an Atlantic gale on a dark winter night. The vast sea is only a few miles away. The john might be a knife wielding maniac for all she knows, there is a chance she may be HIV positive with the amount of injected drugs around in her world. Or it is possible just to turn up somewhere and be mugged or robbed or raped and there is no one much to help. Everything on the road is transactional, driving or chilling out in the motel, and all transactions have on-costs. Does popular American music have on-costs? Many of them are the same, drugs and rehab in the background always, sometimes in the foreground, the struggle for authenticity against the false images in the cave cast by the fire of fame. And maybe nobody is really listening to you, as Bruce says in

'Radio Nowhere'. Maybe that is why it was the first keynote song of the *Magic* album. But if you do a rock bottom job, even nowadays in working-class Bronx or Queens let alone in much poorer black New Jersey, there is not so much time for anything unessential.

Honest work for the American poor is also very long hours, for as Italian-American author Michael Parenti recalls in his autobiography, *Waiting for Yesterday: Pages from a Street Kid's Life*, existence in East Harlem consisted of meagre wages and often long commute travel times, so family life had to be traditional, or the family would collapse. People met on Sunday for a big lunch as they never saw each other the rest of the week. Strong creative mothers, as with both Sinatra and Springsteen, had to hold things together and keep the home fire burning; they were central to everything, and then church on a Sunday, also a female-dominated ritual of attendance with a lot of focus on the venerated Virgin. He writes:

> My father played a more distant role than my mother, as was the usual way in Italian working class families—and in just about any other family where the division of labour is drawn along gender lines. He laboured long hours, sometimes two jobs at a time. Born in Italy he was transported to this country at the age of five.

The word 'transported' is significant. Criminals and slaves are transported, free men and women travel. The United States has always suffered from a chronic labour shortage, and the door at the bottom of the social ladder has always been open to migrants, legal or illegal. Education was not a way out. Immigrants then and now often spent two or three years in the first grade because their English was so poor. Life in the outside world began after surviving until the fifth grade, somehow or other, and into the world of work although with hardly any of the skills needed to get a job. In this world, female relationships became very secondary for boys.

The world of Springsteen is way beyond the immigrant experience, but the traditional family and the male buddy group are still very important. Bruce's forty-year friendship and band relationship with 'Miami' van

Zandt is a classic buddy dialogue, between men and between musicians. And the most important group was the Band, which is not far at a symbolic level from the Mob crew. The E Street Band gives Springsteen's music its massive power, the sweeping rising and falling octaves of contemporary America. But the achievement is not based on over-rigid thinking, despite the Boss's lengthy and often authoritarian rehearsal periods. To achieve success, improvisation is essential, and has long been at the heart of Jersey life. The Band is sure of the order of songs but never quite knows how Bruce is going to lead them.

The term wise guy is a way to see this. A wise guy can mean many things in American English. Starting off in nineteenth-century literature, it could simply mean an educated, successful man, someone with a high school diploma and a route into a white collar job. Then it came to mean more just somebody who was successful, and then faded during Prohibition into Jersey slang as an operator, someone who knows how to fix things to their own advantage, and last of all, a conventional term for someone with Mob connections, someone who covers all the bases and plays all the angles, and fading again into wiseass, someone who is arrogant and cocky. The wise guy improvises, often on the edge of or outside the law.

The old jazz musicians in Newark were famous for improvisation. They are gone forever now, the great names who played the little clubs in the 1930s. A wander down Jersey way then could lead to hearing men and women of real genius, towering figures and close to their public, like Duke Ellington, Ella Fitzgerald, John Coltrane, Sarah Vaughan. The latter was very much a local girl, as Basie was a Jersey product who made his name and first great band in Kansas City. Her voice ranged over four octaves. After listening to her recordings, it is hard to believe that she, like the rest of them, is dead.

Rap and hip hop are alive in Newark music now, the anger of the alienated and unemployed young, attractive energy and anger in the music, unattractive cults of guns, drugs and violence in many of the lyrics, the gangsta lifestyle institutionalized in the mock battles between stars like Kanye West and Fifty Cents, that year photographed eyeball to eyeball on the front cover of *Rolling Stone*, or the earlier blood soaked death of Biggy Smalls, the Notorious B.I.G. Women are not that prominent in this world, nor is Springsteen and the Band. It is rare for anyone black and young in Newark or any of the tough towns along the Passaic River Valley to show any interest in Bruce Springsteen, but this is a long story. He has never played many concerts in the South and disproportionately few in the West or in California, and disproportionately many more in the old north-east and Midwest, hard working-class white America. Most young black people when I asked them once in Patterson had to think who he was, and are also unsure who Frank Sinatra actually was, and the previous generations of great Newark musicians are part of music history and the heritage, not the present. Springsteen is part of the present but a distant present, although it only takes half an hour or so to drive from the ghettos along the Passaic Valley to Freehold or Long Branch and the heart of Springsteenland. American musical sub-cultures have powerful boundaries, invisible borders where you don't need a passport. The same is true of the underworld.

As academics and other students of the subject have pointed out, there have been Jewish, Polish, Russian, black and Latino gangsters who have been extremely successful in America, but it is the Italians who have the label stuck to them and remain deeply embedded in the general culture, criminal and musical. In Sinatra's generation in Jersey, and in the world shown in the hugely successful musical *Jersey Boys*, based on Frankie Valli and the Four Seasons, the Mob were ubiquitous and hard to escape in the most mundane activities of daily life. In the view of some rock historians, Valli is really the inheritor of the Sinatra tradition, not Springsteen in any meaningful sense. Valli, born Francis Stephen Castelluccio in Newark in 1934, and the Four Seasons embodied the style of the juvenile delinquents around the Newark suburb of Belleville, maybe not very seriously criminal in themselves but familiar with the criminal world, and not always in its milder aspects. In a recent interview, Valli observed that he was a lucky young man, after some of his school friends were wasted (killed) in street shootings and knifings, or discovered in the trunk of a car sinking into the mud of the Jersey marshes. In his old age, Valli duly turned his experiences into star value by playing the gangster Rusty Millio in *The Sopranos*, a fading between myth and reality, and Rusty Millio duly died in a hail of gunfire in his final appearance in the show. With his very unusual falsetto voice, Valli was a phenomenon, unique, and has outlived both his violent youth environment and the Four Seasons themselves, and like Britain's national treasures has become a New Jersey state treasure.

These contexts help explain the Springsteen concentration—to his fans—and obsession—to his critics—about cars and driving in his songs, particularly the early numbers. The car is not just a way of getting around; it has the identity of the means of escape. The man with the car can get away from threats and danger, he can disappear, from the old paradigm of crossing the state line but more likely into the hidden recesses of Jersey itself, the dense wilderness of the Pine Barrens only an hour or so driving time from Newark or New York City, the wild and dreary marshlands with their curling winter mists cutting visibility down to a few yards and treacherous unasphalted tracks that the Lenape Native Americans would have recognized. As the *Magic* album opens, 'I was tryin' to find my way home/but all I heard was a drone/bouncing off a satellite/crushin' the last lone American night …'

The all-powerful technical present, with its military echoes, is contrasted with the spiritual isolation of the land within in Jersey, the unchanging landscape with its dramas, strangeness, dark streets and dark secrets. The song is about the fear of the all-powerful state and the intrusion into places where it does not belong, threatening the integrity of the free individual in the traditional landscape. It is a long way from the simple, comforting lyricism of Sinatra and his tradition; it is a full encounter with the world of the Bush administration and its view of America. In the early song 'Jungleland', he sang of the 'opera out on the Turnpike'. The great road has its music, but the essence is a music of escape; as he sings, in perhaps one of his two or three finest classic songs, 'Thunder Road', It's a town full of losers, and I'm pulling out of here to win.'

But leaving is not an option for most, any more than it was at the time of the 1967 riots that left twenty-six people dead and over ten million dollars' worth of damage. If you are poor in Newark, you tend to stay there. The different communities celebrate life as always in their music, and the summer in Newark is a bewildering, wonderful stream of different ethnic music festivals, often outdoors in Newark Museum's garden, or the Lincoln Park music festival, or the concerts of classical music by the Newark-based New Jersey Symphony Orchestra. A highlight is the music of the numerous Puerto Rican citizens, the world Hunter S. Thompson depicted in his early novel *The Rum Diary*, where in one of the great erotic scenes in modern American fiction, the hero and a girl he knows, Chenault, go to a *bomba* music club on the waterfront in Puerto Rico and she is swept away by the wild drumming and horn playing:

> Now as if in some kind of trance, Chenault began to unbutton her blouse. She popped the buttons slowly, like a practised stripper, then flung the blouse aside and pranced there in nothing but her bra and panties. I thought the crowd would go crazy. They howled and pounded on the furniture, shoving and climbing on each other to get a better view. The whole house shook and I thought the floor might cave in. Somewhere across the room I heard the glass breaking
>
> I looked again at Yeamon. He was waving his arms in the air now, trying to get Chenault's attention. But he looked like just another witness, carried away by the spectacle.

This is a world where bands with not-very-distant roots in the rhythms and beat of voodoo ceremonies are wild, hypnotic and with more than a touch of danger. Dancers shake and scream and trumpets howl against the steady beat of the drums. The heritage of voodoo in the unconscious opens doors into a dark and difficult and often violent past echoing across the mundane cut grass and untidy, cash strapped and a little down at heel city of Newark. By day the musician may do a mainstream job and drive a New York City bus or a subway train, a particularly common Newark Puerto Rican occupation for some reason, and then playing in the band at night takes a dive back into a world of superstition, cockfights, blood sprinkled on a Newark backyard, animal sacrifice and the deepest recesses of the cave of memory and obscure images. The music may be *bomba*, with its roots in slaves taken from the Congo region, *plena*, the Creole tradition, and *jíbaro*, linked to the Afro-American *santería* cult, voodoo–lite in the eyes of its critics. Guitar strings shake the flimsy walls of backyard Houses of the Saints, rhythms and drumming bring in the Zombies, well dressed living skeletons, stylish, with black suits, white ties and black hats haunting the streets and maybe coming to visit for a dance. The Puerto Rican kids who go the bad road end up in the Latin Kings or Ñetas, their gangs a spider's web that started in Puerto Rican prisons, bad places. They sometimes wear skull and bones masks when they party. Inspiration might come from Newark's vast sprawling cemeteries, with North Arlington the largest single cemetery in the United States containing 35,747 burial plots, not far from Newark Ridge, a popular vantage point to watch the burning Twin Towers at the time of 9/11.

What is the right number from *Magic* in a Newark motel? It can only be 'Radio Nowhere'. This motel is a dark cave. The song is about non-communication in the age of the internet and the decline of the US media, the end of the great days of rock radio, the exclusion of rock under the dominance of hip hop, and as Springsteen himself put it in an interview for Uncut that fall 2007, 'It's the end of the world scenario, he's seeing the apocalypse':

This is Radio Nowhere,
Is there anyone alive out there?
I was spinnin' 'round a dead dial
Just another lost number in a file
Dancin' down a dark hole
Just searching for a world
With some soul

Bruce Springsteen knows the cave and the prisoners. Unfortunately they are divided into different gangs, as my local paper that week screamed on the front page:

New Jersey
GNG'LND
The Gangster State
Report: Bloods, Crips, Latin Kings, Neta and MS-13 are on the rise, especially in Mercer County (Page5)

Who was, say, MS-13? I didn't know then. But I would soon find out, in time. Jersey is a small crowded place, the most crowded state of all, according to Federal enumeration. Everybody, sooner or later, runs into everybody else, whether they want to or not. It's the American Dream gone wrong in many conventional eyes, the vision of Daniel Boone's pioneer isolation in his own forest gone bust in a mad ant heap of stroppy Joisey people, but *Paradise Lost* with Satan in action is a much more interesting poem than *Paradise Regained.*

In the background on the radio there was some pundit making a spiel about Hillary Clinton and Barack Obama. Hillary's campaign for the nomination had run into problems in Jersey connected with allegations about Democratic Party mismanagement of the state finances, and the usual corruption background. The *Magic* tour was going to exactly coincide on its 100-stop route around the country with the presidential campaign. The word on the street was that Bruce had met Obama somewhere and thrown in his lot with him as he had liked him. But it was hard to see whether it would make any difference to the problems of a place like Newark, as duly turned out to be the case several years into the Obama presidency. Other shadows were falling over the E Street Band.

Although nobody knew it at the time, from the glorious open rehearsal back in September at Asbury Park on the shore to the ominous journey to Pittsburgh I knew was inevitably coming, it would be the last time the classic crew of the E Street Band itself would play together. Danny Federici's death came in April 2008 during the *Magic* tour and inspirational horn player Clarence Clemons was facing serious ill health and mobility issues. His coming demise was maybe already on his mind. Writing in his fine memoir *Big Man*, Clemons says that he thought the August 2008 show to a massive mainly biker audience in Milwaukee was the finest Bruce and the E Street Band concert there had ever been, but there was a sad even tragic undertone for 'every time this band ends a tour, there are no guarantees that they will ever take the stage together again'.

It was the 105th anniversary of the foundation of Harley Davidson. There were hundreds of thousands of motorbikes in town, all having completed the ride home to Milwaukee where they were made. Returning home and defining what it means to do so is a recurrent Springsteen theme. The motorcycles had made it real. The last music on the Milwaukee sound system was 'Born to be Wild'. But the music always lives on. There had been a meeting recently with old friend Bo Diddley:

> I was at this stone crab restaurant one night and Bo Diddley was in there. Everybody's got the mallets, you know, for cracking the crabs. Bo Diddley starts tapping out the Bo Diddley beat. Pretty soon the whole place is doing it, and Bo starts singing.

Big Man gives a unique perspective into the world of old age as a rock musician, playing in the temples of eternal youth, but as he puts it, 'Max [Weinberg, the drummer] is almost always trussed up to support his bad back ... Clarence is held together with bolts and wires and electrodes and is full of plastic and metal in places where bone used to be. He needs new knees.'

Yet the *Magic* album and tour was a triumph even if was the last hurrah of the original E Street Band, in 2007 and 2008 time and yet outside it.

Experience

'Now and almost ever since the war began both you and your enemies have been ruled continuously by that one family.'
Plato, *The Eighth Letter*, 353.[†]

> When people thought of the Mafia in 1994, they most certainly did not think of the DeCavalcante crime family—New Jersey's only homegrown Mafia clan. By the time the protestors started marching outside Vinny Palermo's strip club in Queens, the DeCavalcante crime family had fallen into an almost permanent stupor.[‡]

It is not possible to leave the rule of the Bush administration or the ongoing Iraq War, but it is possible to leave the city. The world of the tough northern suburbs has ways out south. The Springsteen heartland lies just to the south of Newark, as does Sopranoland, another mythical land but also so real it can be touched, like the Soprano family house hired for filming the series with its sweeping operatic driveway and manicured shrubs in a quiet fashionable road in North Caldwell half an hour in the car from Newark and New York City. Myth and reality in Jersey are never far apart, as the revival of the DeCavalcante family under new *capo* Vinny Ocean showed in the years after 1999 when the Soprano family on TV were widely believed to be closely modelled on them. Even for non-fans the series made the *Cosa Nostra* chic. Long-time cornerstone of the E Street Band and near Bruce *alter ego* 'Miami' Steve van Zandt occupies a position in things, as Ed Pilkington has pointed out, exactly like a Mafia *consigliere* to the Boss, whereas in the TV *Sopranos*, he is a *consigliere*

[†] The philosopher is thinking of the war against Carthage, in progress on and off from the end of the fifth century BC.

[‡] See Greg B. Smith, *Made Men: The True Rise-and-Fall Story of a New Jersey Mob Family* (2003) for extensive detail.

to a 'real' Boss, Tony Soprano. New Jersey myth and reality unite in this. The series exploded with the end of the Clinton administration and the arrival of George W. Bush. Suddenly after 1999, women not only in Jersey but across the country were sporting layered gold chains with crosses and Italian horns, not to speak of astronomically expensive sweats over stratospherically expensive underwear. It was the first TV series to make it to the Museum of Modern Art in New York City. Caché store reported spiralling profits because women wanted to dress like Carmela Soprano, sophisticated and sculptured but somewhat over-the-top: that was Carmela, and that was Jersey style. The series has become a way of life with **bada bing** entering the *Oxford English Dictionary*, magisterially explained from the OUP fastnesses at home in Walton Street, far from Jersey, as 'An expression that underscores the idea that something will occur as expected and with ease'.

It was good to think that someone was thinking of the *Sopranos* series etymologies so seriously in my favourite Oxford street, but like the stock market boom, it was driving forward but bound to end, an epic of eight years and six seasons, an end in 2007 as an end was coming to the economic boom. The fact that you can find fairly convincing pasta *ziti* in Oxford is probably a tribute to the series. Would Tony die? The idea seemed fanciful. And there was optimism in the air for the Band in the fall of 2007. The magic glow of the Sopranos on TV was reflected in the acting of long-time buddy and E Street guitarist 'Miami' van Zandt in a masterly portrait of a junior mobster and honcho working for Tony Soprano, just as he worked for the Boss in the band for so many years. He was from the same mixed Italian and Other background as the Boss; his Italian grandfather taught him to sing Italian folk songs before he could walk. A media aura was forming around the achievements in New Jersey popular life unknown since Frank Sinatra and the gangster films of the 1930s. A colleague in the university said I should go up to East Orange and see where Dionne Warwick was born, another possible music pilgrimage. The *Magic* album was starting to motor outside the United States, with rave reviews in Spain, a stronghold of Springsteen fans with tour dates looming in December, and in London, where *The Independent*'s rock critic Andy Gill saw it as 'the most complete and damning denunciation of Bush's foolhardy adventurism in Iraq yet thrown up by rock music... with ruminations on society that make Springsteen the pre-eminent political songwriter of his era.'

But on the Jersey road labyrinth London seemed a long way away. The most obvious escape from the endless complexity of the suburbs is Route 1 to the south, obvious because it was the first main road in American history and linked New York with the new Federal capital city of Washington DC as early as the eighteenth century. An early speculative explanation for the great influence of Princeton alumni in American elite circles was that Princeton was exactly half way between New York City and Washington on this road.

On the car radio there was a learned discussion between theologians about the significance of the Eighth Commandment, 'You Shall not Bear False Witness against Your Neighbour'. It was a normal enough American religious radio programme in one sense, until after a while it became clear that what it really was about was the ethics of becoming an informer for the police or the Feds, the FBI, and the dangers of committing perjury in a court. Jersey theology programmes can be slightly different from many other places. Theology in popular life in Jersey can take some strange directions that would not be common in Greenwich, CT, or Godalming, UK. The theologians on the whole leaned towards discretion and protecting reputations, rather than taking on making something public or talking to the cops or Feds without sufficient evidence, a risk on what maybe ought not to be known. It was a familiar script.

Police informers matter in the state and underlie the carefully constructed media narrative of Fed 'success' in destroying the old Mafia, where those wearing a wire reveal enough to convict the big fish. One inner narrative of the *Sopranos* series is that the family are old-fashioned and in inevitable decline as a result of technology in law enforcement coupled with members talking to the cops. The reality is rather different, as crime commissioners' reports on organized crime in Jersey show every year, and being a Fed informer can be very dangerous indeed, particularly when witness protection plans break down or do not work properly. If they do work, life under a programme may involve breaking all links with your family, your old friends and your locality. You may never see your children or grandchildren again, an unappealing prospect in a close Italian-American family culture. At a Vox Pop level the memory of the fiasco of the Lucchese trial is very much alive in the NJ bars and pizza restaurants where the prominent Italian-American family was subject to major FBI and NYPD attention to break up their alleged criminal stranglehold on the shore south of Newark, but the trial of Jackie (Fat Jack) DiNorscio and other family henchmen in 1988 degenerated into farce and collapsed with the exposure of some witness identities and general acquittals. It is not surprising that crime and knowledge of crime permeates the general NJ culture in a way it may not in some small town in the Midwest, and many outsiders and foreigners see New Jersey as the prototype of American organized crime (rather than the place where the first can of tinned soup was produced, or the first game of organized baseball played, or the first drive-in cinema opened, in Camden, in 1933). The overall perception is just there, and changing it is probably impossible. As Springsteen writes very perceptively in his autobiography *Born to Run*, 'I come from a boardwalk town where almost everything is tinged with a bit of fraud.'

There is also the aspect of events where the Mafia versus the FBI gets reported in the media more as part of the entertainment industry or sports than crime, with colourful local characters, sexy girlfriends and reversals of fortune in courtroom drama. The reality of brutal violence and the damage Class A drugs cause to people are thus obscured by the comforting myth of battles between Mob and Feds like teams in ballgame finals. It is very different with court reporting of some African-American gang cases where individual defendants can get hauled through the papers long before a word has been said in court.

The Springsteen persona is always seeking, an element of the magnetism of the music is the encounter with the changing American landscape itself, the sense that taking the road will lead to a different world, a solution to a problem and ultimately the larger problem of life itself. As in the lyrics of 'Highway 29':

It was a small-town bank, it was a mess
Well I had a gun, you know the rest
Money on the floorboards, shirt was covered in blood
And she was crying, her and me we headed south
On Highway 29

The Route 1 road to the south is very well known and is very rich in popular culture associations. Tony Soprano tried to get a college education nearby at the venerable Seton Hall University in South Orange, one of the best Roman Catholic colleges in the country. But it was not a success. 'I tried Seton Hall but it didn't work out,' he explains in an episode. His crew, the male buddy fellowship, always beckoned. A little way off the road west is Rutgers University, a progressive college with long lists of famous alumni, but Seton Hall was the Soprano *alma mater* insofar as Tony had one.

What is a crew? At one level it is just the Jersey word for a member of a Mob gang, a family. The DeCavalcantes in real life were nicknamed 'The Farmers', a sign of the way old labels from the nineteenth century for Jersey people applied by New Yorkers have stuck a hundred years or more later. New York is the City, Jersey is where people grow vegetables and look after cows. Northern New Jersey is a very hard world if you are poor, or hustling on the street. It is less violent than it used to be, say, thirty years ago, but violence is there nonetheless, along with many words that cannot be heard on mainstream television. *The Sopranos* was an exercise in Zolaesque realism, with David Chase's genius binding together the hard world of his youth and the realities of the suburbs today. A crew had its own internal rules and hierarchies. Made men rule. And you do need to be Italian to be made. As one character, Henry, said, 'Jimmy and I could never be made, because I had Irish blood. It didn't even matter my Mother was Sicilian.'

The bad words do matter to the respectable Jersey suburban majority. 'Profanity' was an issue with the first *Sopranos* series and has remained an issue ever since with some people. Violent images seem to matter much less. Seeing the likes of Frenchy McMahon dead with an arm sticking out of a garbage truck didn't worry the viewers, or Mr Sepe murdered in the meat truck, when he was frozen so stiff it took two days to thaw him out for the autopsy. The Fuck word is the overriding problem for respectable viewers. The reaction of most people to this world, if and when they run into it, is to leave town.

Springsteen's songs are full of these difficult journeys, to find hope where it might not seem likely there is any. It is hard to make money from a bad starting position in the United States without soon running into onerous regulations of some kind, and probably equally soon, contact with those who will help you get round them. If you run a New Jersey café, stolen meat is much cheaper than legal meat. If you sell cars for a living, margins on used vehicles are tight. On recycled stolen cars they are massive. If you have physical property as part of your business, security can be a big issue in bad areas. So a security man is essential; and he may not be all he seems. And even if he or she is, in many areas they are almost certain to know criminals.

What does being 'made' actually mean, in detail? Henry opines, in the same sequence, that it means that you have got to be a hundred per cent Italian so you can trace all your relatives back to the Boot, and it's the highest honour on offer, and it means that nobody can fuck around with you, and it means that you can fuck around with anybody, as long as they are not a member of your crew. Summing up, he observes it is a licence to steal. So that is all that need be said here. It's a licence to steal.

But there are different ways of stealing. Joe Moriaty was the King of the Numbers in Newark and around, he held a great royal realm of numbers; barely literate from a terrible childhood in the Horseshoe in Jersey City, he had it all in his head. Down the road off the Turnpike Exit 8 there is Princeton and Princeton University and there the numbers are written down. Top 1930s mobster Dutch Schultz died the gangster death over problems with a numbers empire, as Beat author William S. Burroughs sets out in his movie script *The Last Words of Dutch Schultz*, a text full of fascination with the numbers as the source of Schultz's vast fortune after Prohibition ended, but with the numbers demystified, showing how dangerous it was to be a city numbers runner and how their protection rackets worked. Schultz cut the runners' percentage from 33 to 25 in exchange for his 'protection'. He was a businessman and, like all gangsters, he was cutting the overheads.

Route 1 is the lowest road number in the United States. But Route 1 is the real Jersey road, a rough bad tempered rush of speeding, interweaving vehicles. Garages will sell you a car with signs up like 'NO CREDIT REFERENCE NECESSARY'.

Endlessly intersecting with other minor and major roads and cross routes, and hidden away off a minor road to Lodi is the Satin Dolls nightclub, the acknowledged model for the Bada Bing lap dancing club on Route 17, and the automobile repair shop run by Big Pussy that does auto repairs and cocaine and the school where Antony Soprano Jr does his vandalism. Satin Dolls is an isolated concrete building lost in a massive car park near the intersections of Route 17 and big Highway 80, and in the series it was perfect for quick exits and getaways into the vastness and strange interconnections of the Jersey suburbs. Nothing more has contributed to international and US domestic understanding of New Jersey than this television show, and myth and reality fade into each other in the endless suburban maze.

Inside Satin Dolls, which runs night and day with its Hot Bartenders and long legged lap dancers, it really is little more than a metaphorical cave, dark and providing instant anonymity but in good taste and with good background security. Nobody gets out of line and does anything illegal or they are out of the door fast, and it is finding its way into Sopranos bus tours of notable sights. Many women come as well as men. It trades heavily on the series, inviting punters to 'party like America's favorite fictional family, the Sopranos, at Satin Dolls, the world famous Bada Bing club, where our girls will make you feel like a kingpin'.

Not every strip club has its mythical archetype in the *Oxford English Dictionary*. The Bada Bing is the place of the male deal where women are only sexy moving images whose bodies reward success. The most successful Mob series in the world achieved classic status long before the different episodes eventually ended and the long and winding tales of a minor Italian-American Mob family have entered contemporary Jersey mythology as a defining image of Italian-American life in the state. It was the first show to perfectly integrate Mob themes with a normal (up to a point) suburban Italian-American family. Some themes are very close to reality indeed, such as the illegal high stakes poker game that Tony Soprano runs in a hotel owned by Hassidic Jews, while in the DeCavalcante world in actuality a high stakes poker game was run out of a community centre— owned by Hassidic Jews. The TV family and the DeCavalcantes both had bosses in prison who continued to run the family operations. Many real DeCavalcante events that were not generally known to the world at large came into Soprano scripts, as Greg B. Smith has revealed. The near-hypnotic cult status the show achieved and sky-high viewing numbers can at least partly be explained by the fact that it told first Americans and then the entire world what was actually happening in the north Jersey suburbs, in a way most escapist 'family' TV shows avoided.

In American television terms the shows broke the final taboos on profane language and a certain kind of neo-realist inscribed imagery of sex, drug taking and random and not so random violence, with superbly written scripts and acting. Unsurprisingly, many Italian-American organizations have not liked it, not on moral grounds, where after all, all that has happened is to bring American TV language conventions to a point European television reached years ago, but because it depicts their community as strange criminal losers, stuck in intractable feuds in New Jersey while the main caravan of American life has moved on elsewhere. The more pedantic members of the community also claim, correctly, that the important Mafias in the United States today are not Italian at all but different Hispanic groups. But in the era of celebrity, taking on Andy Warhol's dictum that everyone is famous for five minutes in the modern

US, Tony Soprano and the crew are anti-celebrities who have achieved celebrity, losers on the run from heat from the Feds, but winners in that they seem to embody the American Dream for many people.

Route 1 is a roughneck of a road, blowharding as it rocks the car dangerously with its often potholed surface, exciting to disappoint and without the vast sweep of the eighteen-lane Turnpike at its grandest. Minor and major roads intersect in a complex spider's web of routes and cross routes, a landscape of myth and legend as much as the arable fields around ancient Troy. In a sense, anything can happen on the road, and often does. Life has no limits other than those made by lack of money, but death may be near. North Jersey has always had this quality, since the days when it was given to the English lords who mostly never set foot there after the Grant of 1680.

In pre-1939 time and pre completion of the Turnpike, Route 1 was the main road in the state, running straight as an arrow between Newark, past Patterson and then to Trenton, so linking the three main centres of the industrial revolution in New Jersey, and later places that were the epitome of scientific progress like Thomas Edison's establishment of the first ever industrial research and development laboratory at Menlo Park. The road has featured in hundreds of films and TV series and the landscape shows as the epitome of northern New Jersey urban sprawl where the urban and the suburban intersect, a concrete wilderness of used car lots, diners and a place to buy Christian books with a plastic church spire on top. Every so often sin intervenes, with sleazy bars, 'juice joints' (strip clubs that often fade into brothels) and lap dancing clubs and the odd gun shop. *The Trentonian's* splash the week before had been 'ALIEN HOOKERS BUSTED' with a picture of three unfortunate Brazilian girls being dragged off from a juice bar.

Style is up front, men always seem to have been born wearing a tough leather jacket, women with bling and attitude. Elizabeth, as the town nestling below the container port and now below the demolition works for the new bridge across to Staten Island, is hard, rough at all edges and the shop traders have no illusions; 'BAD CREDIT IS GOOD CREDIT HERE,' a sign runs. Car dealers can fix a car fast for you but if you don't pay an instalment there won't be a polite reminder letter on the mat but a man in a leather jacket telling you to sell something you own to pay up. If the answer is No, he will just take the car away. Many young men who end up in organized crime start as debt collectors of some sort. The first drug deal is often some random package that has to be sold on from a desperate creditor. Gas stations are popular places to sell on illegal drugs and other seized goods. New Jersey has 3,601 of them and at night they are often deserted apart from an attendant locked into the fortified cabin, and dark side deals are easily done. The gas stations are supplied from Jersey's big refineries, the Valero complex in south Jersey and the massive sprawling Bellway complex. The state knows how to do oil and is second only to Texas in refinery capacity in the United States. In the song,

The highways are jammed with broken heroes
On a Last Chance power drive,
Everybody's out on the run tonight
But there's no place to hide

Big Oil has eyes and ears everywhere in New Jersey. Much of what the series and many of Bruce's songs show as misty, maybe dangerous Sopranoland lies in the shadow of the refineries, and they seem outside time as they run twenty-four hours a day, seven days a week, fifty-two weeks of the year, mainlining on tankers coming in from the Middle East. They churn out much diesel. Many Jersey people buy big SUVs. Sopranoland does not have passports, or borders, or border signs. It is more a state of mind, the mythical Jersey where the endless struggle between Good and Bad, Mobs and Feds goes on every day. Some of the Soprano tour landmarks such as the family home are easy to see and seem in a way very quiet and suburban. The Soprano family house is in a plush road in the suburb of North Caldwell, at 14 Aspen Drive, a place named originally, ironically enough, after a prominent eighteenth-century Presbyterian minister James Caldwell. North Caldwell has also had a more unfortunate recent history in real life, as in 1994 it was the scene of the demise of the 'Unabomber' Theodore Kaczynski who sent a mail bomb to Thomas L. Messer, an advertising executive resident in North Carolina, which killed him. Kaczynski, yet another numbers obsessive, was a Harvard mathematics prodigy who developed 'geometric function theory' and who later turned into a terrorist, a paradigm of the suburban nightmare in so many rock songs of 'growing up all wrong'. He rebelled as an anarchist against what he regarded as the technological slavery of the contemporary United States and the rule of law becoming a tyranny when allied to overwhelming technology, the world of the protest in the *Magic* song 'Radio Nowhere'. But in actuality many other people, neither particularly good nor bad, live in Caldwell now, and lead their normal Middle American and working-class American lives.

Not far south of Elizabeth is Rutherford, also authentic Sopranoland but also the home and working place of one of twentieth-century America's most notable poets, Ezra Pound's friend, William Carlos Williams. For most of his life he worked as a doctor and paediatrician in Rutherford, and was a radical in his life as well as in his art, close to the working people. He had originally met Pound while studying medicine in the University of Pennsylvania and his early work is Imagist, but he later took his material from everyday American life. When he died in 1963, he was buried at nearby Lyndhurst in Bergen County. His grave is a simple oblong granite block with the single word WILLIAMS carved on it. Many consider his epic masterpiece *Paterson* to be about the decline of civilization in one of the homes of America's industrial revolution. Williams was a first rank Modernist poet and friend of T.S. Eliot but also the poet of the damage industrialism did to parts of the state; *Paterson* describes the foul pollution of the Passaic River from the dye works before it was cleaned up:

Half the river red, half steaming purple
from the factory vents, spread out hot,
swirling, bubbling. The dead bank,
shining mud...

Thesis and Antithesis: Morristown

It takes about an hour or so to drive from Paterson to Morristown, a town perched in discreet and well-kept deciduous woods just above the 287 South. The four-lane highway gives a clue: to the shore side it looks over broad acres of flatlands, but to the west it cuts through tough granite hills and there are clearly bigger hills in the farther background. The Appalachian foothills are here in Jersey, hard, uncompromising and poor until suburban development spread up here in the 1930s, and flourished after World War II. Further west on the state line is the lovely if over-touristy river junction at Delaware Water Gap, and the main road into central Pennsylvania. The lakes formed by glacial moraines supply Newark and other lowland places with good clean water, and in the nineteenth century were part of a complex network that fed the Morris Canal that opened in 1831. It linked the Delaware River with the sea at Newark and first boomed, with over 1,200 boats in operation by 1866, and then busted, killed off by far faster railway transport. In early days Morris County had always been industrial, with natural iron ore on the surface in many places, and local burnt charcoal used to make pig iron as early as 1690.

The canal water has long gone, but in some places such as Boonton near Kinnelon a deep empty ditch can still be seen threading through the suburban landscape, now a haven for birds and other wildlife. You drive from Asbury Park, a small town that everyone has heard of because of rock music and Bruce Springsteen, to Morristown, another small town only historians of the United States know much about. But it is useful to visit in order to read into the New Jersey story and understand why the state was so important in the success of the American Revolution. The 287 is a gentle, well ordered and often beautiful road with patterns of light in the evening dappling the asphalt. It comes, sweeping down from the wilds and exposed glacial erratic in the forest on the state line with New York and the rocky, sometimes bleak fastnesses of the Harriman State Park. There is a sense that to the north lies increasing emptiness and the long weary road surveyed by wandering moose and coyotes on the way to Canada. Morristown is reached almost by accident. But as always in the US, there is a sign with a useful slogan to assist: 'WELCOME TO MORRISTOWN—MILITARY CAPITAL OF THE REVOLUTION'.

The phrase has the echo of revolutionary St Petersburg, Paris or the Long March in China, with a distinct old-fashioned Marxist ring to it, although in reality Morristown is now one of the plushest and richest towns in the state, popular among Wall Street people with excellent schools and endless civil society organizations and clubs. This area has always been rich; in the 1930s the stratospherically wealthy Mrs Geraldine Rockefeller conceived the idea of building a vast luxury dogs' home not far away at Denville Township, a canine Manhattan, with luxury kennels named after rooms in the Waldorf Astoria hotel in NYC, one per dog. In New Jersey the rich do strange things, like many other people. Many other people who work in Newark also live in the town and it grew strongly as a result of white flight from Newark in the 1970s, with neat white clapboard houses and equally neat leaf piles blown carefully together in the fall. Only the signs to Historic Sites betray the fact that anything important in the past has ever happened here. The main drag is Elm Street, but with no Nightmare thereon. The railway runs fast into New York City, helping commuting life.

When in 1776 George Washington was looking for winter quarters for his ragtag and half-starved army after the Battle of Princeton, Morristown seemed a perfect refuge. The wilderness and the Wild West began beyond those ubiquitous beech and ash trees. He was fighting a guerrilla war against the British and as in all guerrilla war, position and holding and taking ground is everything. Morristown was far enough above the main Jersey lowlands to offer a safe refuge for winter re-organization and re-equipment, and without his success here, the Colonies might have stayed British. The beginnings of the Appalachians to the west, severe and then without any significant roads at all, were a sure protection from British raids. The disadvantage was that there was little to live off the land, as it was entirely forest apart from the tiny charcoal burning settlements around

Boonton and Kinnelon, and his men ended up eating the horses' food and then the horses themselves to survive. Washington's headquarters remains visible, then a tavern and now an impressive old eighteenth-century family stone house painted white, reached by a short walk up the hill from the Heritage Site car park. In a real sense, free America began here, but it a quiet and modestly understated place, with none of the imposed grandeur of the Gettysburg battle site, just a quiet dignity and peace. It has no Wow factor whatsoever, and it is visited by mostly serious and usually elderly educated Americans, but not all that many of them. There is a good tourist centre and shop with very good books on offer, but it is very small. A visitor is treated like a long lost friend by the high minded volunteers who keep it open. Morristown has not been absorbed into the main narrative of US history as many other later national shrines have been, and is in some senses outside the received wisdom of the civic religion element in the American story.

Terminology is important. The War of Independence is now the usual term for the colonial period conflict and the term War of Revolution vanished from many, maybe most, school history books after 1950. But historical understanding in the US can often be unduly utilitarian, and the common European academic debate about whether it is possible to learn from history does not take place in the same way here. The imposed narrative emanating from the Civil War period effectively dominates popular consciousness in a nation which is still struggling to resolve issues about race from that time. The historic significance of the Obama victory in 2008 was to show, at the time, to many people that those conflicts had been 'superseded' but as professional historians know, supersessionism is a very dangerous and misleading ideological construct and recent events in US cities have in any case cast much doubt on what was actually achieved in the Obama era anyway. There is also the issue of American popular psychology, the love of history on a grand scale. The Civil War involved more or less a whole nation split and under arms but the eighteenth-century conflicts in Jersey and nearby only involved a few tens of thousands of soldiers.

About 10,000 men were encamped at what was then called Jockey Hollow, an area of Morristown, and in a moving memoir a common soldier Joseph Plum Martin, a nineteen-year-old private in the First Connecticut Brigade describes the conditions in December 1799:

> The snow had fallen nearly a foot deep. Now I request the reader to consider our situation at this time naked, fatigued and starved, forced to march many a weary mile in winter, through cold and snow to seek a situation in some (to us unknown) wood to build us habitations to starve and suffer in ... but there was no remedy, we must go through it, and I am yet alive ... sometimes we could procure an armful of buckwheat straw to lie upon, which was deemed a luxury. Provisions, as usual, took up but a small part of our time, though much of our thoughts.

A good part of the subsequent history has not been focussed on these men and women fighters and what they endured to secure the freedom of the United States from British rule, but on the person of Washington himself. Although a great commander deserving his heroic imagery, his portraits, and usually in much later formal army general's uniform and looking vaguely imperial, belie the realities of the war. He was presented in my schooldays as a moral icon, 'the man who could not tell a lie', rather than the ruthless and effective guerrilla commander he actually was. Egalitarian radicals in the Washington leadership group like Worcestershire, UK-descended proto-socialist George Mason have been more or less elided from all but specialized histories of the time. The famous portrait of Washington in Princeton Art Gallery shows him in a resplendent ceremonial uniform in red, white and blue looking remarkably like his British military opponents. It is now certain that in the actual war he never wore anything of the kind while passing through the lonely, misty and dangerous Jersey forests. These distortions in memory are not new; even in the radical 1930s a contemporary guide book talks of 'the air of remote timelessness about the tree bordered streets, blue flagstone sidewalks and picket fences'. The wartime camp, a mile or two from the centre of the town, is an intelligent reconstruction of what may have once existed but could well be something left over from a film set. A modern guide remarks, in slightly speculative tones, 'The Dignitaries who visited Morristown went to the Grand Parade to witness ceremonies involving the entire army ... guards were assigned, orders were issued, and punishment meted out almost every day.'

The latter is certainly true. Washington enforced the most draconian discipline to try to prevent his whole force disintegrating into chaos and mass desertions, but the polished image of a precursor of West Point or the Academy at Annapolis is far from the truth. A tradition has been manufactured to fit the preferred image of the time in modern America, and this mythology finds its way into some of the Springsteen song canon, with a number like 'Independence Day' having little to say about the history, but providing a fixed known backdrop for a critical family event, the past eliding with an oppressive father.

Travelling south of Morristown the journey takes one through rich farming country, and in the time of the War of Independence this was, and in small measure still is, the terrain of the Jersey Dutch, augmented by different phases of dissident German immigration, as at Denville. Dutch reformed churches are still found and one of them, at Westfield, started a Theological Seminary that after various twists and turns in its history eventually became the now venerable and universally respected Rutgers University. In the modern United States, many ostensibly governmental and secular institutions have confessional origins. Many of Springsteen's songs are about belief, belief in oneself and the need to 'stand ground', belief in a particular loved woman, belief in the possibility of a better America. Behind the manicured but inert and apparently anonymous trees marching in their millions by the 295 South is a strong faith and the distilled faiths of the past, in a country where it was possible to escape the faiths of the Old World with their structural links to oppressive and undemocratic government and for individual to begin again and become new in the eyes of God. Unsurprisingly, in modern Jersey the churches in bewildering variety are still there and doing well in their diversity.

Surrounding Morristown are many different small town communities seemingly lost in the woods, often with signs boasting of their foundation as places in the inter-war years. By Kinnelon on Route 23 towards Butler there was then a vast and glittering Harley Davidson showroom, and nearby a classic chromium box American diner, run by a Greek family whose politics, like many round here, are firmly of the Republican right. It is a temple as much as on the Acropolis to eat and hear the unmistakeable bubby roar of the Harley engines as bikes and bikers come and go, as unique and evocative a sound as the rat a tat of an AK-47 semi-automatic rifle in wartime. In both cases, once heard, never forgotten. Harley Davidsons come from Milwaukee, a place for great beer and engineering skills built on numerous German emigrants over the years. A road leads left up into the stylish suburban houses and expensive 24-hour security gated communities of little Kinnelon but suddenly there is drama.

A lady is in the centre of a disturbance going on outside the garage of her pretty house on the edge of the wood, a younger one who looks like her daughter is screaming blue murder and flapping her fleece madly at the open trunk of her car, for no apparent reason. Then a small dark mammal legs it away. The unwanted visitor to her car has left. It was a skunk. Jersey skunks like garages, especially in winter and when the weather gets colder. Then you come into the garage and disturb it and it sprays your shoes and tights and under your skirt with its foul smelling fluid. Yuck. Skunks also like to live under the lee boards of your house. Some people also find them caught in groundhog traps when they get really angry and have a chance to bite you as well as making you smell unimaginably awful. And then you might just fall into the poison ivy, be bitten by a tick left by a wandering deer or meet a black bear in the mini-woodland. Or maybe a wandering coyote, immigrants from Canada a while ago and also flourishing.

There are hundreds of black bears in Jersey, their numbers are growing every year and a limited hunt is allowed. The state Division of Fish and Wildlife puts a leaflet through your door urging you to bear-proof your surroundings this fall. An electric fence is recommended. There is a lot going on in the woods around Kinnelon and Morristown and Boonton and Pompton Lakes and all those lovely echoing place names. The Department has more good advice: use common sense in an encounter with a bear, remain calm and never approach the animal. But it's New Jersey. It may approach you. The woods can be full of symbolic fears as Tony Soprano found obsessing about the ducks in his swimming pool, but the obsessions are also based on real experiences, as its takes Tony's confessor cum therapist, the lovely Jennifer Melfi, quite a while to find out.

Earlier in the year, in March, the last *The Sopranos* series had started on TV. Soap opera characters—and an important dimension of the appeal of the series was that it conformed to most of the demands of the family soap epic—are uninvited guests in our homes and we get to know them very well. Series creator David Chase had commented in an important interview that spring that the attraction of the series was bound up with the fact that it showed the ordinary person in conflicts viewers could understand, Tony's crew against the crew from over the hill. The theme of depersonalization in life is identical to the main themes in the *Magic* album, and affects its sense of time, the immediacy of the present, so watching a *Sopranos* episode is like reading a good newspaper story, a report on conflict in the present day, subverting the conventional narrative of most Mob films and books which are set in the past. It is also about the domestic life of the Mob, something new and meaning that women could figure as large as men and gender issues could be explored, from episode one in series one where Tony seeks to unburden himself to his therapist Jennifer Melfi, a woman who herself has a long family history from the Boot, Italy, to the puzzle of the final episode ending when so many potential assailants line up by Tony's dead body. He is a truly tragic character here, in a way other fictional and real Mob leaders meeting their final demise are not. That episode was seen on TV on 10 June. It was a fateful, sombre day, 10 June 2007.§

---

§ Another sombre day followed a few years later. On a hot day in Rome on 19 June 2013,

Innocence

'*Surely nature longs for the opposites and effects her harmony from them.*'

Aristotle, On the World, 396b7

Innocence in modern America can seem a hard quality to find. Writing in his autobiography, the Boss observes:

> I was the child of Vietnam-era America, of the Kennedy, King and Malcolm X assassinations. The country no longer felt like the innocent place it was said to be in the Eisenhower fifties. Political murder, economic injustice and institutionalized racism were all powerfully and brutally present... This was the new lay of the land and if I was going to put my characters out on that highway, I was going to have to put all these things in the car with them.

For the exhibition in Newark Museum a while ago, the automobile and road were the motifs and it was headlined 'Springsteen, Troubadour of the Highway'. It had some astonishing photographs, like Annie Liebovitz's portrait of Bruce in Asbury Park in 1982, draped elegantly in the back of a sedan in his James Dean mode, too sexy to look at for long, a woman friend of mine said. Perhaps she was thinking of the line in 'Cadillac Ranch', 'James Dean in that Mercury '49', and this was always the case.

Innocence didn't last very long in the pioneering days either. Economic exploitation of New Jersey was important to the British colonial system from the earliest days and this led to pillaging of the natural resources and environment. As early as 1711, an Act of Parliament was passed for the 'preservation of the white pine tree for the masting of her Majesties Navy'. The colonial pre-industrial past was not innocent. Native American life

---

James Gandolfini suddenly died of a heart attack. An era was ending. The series had died five years before. The great film and TV actor who brought Tony Soprano to life and sustained the series throughout was no more. Yet in a final symbol, if it had to happen, it was within sight of the Vatican, which seemed an appropriate place for him to leave the world.

before the colonialists arrived was one of continual, if intermittent, war and fierce competition for territory and resources.

A recurrent theme in Bruce Springsteen's songs is that of an innocent past, not necessarily a better part of the standard Republican Old Glory kind but a sense of loss for a better America, or just a simpler, more comprehensible America. Beneath the stereotypes of Coke, McDonalds and the Empire State Building that every tourist knows and sees is an extraordinarily complicated society and a vast country where few of even the most travelled inhabitants have visited more than a small part. The end of the conscript military has closed a major youth travel avenue for many from poorer backgrounds. Meanwhile science and society have advanced and society grows ever more difficult to know and understand in a country which does not really have national newspapers except for the elite and where it is not always easy to find news and information of good quality on television. The common well-travelled Briton's jibe against Americans is about how many have never been abroad and the high proportion of the population that does not own a passport, but equally relevant is how many have never visited anywhere much in the US outside their home and family orbit, vacation spot and locality. The Springsteen call is often for America to renew itself, but this may be difficult when you are tied to very long hours and average wages in a job and shorter vacations than Europeans. Another factor is the increasing expense and bother of internal air transport, from its days as a near bus service with kerbside check-ins to the heavy security, expense and long travel times of the post 9/11 world.

New Jersey can seem a crowded state where the original innocence and promise of the United States is hard or impossible to find, and is often ridiculed by many Americans and seems an awful place to live. It is not like that at Sandy Hook, 'the Hook' to all Jerseyites, and its nearby seaside town of Highlands, or Atlantic Highlands. Sandy Hook is a strange and beautiful little peninsula formed from ever shifting sand dunes and facing due north into the Atlantic and into Raritan Bay and then beyond that, the Bay or Lower New York itself. It is in the front line for savage north-east gales blowing down from Labrador in the winter and the remnants of hurricanes in late summer. Few people have ever lived there, but it has always been favoured land, an important port in the eighteenth century:

> Sandy Hook, where vessels may arrive almost any weather in over tide from the sea, and find a safe corridor harbour, capacious enough to contain many large ships, is allowed to be as good a port as most on the continent.

The port went decades ago, swallowed by the development of the ports of Newark and Elizabeth and New York itself in the nineteenth century, but it was always a place for relaxation and pleasure, the land in the *Magic* album of

Girls in their summer clothes

A mile or two south is the little estuary of the Navesink River and on it plutocratic Rumson, until recently Springsteen's home beat. It is the best of the New Jersey shore suburbs, in the eyes of some New Yorkers, and what had once been a rather poor and marooned mostly German-American and Irish-American fishing community at the time of World War I boomed in the interwar period and spawned holiday homes for rich city families ranging from Mob dons to respectable stockbrokers. The town bore a heavy burden from 9/11 and the collapse of the Twin Towers with so many Wall Street commuters living there, and there were over 150 funerals in Monmouth County alone. Ferries crossed the water, carrying survivors from the city, grey with ash.

The Hook is, in its way, exquisitely beautiful, with hanging branches of native deciduous trees brushing the sand dunes, a rich birdlife and vast views northwards to New York, Jamaica Bay off Brooklyn and the distant state of Connecticut. The memory of the recent terrible school gun massacre is hard to credit. Birds of prey hunt over the marshes and much of the scenery is the same as the dense shoreline woods the first

European settlers could have seen. Girls in their summer clothes are part of the fabric of life in the warm months, although with a touch of daring: the Hook also hosts the only 'clothing optional' (nudist) beach along the Atlantic Jersey Shore. From the top of the salt grass-covered dunes there is a small concrete viewing platform by the car park, and then, over the dunes, hundreds of acres of wild open beach with thickets of spiky shrubs and an odd oystercatcher pecking about and the moving wilderness of the sea. This is the world of innocence, whereas the New Jersey of the Sopranos is the fabric of difficulty and experience.

Yet it is a world of change. Sandy Hook now may look the same in the vast blue open seascape, but it is geographically nothing like it was when the first Europeans came, or even as it was at the beginning of the twentieth century. The shore is constantly under the pressure of the wind and waves, and the longshore current has been moving sand and silt northwards to broaden and lengthen the Hook for thousands of years. When the first military structure, Fort Hancock, was built in 1764 by the British Army at the northern tip, the Hook was more or less an island, surrounded by marshes and dense marine forests which the Native Americans treasured for the rich berry crop and opportunities to net migrating birds. Recent archaeology on the Hook has revealed the lifestyle of the British colonial garrison officers, with elaborate clay pipes, marble statues and bottles of fine French wines. Early accounts of interaction between the Lenape and the settlers recount Native American complaints about their historic foraging and hunting grounds being eroded by settlers' farms, and the loss of traditional habitat. Although on a deserted shore as far east in the United States as it is possible to be, the dialect of the conflicts of the later West and the obliteration of the Native Americans' traditional lands on the Great Plains was already being played out here on little Sandy Hook and all down the Atlantic Jersey Shore.

The modern world is not far away, however. Driving north along the Hook towards the historic Fort Hancock lighthouse it does not take long before a slightly incongruous looking Nike missile appears sticking out of a roadside plinth, and there are closed military areas nearby. The

Hook is host to various missile batteries that protect the gateway to New York City to the north. The initiated might think that they were placed in the aftermath of 9/11 but in fact the Hook fortifications date back much further, to the birth of American independence, in the form of the little Hancock naval base on the north-west tip, and to the remarkable lighthouse, the oldest in the United States, which was built by the British colonial merchants of pre-independence New York City to aid their ships. The main defences started to develop against the Nazi submarines in World War II. German U-boat submarines were a direct threat to New York City long before the United States entered the war on the side of the Allies. The Nike missile batteries are from the height of the Cold War. The World War II threat to New York was much more real than most Europeans nowadays realize, and evidence of German U-boats lurking underwater near New York was one of the factors that convinced many doubters of the need for US commitment against the Nazi war machine after 1939. Historians of 9/11 will no doubt surmise what might have happened if the Nikes' post-Cold War successors had been able to shoot down one or more of the hijacked 9/11 planes.

Innocence and wildlife are found in the museum with its display cases of racoons and white toed field mice. There is material from the pioneers of the United States Life-Saving Service, a nineteenth-century organization founded by a Congressman Newell after he had watched people drown as a wooden ship broke up on a coastal reef. It later mutated into the modern US Coast Guard. Sandy Hook was notorious for shipwrecks, with the ever-changing sandbanks and shoreline making charts and navigation aids useless, with its exposure to the vicious storms in the congested shipping lanes on the approach to the port of New York. So, as in the song, there is a bittersweet character to the Hook shoreline. Springsteen's 'Girls in their Summer Clothes' is both a simple statement of a man watching pretty women passing along the street or the beach, and a nostalgic reflection, a song written by a man in his sixties who knows he will not always be around and that perhaps he is more interested in the girls than they are in him.

Jersey shores like the Hook are also innocent in another way: money and the power of money is irrelevant. In 2007, when the *Magic* recordings were released, *Forbes* magazine published its annual evaluation of the world's richest people. New Jersey did not do very well. It is seen by the very rich as a high tax state, which it is, and many who make their money there choose not to reside in it. The magazine itself has New Jersey links in that founder Steve Forbes is a Tiger, a Princeton alumnus, and so on. 2007 was in its way perhaps the last year of innocence for the superrich before the banking crisis which loomed in 2008-9 and with it the stock market collapse that late summer. The list of American billionaires has its familiar names, with Bill Gates then at Number 1, followed by master investor Warren Buffett, but what is also interesting is their state residence locations: Washington, Florida, California, Texas for so many, and New Jersey hardly figuring at all until the 58th richest person, Jacqueline Mars, of the confectionary empire, worth about US$10 billion, according to *Forbes* billionaires rankings, the richest resident New Jersey citizen. There are then no New Jersey residents until the 100th richest person, Donald Newhouse, the publisher.

What have all these people got to do with Bruce Springsteen or his fans? Not very much, although among some of the very seriously superrich are also very serious rock fans like Microsoft co-founder Paul Allen, in 2007 worth US$18 billion dollars and sponsor of his own rock and roll museum on the Pacific coast which includes Springsteen guitars and other material in the collections. But there is an inherent egalitarian streak in New Jersey life, the sense that any man or woman is as good as another unless proven otherwise, and the discreet old money of Jersey stays that way, discreet, unlike some of the new money on the West Coast.

So is there no cave on the shores of Sandy Hook? But there are, many. Along the north side of the old military base are picturesque and very ruined old officers' houses, torn and engraved by the wind and rain and sun, and quite empty. The military have long gone here and only the odd groundhog has taken their place. Seagulls and terns quarrel on the roof. No one is chained inside. The military have moved on from most of Fort

Hancock, but are still busy in the great task of defending New York City.

It would be tempting to think of this innocent world as distant from crime and enumeration, greed and theft, threats and murder. There are so many familiar street names, domestic and English, like Cornwall Street, Shrewsbury Avenue, Dover Street and so on. But that would not be true. Made men have walked here. Rum running brought the first big money to Highlands and Hook, as ships came down from Canada heavily laden with whisky and gin and anchored just outside the three-mile enforcement limit offshore. The bootleggers sailed in fast lobster scamps and loaded up at sea, a dangerous, uncertain business, before running the liquor into New York City where there was almost infinite demand. Many of the seamen were Irish men and women and used to dealing with the shoals and dangerous tides off Kerry or Mayo before they came to the Hook's shallows and sandbars. Bahrs Landing restaurant in Highlands is a hundred years old and a famous seafood place that first prospered accommodating bootleggers. Like many newcomers to the Hook around that time, the Bahrs were German and prejudice against them ran high. A song thought to date from around 1910 goes

> Highlands' Miller and Burdge, Parker, Cottrell and Brown
> Maxson, Matthews and Mount, Liming, Hartsgrove and Worth,
> Now Lynch, Scalia, Rosenblum, Irish, Guinea and Jew,
> Damn, the Highlands ain't the Highlands anymore.
> No, the Highlands ain't the Highlands anymore.

The old Monmouth County ascendancy of Good Ol' Boys of Scottish and English Presbyterian descent, the self-appointed Yankees of the shore, were being outnumbered by the cosmopolitan new immigrants of those years. There was little in the way of respected local cultural authority, or government authority of any kind. And after World War I, under pressure from Prohibition, law and order, never in great standing on the shore, was breaking down. Men from the Dark Side were about. The Hook and the Jersey Shore generally was a favoured recreation spot of Joseph Vincent

Moriarty, 'Newsboy Moriarty', the mobster controller of the numbers game in north Jersey. He was a small, nondescript Irish-American, originally from the Galway *Gaeltacht*, an Irish-speaking enclave on the Atlantic Ocean with a long tradition of lawlessness and anti-British rebellion. This spirit was easily transferred to the slums of the United States. Illegal gambling is and was absolutely central to the whole panoply of the efficient survival of organized crime in the US. As a semi-literate Irish immigrant Moriarty knew it as well as a crooked cop turned Fed wire wearer, Ron Previte. Speaking to the State of New Jersey Commission of Investigation in 2004, Mr Previte said that

> As long as you have illegal gambling and that sort of thing, you're going to have the mob, because … there's big money in bookmaking and gambling and it's not going anywhere. I mean real big money. And that, I think, is the backbone of organized crime...

The Hook on the opposite shore reminded Moriarty of his Atlantic boyhood. Irish-American cops could easily be bribed and in places like Five Points or the Horseshoe they were the US state, alone. Square the cops and you were born to steal without hindrance. Joe Moriarty had arrived off the boat in 1910 and before long was living in the dire area in Jersey City called the Horseshoe, inhabited mostly by other very poor Irish immigrants who made a living, just, as day labourers on construction sites. He liked to take the bus over to the Hook and walk the shore on a Sunday after Mass in his nondescript brown church suit. But he was an ambitious young man and hated the poverty in the Horseshoe, where he seemed entombed. Then and now, crime is for many the only way to make very fast bucks and get off the Jersey street. He started as a teenage numbers runner collecting illegal betting slips and joined the street numbers rackets, an obscure game and gambling system brought up from the South in the so called Great Migration of maybe a million Afro-American ex-slaves that took place after the Civil War. Numbers with them was becoming a craze.

The Numbers, or Policy, or Italian Policy as it is sometimes known, was essentially an illegal offshoot of the numerous official lotteries that blossomed in the nineteenth-century South, particularly Louisiana, to help fund infrastructure projects. It was called 'policy' as it seemed to offer insurance, of an odd kind, against bad fortune, through enabling the poor to gamble a very small stake but very occasionally win big. The day's number was decided by derivation from the last number before the decimal in the handle at the racetrack. It swept through the ghettos of the post-World War I period, and vast fortunes were made by policy controllers, in Harlem by Stephanie St Clair, America's most successful black female gangster of all time. She was displaced in the 1930s as the 'Queen of Harlem' and sultana of the numbers by bootlegging magnate 'Dutch' Schultz. St Clair had herself displaced 'Bumpy' Johnson and the other gangland controllers of the several policy rackets operating in Harlem in the early 1920s before being sidelined in her turn.

'Dutch' Schultz built his late-Prohibition period bootlegging empire in New York City in a river of blood on the ruins of Irish gangster Jack 'Legs' Diamond's operations. Schultz was actually German-Jewish before his conversion to Roman Catholicism and at his birth was called Arthur Simon Flegenheimer. Schultz was looking for profitable business opportunities to make up for the loss of revenue after bootlegging alcohol and Prohibition ended in 1933. The numbers racket based on numerous policy banks was vastly profitable as the pay rate was only 600-1 on an odds range of 1000-1 and operators were experienced and streetwise, often barely literate but capable of doing the complex mental arithmetic on the odds with astonishing speed and accuracy. Later, an Irish-speaking outsider like Moriarty could move in at street level in the slums of north Jersey where by tradition there was little respect for the law and build up his own policy 'bank' (actually just an illegal bookmaking institution) quite quickly. He became the Napoleon of the Jersey numbers game just as in a very odd onomastic coincidence Sherlock Holmes's most lethal and final enemy Professor Moriarty in Doyle's great story *The Final Problem* was the 'Napoleon of crime ... organiser of all that is evil and nearly all that is undetected in this great city'.

Conan Doyle was an early exponent of the glamorization of the master criminal, a process many law enforcement staff believe still affects perceptions of the Mafia and leads people who are successful and don't actually need to deal with them to do so. Immensely respectable old ladies from New York suburbs love the Mob court cases, fight for places in the courts and are connoisseurs of beatings, threats, kickings and murders. As always in this period in America, the shadow of Nietzsche falls over the Jersey streets, the master criminal as Superman, the one above the law, 'who sits motionless like a spider at the centre of a web'. Conan Doyle's Professor Moriarty also derived his power from the numbers, as a young man he was a mathematical genius:

> At the age of twenty one he wrote a thesis on the Binomial Theorem, which has had a European vogue. On the strength of it he won the Mathematical Chair at one of the smaller Universities, and had to all appearances a most brilliant career before him. But the man had hereditary tendencies of the most diabolical kind. A criminal strain ran in his blood ... rendered infinitely more dangerous by his extraordinary mental powers.

Policy gambling had existed in the United States since at least 1860. The Jersey region was similarly grabbed in what later was to become Bruce Springsteen's home turf; as the New York paper the *Inter State Tatler* reported in 1927, Asbury Park was 'numbers mad'. A young Joseph Bonanno, later hoodlum Joe Bananas and future boss of the Bonanno crime family, was expanding the Italian version of the illegal lottery all over Brooklyn. Policy gambling was a parallel structure for poor blacks to compensate for the fact they could not take part in the middle-class Wall Street get-rich-quick frenzy of the time. Policy was what ex-Southern blacks knew and the numbers frenzy grew exactly as stocks frenzy did. 'Dutch' Schultz's and later Joe Moriarty's strokes of business genius were to transfer the gambling system off the streets of Harlem and other black districts and make it a regular habit of the white working class, although

Schultz himself did not live long to enjoy his fortune. Even in the early 1930s, as a commentator writes, he was 'a loose cannon out of control, he was a dead man walking'.

The latter Southern metaphor derived from a voodoo zombie fitted well. Schultz was shot down in a gangland feud in 1935 and died in a New York hospital. He had wanted to slot his nemesis, the prosecutor John Dewey, but the Mafia commission didn't allow it and had him killed instead. Joe Moriarty, by comparison, had quite a long life but was busted forty-seven times and died of cancer in 1979 after many spells in gaol. Once, someone finding by chance US$2.6 million in the boot of his car led to his arrest in Jersey City. But Joe was popular, something of a Robin Hood figure who loathed conventional banks and always paid, on time and in full, even if a number had come up badly on the racetrack against him.

In practice, often the only time the US government and state gets a real clear win against mobsters like Moriarty or, most famously, Al Capone is over tax evasion. Moriarty was charged with owing US$1.5 million in back taxes. Nice magazine pieces about him with titles like 'The Honest Bookie who Just Hated Banks' were not much help against the forces of the law. Thinking of him, the Hook afternoon remained beautiful, but was suddenly empty. Were the numbers played now on the Hook? Were vast profits made? Schultz had certainly made them. But then, in the traditional English phrase, 'his number was up'. For most Hook bootleggers it was different. Prohibition had been a party and it was over and the hard years of the Depression and the soup kitchens and food line had taken over. The little fish made is safely back to harbour even if big fish like Schultz moved on to the numbers and then were put away. After 1933, law enforcement lost interest in what was happening along the shore. Tidy packets of illegal money from running whisky into New York in the small boats were hidden away under mattresses or invested in houses so that it could not be traced. In Highlands and as the years wore on the stories got taller and taller as they were shared between old sailors on the windy winter nights. Sometimes they talked of the whisky runs, and how the whole town benefitted from Prohibition, other times mulling over recent local sensations like the murder of Raymond Waddle in Highlands in 1930.

If the talk was slow there was always reminiscence of the most famous Highlander of all, Gertrude Ederle, the first woman to swim the English Channel in 1926. Time moved on. As the Depression worsened, Highlands became full of families who were camping out in their summer cabins after losing their main homes in foreclosures. The atmosphere was very bad and the place seemed to be on the skids. They were refugees on the shore from the Depression as much as Douglas Springsteen was a refugee from the Depression when he left the Appalachians then and started looking for work in Jersey before eventually the army and World War II swept him up. But the place has always appealed to some prominent people, good and bad, in the latter case crime boss Vito Genovese who lived modestly in the Highlands for thirty years, a respected (and feared) local citizen, and there is a close E Street connection, as band drummer and TV star Max Weinberg was also born and grew up here. It is perhaps a sign confirming the views of those who think that Mob culture has so impregnated Jersey life that law enforcement initiatives will ultimately always fail.

A little inland is Paterson, perhaps the antidote to the innocence of Sandy Hook. The old city has a long and quite often troubled history, and frequently a bad press these days, and it is not hard to see why. It is easy to find. Just spin the car along the 78 West for a while and then turn onto the Parkway into the great spider's web of roads towards Paterson and great Victorian mill buildings and the odd minaret and church tower loom in the distance. Established by President Andrew Hamilton in 1791 as a model industrial town, with rapidly developing mills based on water power from the Passaic River waterfalls, its high bridges over the river are deeply familiar to all students of *The Sopranos*, a place where crooked cops can be talked to without the FBI listening, and where the odd corpse can be dropped into the river to be quickly carried away into the sea by the fast flowing waters. The deep river gorge is still a fine place to visit nowadays, and Paterson has more of interest than might first appear, and enjoys fame as the place where in 1836 the legendary Samuel Colt made his first revolver, rivalling his brother Christopher who had opened the first silk mill. The Colt was the gun of the Old West, just as the Beretta, Glock and Luger are nowadays the guns of hundreds of thousands of Jersey car glove boxes, progenitors of TV soap lines like 'if I had a Luger I could drill the bastards,' or 'No Beretta, no waiting room for the crematorium.' And so on.

In those days machine-made silk was a novelty and visitors came from Europe and Asia to Paterson to see this breakthrough and they marvelled at the number of mills and the amount of silk and other cloths that were produced. Yet silk was a peculiarly eighteenth-century product in its way and as the nineteenth century wore on, Paterson was no longer at the forefront of American industry and some strain on the earlier prosperity was showing. In a modern echo, cheap imports from Asia became a problem, and as a result the employers put more and more downward pressure on wages. Paterson quickly became an early centre of first trade union and then socialist organization with the Industrial Workers of the World, the Wobblies, and the scene of some of the most bitterly fought and divisive strikes in the history of the American labour movement. Famous names such as Big Bill Hayward, civil liberties leader Elizabeth Gurley Flynn and Harvard revolutionary John Reed stood on the violent picket lines against Pinkerton private detective-organized strike breakers. In 1910 a picket was killed and Haywood led 15,000 people on a march through Paterson to the cemetery. It was another world, where intelligent people discussed a socialist revolution in the United States as a real possibility.

Paterson employers liked the old methods of production, and made their workers sweat long hours in poor conditions for paltry wages. When technological improvements were introduced, there were mass sackings. As many of the Paterson workers had originally come as political exiles from Germany, Italy, Ireland and Russia, and in most cases had radical traditions of their own, particularly the Jews, it was an explosive mixture. In not so far away New York City there was the United Garment Workers of America, a trade union which was run from top to bottom by Jewish Marxists. In theory help was at hand but it did not suffice. The mass strike was defeated and after World War I the movement never regained its former strength. There was a long and bitter strike in 1924, the mill owners began to close down facilities, and apart from a brief return to former glories making parachute silk in World War II, the final decline began from which in many ways Paterson has never recovered. The dyes used brought serious pollution to the Passaic River, which ended the oyster beds along that part of the Jersey Shore near the estuary. New plants like the huge Wright Aeronautical factory nearby brought a respite, but the old days of mill glory were over.

Many Springsteen songs are near this world, although as always, specific place names are often absent, apart from narratives like that of American industrial decline in 'Youngstown', or the very contemporary echoes in 'Johnny 99', where 'the bank was holding my mortgage and they were taking my house away', but 'The River' says it very succinctly, in a song everybody knows:

I got a job working construction
For the Johnstown Company
But lately there ain't been much work
On account of the economy

The world of the rundown rustbelt Jersey towns is not only a common story of industrial decline, but a story of consequent alienation and dehumanization in relationships, a recurrent Springsteen theme. It is set out as part of the crisis of mid-twentieth century America in William Carlos Williams's great poem *Paterson*.

I reached for the car keys. The weather was an Atlantic storm closing in with drenching rain and it was not a good day to see Neptune City, south of Long Branch and Asbury Park, birthplace of Jack Nicholson in 1937, and Spring Lake, where the Hollywood star later grew up on the so-called 'Irish Riviera'. The shore had nurtured here yet another supremely gifted Jersey cultural icon. Although a classic Jersey Boy rebel, so bad at school after a chaotic childhood with uncertain parentage in a very broken family that Nicholson was in detention every day for a year, he has always carried his state identity with him, if sometimes lightly. When Nicholson was inducted into the New Jersey Hall of Fame in 2010 he said whatever you did afterwards you could never get away from the place and its maverick quality: what other state would celebrate one Gideon Sundback, inventor of the fly zip on men's trousers? And then, chameleon-like as always, he gave a learned disquisition about how Walt Disney Pictures got started in New Jersey before, like all the nascent industry, it moved to California for the sunny shooting weather. And he said he could sing the praises of New Jersey all night; he was a Jersey Boy who had taken the route to Hollywood exile and triumphed.

It was time to think about Bruce Springsteen in Princeton. Would the Boss's father have played the numbers? Did Bruce ever relate to number through gambling, or only through the interaction of words and music? Iris Murdoch has explained more clearly than anyone not just how but why Plato would allow music as an art but users of words in art—the poets—would face exile, or at least be gently escorted to the border of the ideal state. Her key point was to highlight the fact that the ancient philosopher disliked the aspect of art as 'play'. Rock bands just play numbers, in colloquial language terms. Plato saw human life as a journey from appearance to reality, a deeply serious journey. Those who interrupted this process face exclusion and exile.⁋ The Boss had done exile in California but returned home. What did this really mean? Could you go into exile within the United States, or only outside it? What did it mean to leave your home state in the modern United States? Some places in the state are full of voluntary exiles, like Princeton, and Princeton is Number City, home of much modern mathematics and, once, the most famous

---

⁋ See Iris Murdoch, *The Fire and the Sun: Why Plato Banished the Artists* (1977).

exile of the twentieth century, the mathematician Albert Einstein. Or that is how one myth of one cave goes. End of travel text for a while (quite a long while) ... because at the exact time 'Dutch' Schultz and later Newsboy Moriarty took the numbers monopoly away from the black districts, Albert Einstein, loving the college at Christ Church but tired of the formalities of Oxford and political crisis in Europe, was arriving in Princeton. He had broken the numbers between Time and Space. Number, time and space would never be the same again.

6

SERIOUS INCIDENTS IN PRINCETON

Concerning Princeton, beauty and intellectual excellence, privilege and style, and the arrival of MS-13 gangsters in the story

'So now the Beloved is in Love, but with what He cannot Tell.'
Plato, *Phaedrus*, 256

Princeton and its University arouse deep emotions. It expects admiration on its own terms, as no doubt Plato's academicians did. For the foreign visitor or the American wanderer in search of New Jersey history, the governor's residence at Drumthwacket is the first building in Princeton to see, an elegant, magnificent 1834 Greek Revival structure at the edge of a wood, acres of white clapboard with tall Ionic columns and a sense of the sweeping confidence that was the country after the final break with Britain in 1812 and the opening perspectives of the vast wealth of the mines and plains of the West. The governor's mansion is white, white, white, endless white wood and is at its most beautiful in winter snow. In the fall the sunlight on the trees with their reds and yellows and browns needs an Impressionist painter.

Princeton was not itself that week, although it was hard to know why, unless it was the Dow hitting a then all-time high of 14,164 before beginning its decline into the recession and the financial crisis. But numbers are like that, they are all around you but it is often hard to know what they mean at the time you read them. There was a seminar in the Princeton mathematics department that October afternoon, in the little neat tower full of mathematicians half way up the hill running through the wood down to Carnegie Lake. So maybe Princeton is not a long way in space and time from ancient Ionia where, as Walter Pater observed, 'The philosophy of number, of music and proportion, came and has remained, in a cloud of legendary glory.'

The purpose of music was to remould and remaster men's souls, insofar as Plato had inherited the Pythagorean traditions. Perhaps Plato had also taken from the Pythagoreans the idea that the body was a prison; in a rock concert the music helps you escape it for a while. Men jump up and down and punch the air with uncontrollable frenzy. Young women peel down their panties and fling them at the stage with their cell number pinned in. A band plays number after number. How do you do this math? Modern mathematics has parted company with philosophy and surrender to number, with my Oxford colleague Marcus Du Sautoy recently observing in one of his books, 'And the Lottery itself? Hopeless without Numbers.'

The dead leaves were beginning to gently accumulate, but not yet the foot-deep carpet they would be in November as Thanksgiving approached. Numbers were being examined in the little tower, not played, in a language much more complex and difficult than Ancient Greek, as the seminar sheet sets out thus:

> We study the behaviour of the eigenfunction of the laplacian, on a compact negatively curved manifold, and for large eigenvalues. The Quantum Unique Ergodicity conjecture predicts that the probability measures defined by these eigenfuctions should converge weakly to the Riemannian volume. We prove an entropy lower bound on these probability measures, which shows for instance that it is difficult for them to concentrate on closed geodesics.

Playing the numbers in Princeton is different, writing the numbers is different. Numbers are beyond words, like music and love. But humans have had different views on these subjects at different times. It was so in the time of the Lenape Native Americans, who, according to the mythology, thought what we now know as mathematics was largely unnecessary, and their religion rejected the fixed notion of human reason embodied in mathematics. The Algonquin family of tribes had a numeration system based on decimals, a one to one system based on the human digits. An Oneida tribal text from the Midwest states that 'the Creator in his wisdom made polarities so that there would be constant movement, constant interchange.' Numbers meant rigidity and the Native American cosmology was fluid, dynamic. It has remained so to the present day, as a study of contemporary Indians' attitudes to education (not politically incorrect, it is what most tribes still call themselves) notes: 'Among

Native Americans there is a negative image of mathematics, whereby mathematics are perceived as remote, competitive, self-seeking, obsessive and calculating.'

Mathematics has here become an intellectual metaphor for the values of highly competitive American capitalism, the world of derivatives and the algorithm. The first inhabitants of the United States loved harmony, the closest element in mathematics to music, an identical view to the Pythagoreans on the Ionian shores of the ancient Aegean. Modern mathematics has departed a long way from religion and philosophy, the men and women of modern numbers and algorithms have left number mysticism far behind and believe they have achieved reason in the neo-liberal economy, so leaving the Platonic cave. The cave for the Indians is Longhouse religion with its totems and god images, those carried in front of the chained in the Platonic *mythos*.

In contemporary America numbers can mean where you are on the scale, the ladder of failure or success, although no number or planning system can protect the student from having to navigate what Princeton University semi-official historian James Axtell has described as the 'social shoals' in the institution. Even in very rural eighteenth-century New Jersey with its horse and cart society, Princeton always dominated higher education. A traveller in 1765 describes 'Princeton village, where in this last is situate the New Jersey College, a handsome capacious building'.

Everything in modern Princeton can be ranked, from the near Biblical status of the online Zagat restaurant guides to local garages and shops. But it is also possible to rebel against the financial establishment's control of number. Numbers can mean illegal gambling on the street by the poor, just as much as the power of number embodied in atomic physics, in the way the discoveries and work of atomic bomb creators like John von Neumann are seen as part of the 'dilemma of power' the modern scientist faces on all sides. Distinguished rock critic and *Rolling Stone* author Robert Christgau was poised on the step of the Princeton University Humanities building. I did not know him well but he considered both of us to be middle market authors, numerically placed, and so we talked sometimes. He was not optimistic about writing any more about Bruce Springsteen: 'I don't follow him so much these days. He was going down. Now he is having something of a revival.'

This didn't seem very optimistic.

'Penn State has got Springsteen tied up. They had a symposium.'

This was true; it had produced an interesting book.

'To write about Springsteen in the States you have to be a public intellectual. That's it.'

This was interesting, but unclear. All kinds of people have published on Bruce Springsteen, from Harvard professors to Jesuit priests to musicologists, philosophers, people out of therapy because of Bruce, sociologists and fans of all kinds. Springsteen's critics on the secular left see him as the happy beneficiary of a cult, part of the seemingly endless capacity of Americans to integrate semi-religious ideas in secular contexts, always reaching back to a fundamentalist evangelism. In the critics' view, people do not just content themselves with being fans of Bruce; they have to believe in him in a particular way. He almost has a theology.

Then Robert's nearby friend changed the subject and began a disquisition on what it was like to be a visiting scholar at Princeton but not a Princeton alumnus. He had been invited to a gathering in the Princeton Club of New York, which was very good and with really nice staff and he loved the building on West 43rd but it was an alumni reunion day and the Club was full of elderly Tigers in bright orange jackets, and he did not own one and was not entitled to wear one anyway. Their jackets roared wealth and power. He did not feel at ease. He was not a member of the Tiger tribe, let alone a product of one of the famous frat houses along Prospect. He had graduated from Dartmouth College, he said gloomily, nothing to worry about you might think given its distinction and long famous history and US Navy links, but the whole subject was clearly on his mind. I too had seen those jackets. They screamed manic demented orange, orange looking as if it had been on the white powder from Colombia, blowharding Orange at you as if in pain. Yet they were rather wonderful in their way, the University has not lost its traditions despite the endless efforts of its administrators, like Oxford, to make it more like everywhere else. Princeton alumni are not given to understatement in life.

Robert asked me what I was reading and writing. I said I was thinking about a book someone had given me, which among other things had made me compare the modern rock star to a shaman, someone who restores harmony with nature by journeying to the spirit world, making contact with the gods when in an altered state of consciousness, and making reports back on his or her return (in the song lyrics, each a small report) at a rock concert. Places like the Bronx and Newark need that harmony and in practice most people can only find it through music, very ancient Greek. And Mr Plato wouldn't have minded. So was the rock concert in some way a fraud, sold as a method for the fans to share the shaman's journey but in fact not involving the tiring schlep of doing so? The fans just had to dance, do pills, vodka or drugs or whatever to alter their consciousness, and generally chill out and share things with the star. Robert looked interested, and replied, 'Maybe. Maybe not.'

He was a man of few words. Maybe he enumerated them, or maybe not. In one way of interpreting the argument, the struggle to get a Springsteen concert ticket was pointless, futile, as the concert itself, the vast arena, well, that was itself a fraud. It could be seen as the most characteristic Platonic Cave, full of chained but voluntary prisoners. The fans thought they were in touch with the other side, in disharmony with Nature during their daily work and the commute grind and then restoring that harmony through contact with Bruce, the healer, the one who can take away evil spirits causing depression or disease. He is, holding his guitar, at once the sorcerer who can ally with spirits, a priest, interpreting the gods to the world, and commanding respect, even fear, as he is the one who can use the music to travel to the other side and return with news, particularly news about the future, the prophetic role. Under the surface of many great rock bands, the séance, and on the dark side, the voodoo ceremony is never far away, as in the Rolling Stones classic *Voodoo Lounge* album. In the E Street Band, Max Weinberg's magisterial drumming starts the journey of the possessed soul, as the voodoo drummer in the South uses drums to raise the spirits of the dead and invite the zombies, the living dead, to walk abroad. Weinberg has the greatest intellectual coherence of any of the E Street Band in his analysis of what a rock band actually does and he was distraught for some time after the Boss broke up the original relationship with the Band back in 1988. The drummer is the beating heart of a rock band, and working with the E Street Band meant that Springsteen could fill arenas. But the lonely outsider spirit of the Boss did not always want to do that. The prophet needs to shed his closest apostles and go into the wilderness on his own sometimes, encounter God in the desert, as with the *Nebraska* album, and see where he is before returning to his buddies.

So is attending a concert in an arena returning to the religion of the hunter-gatherer era, and helps the fan adherents to experience transcendence first hand? Or as Hunter S. Thompson puts it more simply, 'Just buy the Ticket, Take the Ride.' But that assumes you can buy a ticket, and the scalpers are not in control. Or it is all a fraud, a manipulation of reality without number? From that line, if you are into Springsteen's music you might as well just listen to it on headphones sitting at home, critics might argue. In terms of philosophy, there was no obvious way to analyse the problem, as the phrase 'Do the Math' might suggest. How could you do that math if the place the singer went to experience the gods didn't have any numbers? And modern mathematics with its arid algebraic preoccupations has departed so far from philosophy that it cannot offer help. Maybe a down to earth conversation with someone in Princeton who was nothing to do with the University might be a good idea? It was complex for both of us. As holders of positions we were Princeton staff, and thus eligible to apply for membership of the Princeton Club of New York. In fact I had already done so and been accepted as a member. It was a wonderful institution on West 43rd with a zingy library and great beer. On the other hand, it was equally clear that there were gradations in the Princeton identity and in the last analysis only those who had been through the undergraduate experience and had the magic 'Class of '84' soubriquet, Fred Smith'84 or whatever date it was could claim to be fully Tigers. They were, in the fullest sense, numbered in chronological time, in history.

It was time to talk to someone with a different view of the Princeton identity. Across the street was a small women's rights demonstration, a sign reading 'Take Your Rosaries off our Ovaries'. Whatever might be said about Princeton students, they don't mind saying what they really think and so are champagne to talk to or teach. The numbers were important for black people in the history of the US. Some slaves were just numbered, and only acquired names by default. And the numbers were played—how they were played. There are those with a clear memory of the numbers dominating everybody's lives in the desegregated black area that I now lived in but where many Princeton Afro-American families have continued to live long after segregation was finally abolished in New Jersey in 1948. May, the very aged lady a door or so away, a little short on teeth but long on memory who must have been about ninety years old, was an oral encyclopaedia of Princeton black history and recalls her grandmother talking of the nineteenth-century days when in her childhood she was born into slavery when they lived in Virginia.

One of the shocks of working in the United States and so getting to know black Americans for the first time was to discover how close in family chronology and living memory the slave experience actually is for many people. A short ride on the underground railway of abolitionists from Virginia to Jersey that had helped so many escape north meant that May's family had wound up in Princeton. All around us on her television and mine was Hillary Clinton campaigning and then a largely unknown senator from Chicago called Barack Obama who seemed very pleased with himself. May did not have a high opinion of either, and to my surprise said she normally voted Republican, if she voted at all. Why was this? I had bought into the European stereotype that nearly all black people vote Democrat. May didn't.

'We're Republican. It's Abe Lincoln's party.'

Suddenly a long symphony of American history was being played; the way she said his name out of her near toothless mouth was near holy, sacramental. She supported the same Yankee political party as most of the screaming orange jacket men? It seemed intrusive to ask any more. Most of her neighbours and her family had acquired their now extremely valuable if small houses long ago as sharecroppers, in the way the high-minded citizens of Princeton had tried to do something positive for the freed slave population there after the Civil War and during Reconstruction. And there were some jobs, as now, with the University and if that didn't work out New York City was on the train line not too far away.

How did the numbers in Princeton work? Was it about demystifying the ruler's arithmetic and getting temporary relief from the power of number over daily life? Some mathematicians have what a recent London *Times* obituary of George Spencer-Brown called 'a tenuous grasp on reality' and are prone to eccentricity. Princeton numbers can seem an obscure magical cult, a long way away from the civilizing Golden Mean of number promoted by medieval Italian mathematician Fibonacci, the man who pronounced Zero the empty number. May had heard of the ace numbers mobster Joe Moriarty, everybody in Jersey had. He had brought betting on the numbers out of Harlem and into daily life in Jersey. Then she launched into a lengthy explanation of how you could bet small, real small, a dollar or less and the numbers runner who took the bet was usually an Irish lad from their community in Princeton, or maybe an Italian from the Italian scene in Windsor Township a bicycle ride away. There wasn't much police interest, the black community in Princeton was law abiding and with all the serious things the NJPD had to worry about, illegal betting slips were not top of their list. Was it a sucker's game?

'Nope. Everybody knew the big number from the racetrack that day.'

This was not what I meant. Did the punters know they were being ripped off by the numbers runners and maybe creaming off 20 per cent or more of the take on a good day from them?

'No, we sure didn't. Nobody thought about that.'

It was the same as down on the shore trying to get a ticket for the performance of Bruce and the Band. Nobody who goes down thinks rationally what a small chance there is of your number being drawn right. So playing the numbers was about taking part and being a regular guy?

'It was what all the men did. Some got lucky sometimes.'

So it was the American Dream, the numbers game. The gamble was worth it; if you didn't play the numbers in some form, you weren't really an American. Looking across the street at a couple of children playing with a ball, it suddenly occurred to me what the issue of number here was all about. If you were playing the numbers, well, that is what you were doing, playing. And playing with number, a small gamble was not just play, fun, it was also a way of saying to yourself, hey, I am playing the numbers for fun, number is fun, it is not the ultimate and very serious organizing principle of the rational capitalist state centred on DC. Number is mine for a while, and it's chancy, just fate, just rolling the bones, just putting a hand on the bare leg of the Goddess Fortuna, *mutabile et lubricia*, according to a Renaissance writer, changeable and sexy. If you win big you lie down with her, she is happy to fuck you. This gambling method, simple and reliable, wasn't confined to the black communities, or to men. The Italian-American author Janet Zandy writes in her memoir *Liberating Memory*:

> They were gamblers. The aunts played the numbers. They would call each other and discuss numbers that figured in their dreams. Every once in a while, a number hit—for a few dollars. The uncles played the horses... I remember one uncle giving me a tightly folded piece of paper to take to a local candy store. The guy behind the counter of this tiny dirty shop was fat, cigar chewing and not particularly delighted to see children. I handed the paper to him. Sometimes I got a Three Musketeers candy bar for my efforts, most times not. Such was my short career as a numbers runner.

May's grandson Harold appeared. He had a small building repair business and parked his pickup truck at night in Quarry Street. He was a nice quiet man. Did he know anyone who played the numbers in the old way nowadays?

'Oh no. That was for poor people, in the old days. Then. Not now.'

Then there was a long disquisition about the evils of gambling that the original Scottish Presbyterian founding fathers of Princeton would have strongly endorsed, in Harold's case straight from the pulpit of the rigid socially conservative black church he attended with his children every Sunday. Gambling destroyed serious respect for money that might through wise investment, frugality and hard work become Capital, and the owner of it a Capitalist, so gambling of any kind was very bad. He was a true American, where free market economics become a branch of theology. He didn't plan to vote for anyone in the primary, but then said he always told the suits in City Hall in Trenton he was a Democrat, as that helped with getting contracts for repair jobs. I liked Harold, he was friendly and a very good neighbour but he had a slight reserve about the University. He had clearly seen an awful lot of students and faculty, who came and went, but his family had been around in Quarry Street area since Reconstruction. He was a cautious man and seemed to save in a small bank that had connections to his church. He didn't buy stocks or bonds. But he was well set in the capitalist world, nonetheless, as the value of the small houses had soared with the Princeton housing boom and many of his friends nearby had taken advantage of it to move out to a more modern and bigger house somewhere else and then let out the original small house to numerous Mexican and other Hispanic workers, sometimes fifteen or twenty to a house, stacked like tinned fish in a can. They kept Princeton's lawns manicured and the hedges neatly clipped, and meant that no one who didn't want to did any manual work whatsoever: the Princetonians as ancient Athenians. It was very unusual to meet anyone in the Princeton faculty or the town who did anything serious in the way of gardening themselves. Growing vegetables was an unknown sacred mystery and best not risked. In the case of some you felt it might have nearly killed them to try.

Ours was a mixed street; there was a two-million dollar home opposite under refurbishment, an old shell swathed in white insulating material and wood panelling just like a pampered and swaddled baby. A dollar mountain of Wall Street money was being spent to make the house green, but there was so much moolah around in those 2007 days as it was the last good year before the banking crash, and you had to spend it on something or other. It was difficult for some people to know what to do with it all. This house was supposed to be something to do with Lawrenceville School, one of the most expensive private schools in the entire United States, a few miles south of Princeton. May the wise onlooker watched it all and did not seem to draw moral let alone political judgements. There had always been the very rich in Princeton. They were always white, and sometimes one or two students I knew came from southern families which in May's grandmother's time had been in businesses nobody nowadays seemed too keen to talk about. So bankers by comparison didn't seem so bad. Banking does not involve the whip, the field guard or the chain gang. She was like Tiresias in T.S. Eliot's *The Waste Land*. She had seen pretty well everything in Princeton in her nearly hundred years. She saw and was gentle and female and wise and still liked a mean mint julep.

Talking to May brought to mind the seemingly endless, intractable problem of the history of Princeton itself. The University owed its original establishment and then eminence to Dissenting Scottish divines like John Witherspoon who as soon as they arrived from Scotland became enthusiastic Americans. Witherspoon particularly admired in 1767 the lack of beggars, the high standard of living and the invigorating climate, and he and others like him later played very active parts in the Revolution. They may have wished to set up the Platonic Academy but in their lives were pushed into Aristotelian problem definition and practical empirical action. Witherspoon and his Princeton successors were acutely aware of the centrality of their new institution and its history to that of the American colonies generally. This remains the case today.

In the bookshops there were books on almost any aspect of Princeton life and history that you can think of, and some that you may not have done. A book on Princeton drain covers, paving stones or lampposts is about all that is missing. In one sense, the history of the black community had once been the secret history of Princeton, to oppose to the official history that of the old days when history was written by privileged white males to be read by other privileged white males. But the bookshop and the faculty now have black community history pretty well covered, and distinguished Afro-American scholars with jobs, so was there no Procopius secret history unless the history of the Mexicans in town counted as that? That seemed hard to imagine.

Many Princetonians inside and outside the University seemed to see the Mexican and Hispanic illegals as something like the weather, just there and of little interest, like the decorative peasants painted into an eighteenth-century century landscape painting, without any history. They were small, sometimes very small, squat people, and were usually openly deferential, and plodded along the long street near Quarry they seemed to have colonized with blank, expressionless faces. And many people believe the Mexs did the drugs and so were better avoided. As always, the drug issue was the silent ghost in the machine, the zombie whom no one sees walking out. There was a Mex shop with very cheap great piles of limes, different bags of beans and a special telephone to make cheap calls back home. Were they Princetonians too? May thought they were very funny people, Mexicans, her creased and lined black face breaking into a big smile and half laugh at any mention of them. Her nephew reckoned that new people in the US never made it unless they did some sports and Mexicans were too small to succeed at any US sports. So QED in his opinion although he was wrong; some Mexicans are very good at boxing, pint sized tearaway fighting machines. There is a Springsteen song to illuminate things, the rarely performed and little known 'Sinaloa Cowboys', telling of two brothers who venture north to try to make their fortunes in the US, but one, tired of the poor wages on the land gets into drug production and blows himself up, fulfilling their father's prediction in the song:

Their father said 'My sons one thing you will learn
For everything the North gives it extracts a price in return'

In these situations of existential doubt and uncertainty about who is American in the US and who is not, there is one easy remedy, the car keys. You can take a drive around and get the measure of things that way, see the competing histories from the car window, the field where the Battle of Princeton took place—from fighting the British redcoats with smoking muskets to the broad open grass in front of the Institute of Advanced Study where the mathematics of the atomic bomb were finalized. It is evocative for the visitor but hardly usable history for most Americans, the revolutionary nature of Washington's amateur guerrilla army much less easy to utilize for contemporary social engineering purposes than the verities of the Civil War period and, above all, Gettysburg. And then there was the narrow and certainly not broad or open small garden in front of Albert Einstein's old house on Mercer Street. Or in the *Magic* album song, 'We took the highway till the road went black.'

Einstein said Princeton is Utopia. But Utopia is not always easy to understand. Nor the history. The 206 North enters Princeton through a long shady wood, with a sharp turn to the right to continue towards state capital Trenton. Princeton can be very beautiful, in the sunlight a realm of Apollo where the escaped prisoner can receive enlightenment, seeking the world of reason he steps very lightly in the streets, a man who has left the cave far behind him. (But has he/she?) Hang a left and you are in Nassau Street. Across the road is the Nassau Club, a stronghold of

Republicanism and what in the faculties goes by the coded euphemism of 'Old Princeton'. There were always rumours around the University that senior Bush administration Tigers like Senate Majority leader Bill Frist '74, Defence Secretary Donald Rumsfeld '54, and older generation ex-National Security expert Frank Carlucci '52 from the inner circle of the 'Vulcans' in the Bush administration liked to retreat and go into conclave in the Nassau Club. Rumsfeld had been an ace wrestler as a Princeton undergraduate, clearly useful in dealings with Washington opponents in later life. He was said to be a very nice and friendly man personally, whatever you thought of the Bushistas, and his famous ruminations on Known Unknowns and Unknown Knowns show a strong private sense of self-awareness of the limits of intelligence in government that clearly began with his student philosophy studies. It is a pity he did not apply them to more of the thinking behind the Iraq War.

There certainly were many, many Tigers around George Bush. Frists had been at Princeton for generations, from Old Tennessee money. Bill Frist was a very generous donor to the University, and although regarded as only a far-right Bush apparatchik by many students, he was in reality a distinguished heart and lung transplant surgeon, with a long record of scholarly research. In 2007 he was about to wind up his two terms in the Senate after a prominent career. At first sight, to put it mildly, nobody here has anything in common with most characters in Springsteen's songs and characters from blue collar America. Protocol in the club is important; on one visit Bill—genial, but a man never slow to point out the faults of others—queried my tie as possibly tied incorrectly. It was not. I then received a friendly glare from the Majority leader, a lot better than many Democrats in the Senate often received, I thought afterwards. He was the leader of the elected assembly in the most powerful country in the world but clothing etiquette was important to him: how very Princeton. There is a lyric sense of pleasure and contentment in Republican life here, a beauty that is very unusual, that still embodies gilded youth, Pindaric in athletic prowess and Platonic in its ideals. Thus the character in John Dos Passos's novel *1919*:

At Princeton he was the young collegian, editor of The Tiger, drank a lot, didn't deny he ran round after girls, made a brilliant scholastic record, and was a thorn in the flesh of the godly. The natural course for a young man of his class and position was to study law.

The novelist could have added that after law he would become a political leader. Tigers are the Guardians, in one sense children of Plato's Republic, but in the actual philosophy of the 1920s Nietzsche is perhaps more important in understanding them: the young hero living outside normal human limitations as *Superman*. Princetonians saw themselves then like those in Tolstoy, men without limits living in Moscow, the city without limits where anything can happen, as they surveyed sudden American world *Macht*, overwhelming power after World War I under the leadership of ex-Princeton Provost Woodrow Wilson. This has continued in many ways. A significant event in the Princeton year is the analysis of the *Forbes* magazine list of the 400 wealthiest Americans, in 2007 revealing that the richest Tiger among the various alumni billionaires was activist investor Carl Icahn '57, a relentlessly generous donor to the University from his US$14.5 billion fortune. He was once a philosophy major in his time as a student who won the McCosh Prize for the best thesis of his year. In more recent years he has been way overtaken by Amazon.com founder Jeff Bezos '86, in 2017 worth US$95 billion dollars and the richest person in the world. As the University newspaper *The Daily Princetonian* pointed out ten years before, Princeton alumni are not known for taking vows of poverty. In Number City, *Forbes* numbers are important numbers. In the view of the University establishment, the extraordinary worldly success of so many Tigers is due to the excellence of the teaching, the staff, the libraries, a familiar script. But it is also hard not to believe that Princeton turns out Jersey Boys and Girls as much as a local liberal arts college, a crew in the Mob sense, fiercely loyal to each other, worldly wise, success-oriented, ruthless and knowing how to use their elbows if required on Wall Street.

A good time to drive into the Tiger myth is a damp early fall evening when the leaves on the trees are fading and changing colour and the town is at its most beautiful and seductive. Scott Fitzgerald concluded in *This Side of Paradise* in 1919:

Long after midnight the towers and spires of Princeton were visible, with here and there a late-burning light—and suddenly out of the clear darkness the sound of bells. As an endless dream it went on; the spirit of the past brooding over a new generation, the chosen youth from the muddled, unchastened world, still fed romantically on the mistakes and half- forgotten dreams of dead statesmen and poets. Here was a new generation, shouting the old cries, learning the old creeds, through a revery of long days and nights, destined finally to go out into that dirty gray turmoil to follow love and pride; a new generation dedicated more than the last to the fear of poverty and the worship of success; grown up to find all Gods dead, all wars fought, all faiths in man shaken.

It seems as though the University has a purity of thought and purpose for the author of *The Great Gatsby* that is often absent from universities elsewhere. Scott Fitzgerald was perhaps typical of many, maybe all academics and students who have passed part of their lives in Princeton in finding it an inescapable part of himself. As his Boswell Matthew J. Bruccoli observes in his monumental biographical work *Some Sort of Epic Grandeur*, the novelist, despite failing his history papers and having a mediocre (at best) academic record, could not escape from the aura of the University for the rest of his life: 'His poor academic record does not betray indifference to Princeton. He loved it and became almost a caricature of the loyal alumnus. For the rest of his life he returned to Princeton as though looking for some irreconcilable part of himself.'

Albert Einstein also became a model Princeton citizen, sailing his boat on the Carnegie Lake as his gentle recreation and making himself available on Friday afternoons to help local children with their maths lessons. He endorsed the Princeton ideal of enlightened democratic intellectualism, and saw the University as a repository of the best of American values, when so much of the world was disappearing into the bloody maw of Nazism. It is a deeply moving story when seen on the spot, as in the informal but beautifully assembled Einstein museum in his friend Jacob Landau's clothes shop, still going strong today on Nassau Street. He did not, of course, achieve the near-magical 'date' after his name indicating his year of graduation by which Princeton alumni always designate themselves. Albert Einstein '97 cannot exist, like anti-matter in the universe. Yet in another sense, more than any other individual, even Woodrow Wilson, Einstein is modern Princeton.

Yet the recent publication of many of his letters and private papers gives a much more nuanced picture of his view of America generally. He was feted as a genius, American by adoption, but in reality his groundbreaking work had nearly all been done in Switzerland, many years before, in Zurich and in Berne, with his *General Theory of Relativity* published there in 1916. Would Einstein have emigrated to America without fascism? Probably not, and his view of American capitalism is very different from the public image of Einstein as the great Princeton brand, his face on thousands of University T-shirts. He wrote to a friend, Frank Kingdon, in 1942 that 'The United States has a government controlled to a large degree by the financiers, the mentality of whom is near to the fascist frame of mind. If Hitler were not a lunatic, he could have easily have avoided the hostility of the Western Powers.'

Princeton was a perfect island within an uncertain nation, 'a banishment to Paradise', as he told another, noting that although 'Americans are less scholarly than Germans they do have more enthusiasm and energy, causing a wider dissemination of new ideas among the people', but at the same time warning of the threat of a mass society, where 'the individual is lost among the achievements of the many'. He never abandoned his Swiss socialist ideas and so came to the attention of the FBI in the Hoover era, and became one of the founders of the Pugwash organization of concerned scientists who became increasingly critical of American uses of the knowledge of atomic power that his mathematics had made possible. In this, he was very different from his Princeton Institute of Advanced Study colleague and fellow radical émigré Jewish mathematician John von Neumann, a key architect of the Cold War. Van Neumann embraced the unity of US military power and atomic physics with enthusiasm, seeing it as a decisive and final weapon in the fight against communism, which in his case had started in the Hungarian Soviet Republic of March 1919 when his rich mercantile family had been forced to flee to Vienna. Fellow physicist and eventual Nazi fellow traveller Werner Heisenberg had, according to one commentator, as an undergraduate, been shocked to discover the view in Plato's *Timaeus* that atoms had geometric forms, and came to have a 'distaste for visualising unnumerable events'. The very opposite was true of van Neumann, who visualized through the victory of his physics based on the final power of number complete American world domination. At a personal level he took part with enthusiasm in the management of the development of the hydrogen bomb, along with fellow Hungarian physicist Edward Teller. Their politics were very different from the nuanced radicalism of Einstein and Institute Director Robert Oppenheimer, who came under suspicion as an alleged Soviet agent in the Cold War era. Intense political contradictions lay underneath the apparently united and magnificent achievements of the Institute's physics and mathematics.

Clearly other Ivy League colleges had many twentieth-century achievements, but few have broken as much new ground or pushed back the boundaries of mathematical knowledge so far. Some things can be described very simply. Near Nassau Street, the 1950s mathematician and astrophysicist John Wheeler first coined the term 'black hole', now part of everyday speech in every Anglophone country. Black holes can eat stars, a long dormant monster black hole suddenly sucking a star into oblivion at an immeasurable, theoretically impossible rapid speed. Thinking of these matters, Princeton staff have unsurprisingly won many prizes, from Nobels to Fields Medals for mathematics. A recent landmark was the 1994 proof of the centuries-old problem of Fermat's Last Theorem in which Oxford don and sometime Princeton mathematician (now returned to Oxford) Andrew Wiles solved an issue that had haunted mathematicians for 358 years He spent six years working secretly on it in Princeton. But success does not always bring admiration. The inhabitants, the denizens of Princeton University, F. Scott Fitzgerald's 'pleasantest country club in America', are not always very popular elsewhere.

At a dinner in Washington one night, the young lady who had just finished her PhD at Georgetown was told I was returning to Princeton that night. This information did not inspire warm thoughts. 'Are they as insufferable up there as people say?' she asked, turning over the rice in her Thai meal as if to check there was nothing from Princeton, NJ, among the ingredients. The authoritative *Rough Guide to the USA* puts it more succinctly but with the same mild anti-elitist rancour, observing that Princeton is a very 'self-satisfied' place. Princeton does not seem natural Springsteen country and as far as I am aware there is no mention of the city in any Springsteen song, although he has many fans there. Or perhaps Princeton is just a well cut diamond with many multiple faces. Business is always there in the background, and in the astonishing scale of the Tiger wealth created in the last generation. Many of the new technology superrich are recent alumni of which Jeff Bezos '86, Meg Whitman '77 of eBay and Eric Schmidt '76 of Google are only some of the best known. In the state, outside the academic and scholarly community, Princeton is often just seen as a pretty little town, which indeed it is with its neat rows of nineteenth- and early twentieth-century town houses, always white clapboard enclosed like a Presbyterian fortress of virtue with the granite fastnesses of the University central buildings. They still stand solid with a sense of the tough Scottish clerics who founded the college in 1746, but have spawned a successor, the centre of what the Oxford geographer Jean Gottman has described as a 'brains town' within a 'Megalopolis', several satellite towns which more or less join each other all the way down to Hamilton in the south, Windsor in the east and with Rutgers University and Edison towards New York City to the north.

Princeton, in Gottman's view (and certainly its own), is part of the 'edgeless city', with its financial centre in New York, as much part of the wider Jersey as the randy, shopping-obsessed ladies who never read anything apart from celebrity mags in TV's *Real Housewives of New Jersey* or the mathematical melodies and nuances of Einstein or von Neumann's writings. The TV show has zany, racy scenes with husbands and boyfriends; its star Teresa Giudice has been under investigation for mail and wire fraud and bank fraud. She has had problems with her numbers. She is not the only one, and the state charges steep taxes to live in it and is often on the verge of financial crisis. As Gottman points out:

> It costs a great deal of money to devour space as residential sprawl has in the last twenty years. The cost is not paid up when the essential plant is in place. Maintenance is necessary for houses and highways, and the latter must be widened or improved as traffic swells. Schools must be expanded and more parking facilities and more parks must be provided … this means upward revision of rates of servicing, and in the long run more taxation …

So Utopia has its difficulties. There are the critics of Princeton within New Jersey itself, like the distinguished poet William Carlos Williams, who wrote to his friend Jim Laughlin in 1942 that 'The thing is that the academic mind is at its most arrogant and fatally deficient stage. The whole Princeton faculty, as a group, is the prime example in America, worse by far than Harvard.' Yet this was the same Williams who years earlier in 1921, when Einstein made his first triumphant American tour, wrote in 'St. Francis Einstein of the Daffodils':

> Sweet Land of Liberty,
> At last, in the end of time,
> Einstein has come by force of
> complicated mathematics
> among the tormented fruit trees
> to buy freedom
> for the daffodils

If you are in the Princeton faculty, there is no one to blame if you do not excel, given the superb working conditions, high salaries and top quality students. The Firestone Library is one of the great libraries of the world, and has excellent staff. There is no space for failure or lack of success. Most academics belong to the standard liberal consensus and the Woodrow Wilson School of Public and International Affairs is a machine, elegant and efficient, for the production of graduates to build an American-dominated globalized world, however much that vision also embodies abolishing poverty and promoting international development and democracy. But many of the students are much more conservative than the faculty and do not entirely share the overwhelmingly politically correct atmosphere around many of their teachers. In modernity, Princeton has always been identified with extreme social conservatism, with every provost from future President of the United States Woodrow Wilson to current female incumbents trying to change the University, reduce the networking power of the frat houses on Prospect and open up the entry procedures but often failing to do so. When Princeton students eventually began to get involved in the anti-Vietnam war campaigns in the 1960s, they marched under a large banner saying 'Even Princeton'.

Money does not cooperate. It was Princeton networking with Wall Street Tiger alumni that secured the initial financing for the massive internet companies and later mega-wealth. President Barack Obama's wife Michelle had her difficulties over race as an undergraduate, finding prejudice still very much alive below the surface with some people, although others have ascribed some of her difficulties to her combative personality. Modern Princeton contains many contradictions. Until 1939 there were very Jews or Roman Catholics at all (the latter still sometimes known as 'Roman Candles' on campus). One of the main reasons for the creation of the Institute for Advanced Study was the faculty's unwillingness to accept the numerous Jewish scholars who were in exile from European fascism, although the US government certainly welcomed them. The time of great change came after World War II when the Holocaust and the achievements of the often Jewish mathematicians and physicists at the Institute for Advanced Study meant the de facto quota on Jews could no longer be maintained.

Yet without the physics of the Institute for Advanced Study, in its sober brick building on the edge of a wood near the Battle of Princeton site, the nuclear age, for good or ill, might not have begun. It is the part of New Jersey most concerned with the future, and the University nowadays prides itself on its global mission and service to the world not only in the advance of traditional learning but also in introducing important scientific research to solve problems like global warming and epidemic diseases. Or so the positivist story goes, and the future will be better than the present. This vision has little resonance in much of the wider state. In the *Magic* collection, the song that comes nearest to the complexity of Princeton is 'Livin' In The Future' with its millennial vision of the end of the world echoing some images from the Book of Revelation, the day after election day, and its thinly disguised glance at the arrival of the Bush administration back in power in 2004, three years before: 'The earth it gave away/ The sea rose toward the sun/ ... my ship Liberty sailed away on a bloody red horizon'.

This is not the world of 'normal' American optimism, the victory over communism at the end of the Cold War, let alone the messianic belief in technology and American globalization that endlessly floods out of universities like Stanford and Harvard like water from a burst pipe. The very words might not come from the twentieth century at all but would have been convincing from a Jersey Shore Primitive Methodist or other revivalist preacher in the eighteenth or nineteenth century, threatening the punters with immediate perdition if they did not mend their ways.

Princeton is Number City. If the mathematics of Princeton led to the atomic bomb, number is certainly in charge, as it is everywhere in what is touched by the United States government. Mathematics or algebra in the form of algorithms are certainly in charge in Wall Street, Silicon Valley and the other West Coast homes of the internet. America is infatuated with numbers, as the prominent philosopher Michael Mack has written, leading to the prevalence of pseudo-scientific habits of thought pervading many disciplines—even theology—under the illusion that they possess scientific objectivity or 'rationality'. Numbers lead to economics becoming the queen of the sciences, perhaps the only real science in the eyes of modern governments. An algorithm like a slot machine sets its own rules and you cannot answer back. Modern neo-liberal governments approve.

One night one of the most eminent historians of his time was reflecting on glass, not number.

> When I came to Princeton I spent the first year thinking about audience. Had I given up an audience in England to come here? There was always the problem of audience. If you come here you will think your audience is way away and through a sheet of glass.

He moved the ice in his gin and tonic and began to talk of the early Russian and Orthodox emigrants in New Jersey, of a beautiful church in Lakewood. The gentle, long-distant Anglo-Irish burr and effortless and famous charm brought visions of onion domes, ikons and Byzantium, the Third Rome come to New Jersey. Then he went home; he ate early with his American wife, he was very naturalized now and he read ever more deeply in the evenings. Then there was my short walk to a cigar store. Not many of the guys were in but the black policeman came in, a religious man, although of what church was hard to follow or designate. I was on a Padron 2000, biting but poetic Nicaraguan tobacco, he smoked long mild Dominicans. Like the town that night, he was tense. He had a killing on his mind.

'A life is a life, you know. In this job you always have to remember that.'
I asked him if it was difficult.

'Sometimes. It's the grime. I deal with some grimy people. Ever since
I was a state trooper.'

It was a tough subject. I dried and didn't say anything. The line from
the Boss's song 'State Trooper' was in my head:

New Jersey Turnpike ridin' on a wet night 'neath the refinery's glow,
Out where the great black rivers flow

There was a world out there and nearby that didn't have anything
much in common with the faculty or the cigar store. Our police friend
had a single dream, of a law abiding New Jersey, and as William. S.
Burroughs has written in *The Adding Machine*, to live by a single
dream in America can be very dangerous. The more self-aware people
knew it very well. A distinguished elderly Classics professor who was
a ceaseless activist for Israel shared a cigarette with me one day before
that and said she felt she had little or nothing in common with most of
the people of her adopted country, having come as a Holocaust child
many years ago. Her dream was of a perfect and secure Israel.

In the cigar store lounge, guarded by a wooden Native American,
we all knew our police friend risked his life for society more or less daily
following the gangs in the gang suppression unit, and they were very grimy
indeed. The day before, the paper had reported a gun battle in Hamilton
where three Ñeta gang members had gunned down a Latin King, cartoon
strip names bringing blood running onto the sidewalk. A Latin King,
'Ace' Hernandez, had been convicted the week before for the murder of
a Latin 'Queen' Jeri-Lynn Dotson, back in 2004. Life can be very cheap
in some parts of Jersey, and with the murder rate in the state having risen
for the third year running, everyone outside the ghetto had huge personal
respect for a NJPD cop, whatever reservations many people have about
their organization. The Bush administration had cut more than 90,000
police positions since 2000 throughout the country. The Feds were seen

as different, sometimes odd people, often not Jersey boys or girls and these days said to include a plethora of Mormons. Many people in Jersey are prejudiced against Mormons for a variety of reasons and it is not a state where they have as much influence as in some others. Feds seemed to rarely appear in Princeton. Maybe this was true, or maybe just an urban

myth.

The cigar store with its comforting aromas was a needed cave, small but with good company and an unspoken house rule that you listened sympathetically to other prisoners and talked yourself but didn't probe too far beneath the surface—so just like an Oxford High Table. Tom had come in, Tom who loved France. I hadn't noticed him. That was good. Tom always brought cheerfulness and stability to the atmosphere of the cigar store. A cigar lounge can be destabilized by a single awkward person. He nimbly changed the subject, as he always did.

Someone once said to me that you don't have to have a lot of money to have a nice life in Princeton. Tom proved that. He could be very down to earth. Once he asked me how the University was, and then answered himself, that it was a good college. You might as well say Bruce sings good songs. He does but there was rather more to both than that. He asked where Brett was. Nobody knew exactly, but nobody ever did. Brett had a mountain of money and had flown down to go sea fishing in Baja California. Nobody said the word Mexico much in the store, it was uncool, the guys preferred Lower California. Brett loved going after the marlin and, by repute also, the Mexican ladies. He hooked both. For those in the lounge too old to chase ladies much, he was the American Dream in that respect.

Then Holly came in, and had a laugh with John at the desk over something. She was a regular, and fun. She had made a pile of money gambling in dot com stocks and had sold out before the 2000 price crash. She had read the numbers right and had a hobby dress shop, a neat bottom and lots of long blond hair. She smoked strange herbal cigarettes as well as small cigars. Holly was a nice woman but said Princeton was provincial and socialized mostly on Long Island with her boyfriend. Socializing on Long Island is usually seen as bad news in the state. The unpopular Governor Corzine had held a big party there earlier in the fall with both the Boss and Bon Jovi on the A List, which had brought general opprobrium in the store about all concerned and a caustic write up of the event in *The Trentonian*. Her man was very well off, inevitably, and for all the knowledge anyone had, he had never been known to do a day's work of any kind, not one. He was maybe not the Great Gatsby but a decent Small Gatsby, a sexy toy boy Gatsby. He drove a Porsche 911, equally inevitably.

And Must, too, now he was in. Suddenly we were getting full. Must was from India a very long way back but was very Princeton now and did trading zinc and zinc futures day and probably night on his laptop. He didn't do algorithms and just traded by the seat of his pants, so he was our real postmodern. Maybe he slept in a zinc bed for trading inspiration while he dreamed of the mine production data. He also followed cricket very closely, although many of our number may not have known what the game is, let alone how it is played. It was like Eugene O'Neill's great play, *A Touch of the Poet*, a ship of souls becoming American except that the ship was a cigar store and not O'Neill's Irish shebeen in Massachusetts. Then someone's thoughts drifted off back to police work, crime. It was a perennial topic.

'Know there was a bad night in Hamilton?'

'Nope.'

'Hamilton can be bad now.'

'Thought it always was.'

The glass wall was across the middle of the lounge, as much as the collective fragrant smoke. University people knew so little about what was going on around them in New Jersey. I had a dim memory that Hamilton was a suburb or satellite town of Trenton. They might as well otherwise have been talking in code, or Chinese. The one person who would definitely know wasn't around. Hannigan worked in the state law administration, as generations of his sprawling Irish-American family always had. There were generations of them who had been sheriffs, top cops, court officers and all the ladder jobs. It was Jersey: once in law enforcement, never out of it. He was a fun man, a lovely sense of humour, always good company. I once asked him if it was hard to follow so many other Hannigans.

'No. They elect us to keep the Italians out. And the Italians vote for us or the Albanians will be sleeping in their beds.'

In translation this meant that that the Italians had had to look for allies in the great battles to try to stop the blacks getting control of the Democratic Party in the state capital after the turmoil in the party following the race riots in 1968. Before that, Trenton was an Italian political fiefdom but the Irish ran the police. It was a tribal world then, warring tribes under the Stars and Stripes. Law enforcement was on the surface humane, modern and progressive but de facto might as well be dealing with warring Mohawks against the Iroquois. The powerful Albanians were spreading out of their original strongholds in the Bronx and Staten Island into Jersey and were rivals to the Italians in a lot of minor scams and not so minor local rackets. They thought, and think, the Italians have gone soft. As in the denouement of *The Sopranos*, 'the feds crack a Mob only because an Italian-American talked.' It is certainly true that the Albanians don't usually talk and hardly anyone in law enforcement can understand their language, even if caught on wiretaps. They are the only white group who have the respect of the black and Hispanic gangs, so get a lot of work protecting businesses in marginal areas and suchlike. Suddenly the Balkans had entered the lounge, and the memory, a long time ago, of asking someone if they watched *The Sopranos.* It turned out to be a silly question.

'Why should I? We live it every day round here.'

He lived in New Brunswick, on Route 1. For Jersey boys and girls, Route 1 is the real Jersey highway; the Turnpike is a Federal imposition. The gap between the world of the University and New Jersey society suddenly seemed to widen to a yawning chasm, like looking across the Grand Canyon. And it was time to get something to eat and do some reading and writing. I never learned anything more about the homicide in Hamilton.

The song in the *Magic* album is 'Long Walk Home'. It was a short walk home to the apartment. The town was certainly tense. On the newsstand *The Trentonian* newspaper was leading on the gang war between MS-13 and the Ñetas. A strange number. Why was a nationwide drug organization called number 13? MS stands for Mara Salvatrucha and is a sprawling international gang with origins some way back in El Salvador immigration to California. They were good with light sub-machine guns because many of them had been communist guerrillas in the Salvadoran civil war. They became effectively subcontractors for wholesale drug distribution to the Mexican Sinaloa drug cartel, opponents of Los Zetas in the bloody gang wars south of the Mexican border that is reducing northern Mexico to a blood soaked failed state. *Mara* means 'gang' in Mexican *Caliche* slang, and is also, by coincidence, the name of a fierce biting ant. MS-13 have a strong presence in Jersey and area dominating presence in the Hispanic gang world of the Deep South.

What was a Ñeta? And what did MS-13 do in Princeton? Unusually, an open police car was parked outside the Public Library, and what seemed to be an unmarked cop or FBI car the other side of the road with dark windows. The Feds favoured hunky black SUVs, more or less identical to Mr Tony Soprano's favoured vehicle. The city of numbers and the city of light had dark edges. Maybe I was near the edge here even on the way home in lovely civilized Witherspoon Street. 'Darkness on the Edge of Town' is a Springsteen classic everybody knows. The poetry of his lyrics comes from deep in Jersey life. It was the right song to hear tonight. The little house opposite my window was rented out to Mexican workers. It was in semi-darkness, but I saw a tall man fiddling with something in the woodpile out the back. It was strange but I thought no more about it then. Maybe he had an illegal piece and kept it out there. The cops came down hard on

Mexicans they found with guns, reasoning that their purpose was bound up with drug deals. It was a futile pastime for all concerned. There are so many guns around, legal and illegal in New Jersey that one more or less would make no difference to anything. Respectable Princetonians and Windsorites kept theirs in the car just as many as sponges kept to clean the windshield, although in Jersey they are usually small, discreet numbers (as you might say) kept in the glove box, unlike the heavy stuff allowed in many other places. It was very different in the 1776 Battle of Princeton when in the aftermath of George Washington's brilliant and daring night-time crossing of the frozen Delaware River the British Crown forces were surprised and scattered. Then black powder muskets were the weapon of the time.

The next day was a bright morning, the light on the trees around Scheide Caldwell House making patterns in green and brown. Hellenic Studies, with its generous funding from the Stanley Seeger endowment, was centred there. Morning was early nineteenth-century neo-classicism texts and studying nineteenth-century antiquarian William Martin Leake in Firestone and then a walk back along Nassau. On the stand *The Trentonian* headlined the MS-13 arrests and reported a police statement that the gang had been fully busted. But this was rubbish. On the street MS was approaching. A taller than average Hispanic man whom I did not recognize was flanked by two small Mexicans. They bore down on me and stopped and surrounded me. This was ridiculous, it was broad daylight at midday in the middle of Nassau Street and I was going to be shaken down. There was even a University security police car parked over the road, although what this force actually did I never ascertained. Their outfit was said to be an Irish fiefdom. I think this was myth. But then I was OK.

The tall man had eyes that burnt anger but just lifted his lower forearm and pointed at an elaborate tattoo which included a warlike, much underdressed Virgin holding a sidearm. Not a word was said.

He was acting without rules, but he was showing me the power of his tribe—they had both the Virgin and tooled-up hardware. What else do you need? It looked like a Heckler. A Heckler is no water pistol, you can do real damage to a lot of people very quickly with one. What else do you need? The Virgin was, as always, a busy lady in Jersey, with many appointments in her Filofax, but my name was down for a special appointment, one for the Next World. That was the SMS on the forearm. Then a flash of a lot of gold teeth, somebody pinched my arm hard and Mr MS and his honchos walked away towards the little cinema, past my favourite pizza place. MS-13 didn't need iPhones to send messages, they had other methods. It was like being in a film, like so much Jersey street life. It was lovely Jersey; the unexpected and seriously dangerous could coexist a hundred yards away from the brilliant academic life and manicured lawns and shrubs.

Was there any rational explanation? They must have thought my witnessing the woodpile incident was a sign that I was eyes for the cops and that it had led to the arrests. The exact opposite was the truth. After years of the Balkan street as a journalist and academic I avoided most police in most circumstances, and the lawyer parasites who rode on their backs. Life in Milosevic's Serbia had been a particularly hard school. Eyes and mouths for the cops did not last long. It was the same in the US. There was the old Jersey legend that was not wholly untrue that the night after Vito Genovese was arrested all fourteen police informers in Lodz and Garfield were shot in the head, usually in front of their families. I liked Garfield. I had given a talk there about my books at a social club that met in the mosque community centre hall; it was a friendly, democratic sort of place. I later learned from a scientist I knew who had had a run in with a gang member that it was usual for MS-13 to dump bodies of police informers they had taken into the Delaware and Raritan Canal, a new variation of feeding enemies to the fishes. Were there predators in the Raritan

Canal? Who knew?

So what was actually happening in Princeton? It was abundantly clear that whoever had been arrested were not the main people; according to *The Trentonian*, only three young lads, and they weren't even from Mexico but from Guatemala. This is what the paper said. And that was interesting in itself. Here is how the copy read:

PRINCETON — Police have arrested three suspects in connection with a string of burglaries, and all three are illegal aliens believed to be members of the dangerous MS-13 street gang. The trio was picked up Friday by a surveillance detail created by Princeton Borough Police in response to a number of break-ins there, in the Township and on the University's campus. Arrested were Saul Eduardo Palma-Chajon, 22, of Birch Avenue; Byron Diaz, 18, of Witherspoon Street; and a 16-year-old Latino male, who also lives in Princeton.

Police said all three were Guatemalan nationals residing here illegally, and evidence points to their membership in MS-13, or Mara Salvatrucha.

The gang is considered by the FBI to be the most violent of all U.S. street gangs with about 10,000 members nationwide and many more throughout Central America and Mexico. Experts have warned of the gang's spread into New Jersey, but it hasn't seemed to have establish [sic] a stronghold in this region yet.

Translated into reality English, what was behind the report? In the never ending high quality seminar on Jersey life that was held in the cigar store, I had learned certain things. One was always to watch for the Nicaraguan factor. Nicaraguans were seen as mattering, ruthless, competent, heavily tooled up with advanced weapons and very dangerous to cross. Mexicans were by comparison just cannon fodder, zeroes who ate too much burrito and whose women would open their legs for cigarette money. The only sure more or less fact was that the guys arrested were Nicaraguan. It was a law of the Medes and Persians in the street world that all other groups were terrified of the Nicaraguans, who worked closely with the Colombian cartels for the transport of cocaine into Jersey. They were said to break up the big wholesale packages into small lots for the street gangs to sell, along with everything else they sold. This wholesaling often took place in Camden, New Jersey, actually the Jersey part of Philly on the east bank of the Delaware River, dirt poor and in a recent year, according to the homicide rate, the most dangerous city in the entire United States.

Maybe reaching for Derrida would be useful. This story could be read in so many different ways. How do you read text, even just a newspaper report, about the drug business when the drug business is walking the street and bothering you? At one level it was just about three small fish being netted for breaking into people's houses. But it would not be read that way on the street. There it had a message: the cops were moving against the Nicaraguans, firing a warning shot, but maybe not too much. Mayhem and blood was what was expected in places like Camden, but there was no question of it going on in Princeton. But that was only one reading. Another was that it was just PR for law enforcement, a ritual gesture when in reality cocaine was a more or less accepted drug in the University, which unlike many other colleges had numerous wealthy students who could afford to indulge in the white powder for big party nights. Only the previous week I had overheard a student planning to go down to Hamilton for a stash for a party to celebrate graduation.

Many different agencies are involved in narcotics enforcement. The prevailing opinion throughout Jersey was that one and all were only interested in moving against large shipments. From the ordinary cop's point of view this was done in more or less paramilitary scale operations where, unlike a single cop doing something on his or her own on the street, there was much less chance of getting killed. If you want to go to the cemetery in quick time do a drug bust on your own and get drilled through the car window. Reports of big seizures looked good in the media, and kept the police commissioner happy. And if the police commissioner is happy, the politicians are happy and police budgets don't get chopped.

This was a common sense policy, and the large amount of drugs that turned up in ordinary policing meant that seizure data for the state didn't usually look too bad without individual cops having to risk too much. With a small stash there was also the matter of disposal. It was supposed to be incinerated but maybe not all of it is, and that is very profitable. Underlying it all was the scale of the drug issue, with, according to a Monmouth County newspaper, some 10,000 packets of heroin sold every day in a small area of the state. Class A drug deals are, suggests financial data, one of the largest industries in the United States. But maybe understandably, nobody liked to talk about it too much. High minded liberal members of faculty in particular, as on many other issues, only saw around them what they wanted to see, while the densely populated and opaque world of the Hispanic slums provided an alibi for the rest of the population.

Penalties for involvement in the drugs business, or even just minor consumption, are very severe in the United States. As a result most prisons in Jersey are full of drug offenders, or criminals who committed other crimes connected with drugs. They also function as universities of drug dealing. After a while many prisoners get shipped off to gaols all over the US, literally millions of people, so that in a state like Utah prisons are the largest employer and a pillar of the economy. Yet the severity of the regime and the long sentences handed out by the courts do not seem to deter, and the industry is booming, if it can be called an industry, a nightmare in the heart of the country stretching from the jungles of Peru, Colombia and Laos across the world to the small towns and suburbs of Monmouth County, NJ. It is without number as nobody can quantify how many people are involved, or their economic burden. It also stretches into the heart of the music business, where opiates are semi-accepted and have been for a long time. In his moving tribute to long time and keystone E Street Band member Danny Federici, who died of cancer in April 2008, with the tour still on the road, Bruce Springsteen said,

> I watched Danny fight and conquer some tough addictions. I watched him struggle to put his life together and in the last decade when the band had reunited, thrive on sitting on his seat behind that big B-3, filled with life and yes, a new maturity, passion for his job, his family and his home in the brotherhood and sisterhood of our band... If we didn't play together the E Street Band at this point would probably not know one another. We probably wouldn't be in this room together. But we do ... we do play together. And every night at 8pm we walk out on stage together and that my friends, is where miracles occur... old and new miracles. And those you are with, in the presence of miracles, those you never forget. Life does not separate you. Death does not separate you. Those you are with who create miracles for you, like Danny did for me every night, you are honoured to be amongst ... of course, we all grow up and know 'it's only rock and roll'... but it's not.

A band member from 1972, Federici had seen everything for thirty-five years, a life's work. He was a chemically pure Jersey homeboy, born and growing up in Flemington, a nice town not far from the Delaware River in the east of the state. It has never been very big, although bigger than in the days of the 1930s official guide to the state which describes it as a 'village'. It had brief notoriety in 1935 over the trial of Bruno Hauptmann for the murder of Charles Lindberg Jr, when local Good Ol' Boys in this then conservative stronghold exploded with anger at all the media strangers the trial had brought into town. Then it lived off the rich nearby agriculture, particularly the invention of modern battery hen egg production, like Delaware. the outlet mall is the best in the state. Flemington is a nice town, on the cusp of the state where it veers near the Delaware River and the well farmed land and neat shops starts to resemble rural Pennsylvania. There is even the odd English-style hedge, neatly trimmed. There are two religions, Christianity and golf. A few miles west on the river is Lambertville, a slinky, fashionable little place with endless art galleries, many attractive women, cafés and used bookstores and pretty nineteen-century houses. It had never been dry, unlike some nearby towns like New Hope with its towering, elegant Baptist church and other places of worship.

Lambertville was a centre of civilized, mildly bohemian life and democratic radicalism, a good place for a future E Street Band musician to grow up nearby. The town grew as a minor industrial centre and ferry terminal across the Delaware River after the War of 1812, the waters being quiet here, but just above the foaming rapids on the river half a mile south. George Washington himself had lived in the town for a while during the Revolutionary War. His ragamuffin army was to drive the British out of New Jersey and open the way to American independence by soldiers often with no boots whose path could be traced by the bloody footprints in the 1776 snow. Its buildings spoke solid American righteousness, competence; rock solid good values just as Danny's keyboard had the same solidity in the Band. Its twin town on the other side of the river across a wonderful narrow old nineteenth-century bridge is New Hope, Pennsylvania, a pretty Quaker foundation now beloved by serious bikers and dense with chrome-heavy Harleys and burly middle-aged men and women squeezed in to the leathers of their youth in the summer. Americans love twin towns on important rivers, like Minneapolis/St Paul. Lamberville/New Hope is not important, but is very pretty. Yet it is a very small town and when he was growing up was very conservative, and Danny as a teenager escaped to the shore and the Stone Pony and all that meant for his future. As ever, the shore and the ocean breed rebellion.

American second-hand bookstores used to be wonderful. I remember Atlanta in 1992, a tough Balkan conference as the war was intensifying and European Union incapacity was worse than usual. It was held at the Carter Center in Atlanta. I was charmed by Jimmy Carter himself, met media figures from the Carter orbit like Larry King, and had difficult, acrimonious exchanges over my views on Macedonian problems (not with him). Jimmy Carter had had a hard time because of untidy, over-optimistic foreign policy and the Tehran hostage crisis but he didn't let it set back his good humanitarian works. You could retreat to get away from some of the delegates to books. There were so many Atlanta bookstores that took up all the interior of big houses, treasure troves, now more or less destroyed by the internet in the name of progress. Another place nearby here has fine used bookstores and many other things, and in its small way is one of the Wonders of New Jersey and as good a place to reflect on the history as any. It is Bordentown, city of Tom Paine, and near Trenton. It in many ways is part of Trenton and yet it is not; they have had a very long complex on-off relationship and much shared history.

There are different ways to drive there. It is New Jersey, so maybe slip down Route 1 a while and then round Trenton on the 29 East, a real Jersey way to go, from Number City to Paine's City. There is every opportunity to get lost east of Trenton and find yourself somewhere you don't know and may not like, but both are Cities of Reason (or that is how they like to see themselves). Towns and Cities of Reason and of Numbers are not the same thing. Driving in Jersey and trying to find where you want to go, you leave the realm of Reason and enter the realm of Chance, just like a casino. Or as Albert Einstein observed, 'God does not play dice but men do.' You may have to pay a toll to drive on some roads, like the money the casino owners cream off from your bet so that you can actually play on their tables. Or as the Greek saying goes, 'You Get What You Get'.

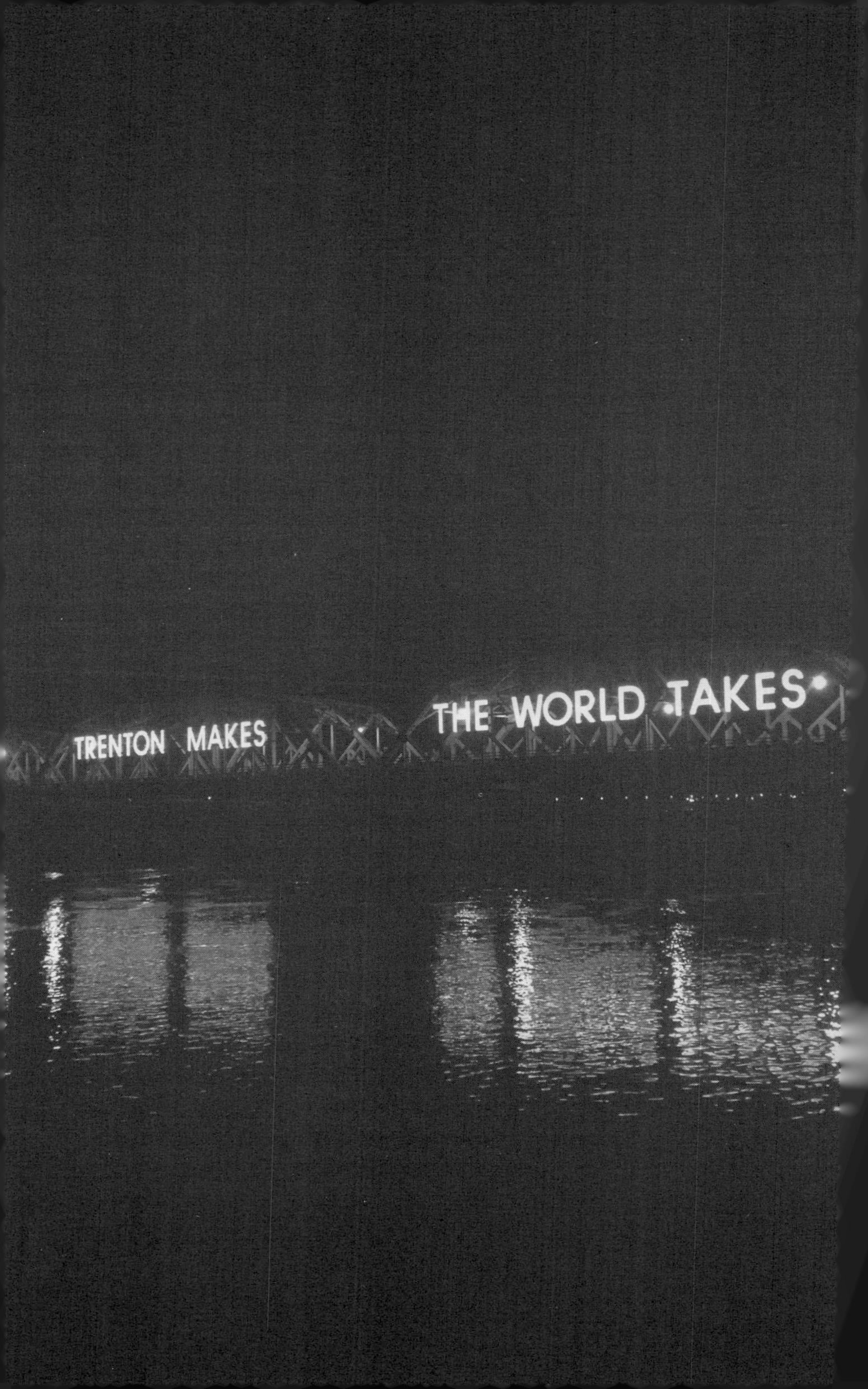
TRENTON MAKES
THE WORLD TAKES

7

TRENTON, BORDENTOWN AND THE LIMITS OF REASON

Concerning Plato versus the Drano Bomber (that Fake News Contest) and Mr Tom Paine and his fine statue in old Bordentown

Philosophy, as Done in the Burg*

> There are some men who enter a woman's life and screw it up forever. Joseph Morelli did this to me—not forever, but periodically.
>
> Morelli and I were both raised in a blue collar suburb of Trenton called the Burg. Houses were attached and narrow. Yards were small. Cars were American. The people were mostly of Italian descent, with enough Hungarians and Germans thrown in to offset inbreeding. It was a good place to buy calzone or play the numbers. And if you had to live in Trenton anyway, it was an okay place to raise a family.
>
> Janet Evanovich, *One for the Money*

Princeton was echoing every day that week with news of the troubles in Hamilton, but Hamilton was not Bordentown although both are on the Trenton borders. Bordentown was the home of the Biles Island Lottery and it had become part of my secret history of the state that was forming, the history of the underground world that Springsteen so often explores in his songs but which hardly ever reaches the mainstream history books. Bordentown also seemed a good place to stock up on Janet Evanovich and learn whether bail bond heroine Stephanie Plum had managed to get it together and enjoy herself in bed with the charming but difficult Joe Morelli. In the past Trenton was about war, not love. And making things, not attractive men, with its famous slogan: 'TRENTON MAKES—THE WORLD TAKES'.

That great sign on the old railway bridge over the Delaware in a way says it all. Trenton was as important to the industrial revolution and the opening up of the West in the United States as anywhere except Paterson. Manufacturing there had been above all the German immigrant-founded factory town of John A. Roebling Sons Company. The Roebling invention

---

* In the past called Chambersburg, originally a German district of south Trenton, which became a Little Italy.

of massive-scale spun wire cable made the construction of the Brooklyn and Golden Gate and America's road bridges possible. The roads built as a consequence that ran between them became the arteries of American life. The Roebling revolution in bridge building led to the construction of the first bridge across the Niagara Falls in 1854, held up by Trenton-made cables, and a new town ten miles south of Trenton was named after the firm. Trenton was the heart of the American Revolution in the state but regarded in Princeton as the heart of the NJ organized crime world. Things happened at Trenton. George Washington had fought heroically there and the city had been almost completely destroyed by a tornado in 1902. The history was dramatic. I had put off going there as, with its dire reputation in Princeton, I had not felt confident enough to do so, but now thanks to my MS-13 initiation I did. I must have been one of the few people in the state that fall with any reason to be grateful to MS-13. ·

Bordentown was in its a way a Number City, as the very complete records have survived of one of the earliest successful public lotteries in New Jersey, the oddly baptized 'Biles Island Lottery', named after a bleak little island in the River Delaware, uninhabited and nowadays used as a dump for sludge and dredged materials from the river bed. The 567- acre island was known in the Lenape language as Minachkonk, and was bought from the Native Americans by one William Biles in 1680. An English immigrant and graduate of Exeter College, Oxford, who had endured persecution as a Quaker, Biles thrived in pre-revolutionary Pennsylvania and made a fortune from land deals

In the 1755 lottery, which was run to finance Bordentown Baptist Church, extraordinarily exact records of the winning numbers of prize winners survive. Some educated gentleman in 1755 must have thought that carefully recording these numbers mattered very much. In the world of intense personalist Protestantism of the day, perhaps he thought the Lord was looking over his shoulder and down onto his quill pen as he did so. Number is inescapable in thinking about US history and the fiercely respectable religious dissenters of colonial Jersey and Philly had no scruples at all in using gambling instincts to provide new religious buildings.

Yet it was a tough sandwich morning and maybe also not the happiest over the Springsteen breakfast table in Colts Neck district up in Monmouth County. The 24 October *Village Voice* had just come out in New York City and the review by Rob Harvilla of the *Magic* tour performance there was not altogether what Jon Landau and the Boss and the Band might welcome. After observing that 'There's something so pure, so sweet so indelible about the sight of Bruce Springsteen and Little Steven van Zandt sharing a microphone, both wielding guitars and beatific smiles, the Boss joyfully bellowing jowl to jowl with his quirkiest minion', he went on to say, 'Madison Square was laden with lustily hooting, wantonly fist pumping disciples.' The concert was presented as an exercise in not wholly successful nostalgia with too much anti-Bush political preaching. Bruce must sometimes wish he was not the only rock star around in Jersey, which of course he is not.

On Route 206 South with its sweepingly perfect manicured forests and sense of a hidden way down to Maryland there was Bon Jovi on the radio, a good song from his original *New Jersey* album dating from as long ago as 1988. It was a good channel. The crisis in rock radio in Jersey had started in about 2005 and was not over, in fact was getting worse. But this station still breathed. Jovi is a fine singer and has always been 'the other guy from New Jersey', who is not Bruce Springsteen, without the Boss's edge and sense of unpredictability and danger, reliably melodic and a superbly professional musician. He was born just south of New York City in seaside Perth Amboy, once home of the British colonial garrison, now a quiet bay full of Portuguese exiles but a little too close to the Hudson Estuary for good beach life and swimming. There are a lot of 'beach whistles' on the sand, tampon applicators. The rubbish generated in New York pollutes New Jersey, as it always has done, although New Yorkers are not usually slow to criticize the appearance of the grotty side of the Jersey landscape with its recycling plants and scrap yards, even though they are the cause of much of the waste. The dialectic in *The Sopranos*' storylines is between Tony Soprano's legitimate identity in waste management disposal and his illegitimate business methods. Bon Jovi in his music lets it all wash over him; he is cheerful, if sometimes predictable.

The lights of Trenton ahead through the fall rain and mist and windscreen wipers are not predictable, but uncertain and possibly dangerous. A particular Boss song was in my head and had been ever since I first started thinking about going to Trenton. In 'Factory' he sings:

It's the working, the working, just the working life

When that song was written, long before 2007 and the intoxicating days of *Magic*, there had still been some heavy industry in Jersey to write about. After all, the first porcelain toilet was manufactured in Trenton. Now there wasn't any much, and a Princeton history faculty friend from Birmingham, a solid Byzantinist and Marxist, had said the day before that I would find nothing there except rust and broken down old cars. Today had been an odd day. The tabloids were full of a story about a wild turkey that had broken into a house and done US$5,000 worth of damage. It was a wild turkey damage record. New Jersey holds many records for many things, part of the numerical obsessions of the government in Trenton, and the local media were also full of news of this weird record being set. Jersey people love the word 'weird' and use it a lot; there is even a magazine called *Weird NJ*. Moreover, a huge, abnormal record size Grey Tilefish had been caught off Tom's Canyon, weighing in at no less than 18 pounds 7 ounces. My knowledge of the Grey Tilefish was non-existent, but it turned out that it was really a visitor to the shore, not a Jersey Girl or Boy, and generally liked to live at depths of over 300 feet deep south of Cape Hatteras in North Carolina where they dig burrows in the seabed.

Listening to some white Mercer and Burlington County people, the poorer Afro-American inhabitants of Trenton might as well live in burrows in the ground, too. There are all kinds of good and bad reasons to visit or nor visit Trenton but one good one is to soon realize how American politics is still determined by unresolved issues left over from the Civil

War period that all the work of social and political reformers has yet to fully resolve. At least the State Fish is colour-neutral but the Tilefish is not the State Fish. That honour goes to the brook trout, *Salvelinus fontinalis.* He or She is, you could say, the Boss fish, and was designated State Fish as long ago as 1991, to join the State Bird, the Eastern Goldfinch, the State Flower, a kind of violet, and the State Shellfish, the Knobbed Whelk. Why are there these designated State creatures? Who chose them? I discovered that the common blue violet (*Viola sororia*) had been designated as early as 1913, but it took until 1971 to complete the designation of the little blue eyed girl creeping along the edge of your path as a State symbol. It all seemed a symbol of no doubt well-meaning but arbitrary and sometimes distinctly odd authority in Trenton, and general perceptions were not improved by the appointment by a recent governor of his poet lover as his national security adviser. His knowledge of security work was believed to be small. The violet was also a metaphor, dealing with the state government: things take time.

It was a strange world, Trenton. One of the best recent state governors, Richard J. Codey, actually wrote a book about the manifold difficulties of running New Jersey, a good honest account, called *Me, Governor?* He never expected (wanted?) the job. Most of the time he did it the opinion polls show a majority of NJ citizens had never heard of him. This was not the case with everybody prominent. A survey I saw recorded that of 'public figures' in Jersey one of the highest name recognition scores went to one Gaetano Badalamenti, a long-time head of the Mafia in Cinisi in Sicily, originally an Albanian exile community which had extensive activity in New Jersey in the days before Codey became governor. In his trade (pizza distribution) Badalamenti was an innovator and set up the systems that still work well for those people today, using pizza delivery boys and girls to sell drugs. As the Bronx phrase goes, you're nobody without a restaurant.

Nobody in Princeton seemed to know anything about the state symbols either; there is always something odd to distract you in New Jersey. More interesting than these bureaucratic inventions is the mythical but also psychologically real Jersey Devil, the mobster of the ancient pine woods. He belongs to the mythology of past centuries, and some think was a transposition from Native American belief systems. In his modern guise he is a product of colonial settlement, born to a lady in Estellville called Mrs Leeds, and arriving on her no doubt capacious lap an angry purple-faced *diabolis* tied up in a tablecloth. He spent his adolescence wandering in the forests and swamplands, and when he was an adult started causing trouble. There seems to be something familiar here. According to those who claim to have seen him, he lives in the Pine Barrens and is white skinned, cloven footed and has the head of a dog, the wings of a vampire bat and the features of a pony. His appearance is an omen of war, so maybe this year with Iraq in full flow is a good time to look out for him on his strange nocturnal wanderings. He lives a long way away from the world of Reason and Number.

The harmless whimsy of state wildlife and local mythology seems a long way from the preoccupations of Trenton, where for maybe a third of the population life is a daily battle for survival. In Washington the main news seemed to be the administration's rigid stand against stem cell research, where there might be arguments on either side, but everybody on the inside or near the inside thought the negative decision was a product of the president's over-close relationship with the fundamentalist Roman Catholic lobby around a prominent cardinal in DC, a little known figure at the time but a sign of the political influence of the Vatican at that stage over the Bush administration.

The old Lincoln was running low on gas. That was bad. The turn out to the south-east I was thinking of taking had been too risky without more gas, to see a little of the Pine Barrens and reflect on the lost world there where the last elements of the 'primitive' (alternative?) lifestyles of the nineteenth-century New Jersey outsiders persisted well into the twentieth century. The vast and now largely empty pine forests stretching right across the middle of the state in Burlington and Atlantic Counties were once the domain of the charcoal burner, the fugitive and the solitary logger, and virtually nobody else. The dwarf pines that grow are of little economic value and in a wet winter the entire region turns into something resembling the Norfolk Broads or undrained East Anglian Fens in medieval England. Old stage coach routes can be seen for a while and then disappear into a mass of clinging vegetation and muddy pools of water. The normal rules of virtuous settler life did not prevail, with polygamy and holding women in common was a particular problem that troubled critics of the Pineys, as the Barrens dwellers were known. Some early inhabitants were deserting British or Loyalist soldiers after 1778 who just escaped to the Barrens and took up with whatever women they could find. The women were themselves often cast out from their community by a teenage pregnancy or death of the breadwinner in the family, and a little settlement like the bizarrely named Ong's Hat was for decades little more than a large crazy horse-type saloon in the woods, with wild square dancing, illegal gambling and general dissipation as its means of earning a living. For the justices of Trenton, who spent much of their time punishing transgressors who lived there, it was the heart of darkness, a land beyond the law—and that is something that is taken very seriously by the official United States. Prize fighting and linked rioting were also a particular issue. The entire social history of the country could, at a pinch, be written through the regulation of boxing and this remains so today, with boxing centred on major ex-'sin cities' like Las Vegas. Illegal bare knuckle fist-fights and cock fighting constituted an important threat to social peace in this world, where schools were virtually non-existent, as were law enforcement officers, and the lack of usable roads made deployment of militia troops from the cities very slow and inefficient. Murders were frequent, and the first legendary Burlington county detective Ellis Parker made his reputation on these cases. The historian of the Barrens, Henry Charlton Beck, writes of a world where

> Battlers, attracted by the prospect of fat purses, corn liquor and pretty dull-eyed damsels, tackled each other for a decision which was often in turn fought over by the crowd, out there in the middle of nowhere.

The hundreds of thousands of nineteenth-century Irish immigrants to Jersey were particularly keen participants in these mass punch-ups in the Pine Barrens, recalling the Hooleys and pitched battles between hundreds of men armed with clubs and staves that were a feature of rural Irish life until the twentieth century, where, say, the men of Galway fought the men of Mayo for days on end in remote countryside with numerous casualties. Some Piney individuals became bandits following on the trade of highwaymen that they may have learnt in the bogs of Ireland or the hills of Calabria or Sicily, or like all soldiers in losing side armies turned to an illegal life as many Confederates also did after 1865. Joe Mulliner from an Irish colonial family was hanged in 1781 at Burlington for banditry and treason but has always been remembered as a Robin Hood figure who helped the poor and 'was polite to all that cared to associate with him'.

The world of the Pineys carried on more or less unchanged until World War I, and the wild and uncouth inhabitants were the despair of social reformers of the Progressive era who believed 'moronism' and 'degeneracy' were rampant there. A study by one Elizabeth S. Kite in 1913 deplored the inbreeding and segregated life in the Barrens, the hovel-like houses and wretched roads and marshland tracks. She also noted the easy attitude to sexual relations where a woman might leave a man as she pleased, and men numbered the various 'wives' they had had as 'John No 1., John No. 2, or John No.3', according to the state of their attachments in yet another example of the fertility of number in American life. In the 1930s the Federal literature suggests that about 5,000 people continued to live in the old way, and in squalor. Some first learned the use of money and wages when working on wartime construction projects when the nearby giant military base at Fort Dix was built. The treatment of the Pineys also illuminates the difficulty progressive mainstream America has often had with the concept of 'the wilderness', being happy to have it exist to look at and harbour wildlife, but also as an irresistible temptation to economic exploitation, above all the irresponsible building over so much Jersey forest land in the last twenty years.

It is perhaps not entirely a coincidence that New Jersey-born James Fenimore Cooper, the novelist whose books helped form the mythology of the Wild West, was a man of Burlington County and when he was born in 1789 the locality on his doorstep was rent by these early struggles between the authority of the new US government and the traditions of the frontier. Frontier-type life outside the rule of law was carrying on in the remote areas of Jersey only a few miles outside towns like Burlington, Trenton and Princeton. Cynics might say a similar situation still exists in the relationship of the prosperous white majority cities with the Afro-Caribbean slums in contemporary Jersey nowadays, where groups based on ethnicity with completely different values and wild disparities in wealth carry on as always. Cooper inherited a substantial fortune from his father whose family came from Warwickshire Quaker roots and who had expropriated Iroquois lands in New York State. He had a broader experience of life than many of his contemporaries, with a brave and distinguished stint in the US Navy and a relatively progressive outlook. His daughter Susan Fenimore Cooper was an early feminist and supporter of female suffrage. Cooper's historical romances of frontier life are set in the Far West, but the uncertain frontiers of the rule of law were everywhere at that time. His novels are little read or studied nowadays, mainly thanks to his use of the racial typology of the time (red men versus white men), as in *The Prairie*, where

> The leader of the emigrants steadily pursued his way, with no other guide than the sun, turning his back resolutely on the abodes of civilization, and plunging at each step more deeply, if not irretrievably, into the haunts of the barbarous and savage occupants of the country.

Antitheses derived from ancient writers read in his schooldays lies behind much of his thinking, but Cooper's actual narratives show that the 'barbarous' in behaviour are often the white settlers, and he highlights the positive values and tragic destiny of the Native Americans. Yet in the politically correct world of many college literature departments nowadays this has not prevented his works from being consigned to neglect, even oblivion.

In the twentieth century Prohibition gave a new boost to these remote areas surviving from the eighteenth century. Only the arrival of the fifty-five acres of Fort Dix disturbed the empty dwarf pine and swamp landscape, a facility that became a focus for conflict during the anti-Vietnam war campaign and became known as The Stockade thanks to its use for jailing dissident members of the armed forces. In June 1969 250 men rioted to protest the humiliating conditions in the stockade part of the camp. The dissidents had joined the outcast Pineys in spirit, for this was always a place for the rebel. The Jersey Pine Barrens could have been purpose-built for smuggling, close to the sea, an unmapped labyrinth, a maze of shifting marshland and forest where a decent path one summer can disappear forever with the winter gales, hurricane-inspired storms and the towering waves wiping out landmarks shown on maps. In terms of middle-class Americans' mythology, which still influences much school and college historiography, behaviour that was supposed to have died out in Jersey and was confined to the wilderness and the Wild West was continuing in their own state, and in terms of illegal opiate transfers still does as a glance at the crime records of the nearby coastal maze of islands and beaches indicates. Or as Springsteen writes in the song 'With Every Wish':

> *These days I sit around and laugh*
> *At every river I've crossed*
> *But on the far banks there's always another forest*
> *Where a man can get lost*

For many Americans, and not only New Jersey citizens, Trenton is now the heart of darkness, and the violent race riots there after Martin Luther King's death in April 1968 have not been forgotten. Hundreds of shops and businesses were burnt out and many never came back to life afterwards. It used to be a Little Italy but the most common word on premises now is *abierto*, Spanish for open. The explosive growth in Trenton's population between 1880 and 1900, when over 100,000 people moved there, foreigners and Southern blacks, also coincided with the high tide of Italian immigration generally. It was a hot place to eat some of the best Italian food in the state but now has only Guatemalan and Costa Rican cafés in many streets. The obvious explanation for this sentiment might seem to be that it is, on occasion, a dangerous city, by repute and by the homicide rate per head of the population in some years, although thanks to the efforts of the NJPD things have improved recently. There is nevertheless a steady flow of violent deaths, mostly of young men gunned down in gang wars. Murders are the prime cause of death of young black men aged between fifteen and thirty-five. In the middle of Trenton is the massive New Jersey State Prison, an American fortress hoosegow where internal temperatures can soar in to well over 40°C in high summer and worse when trouble beckons and a cell lockdown is imposed.

A second explanation for its bad image is that it is the state capital city, seat of the governor and source of the high tax bills (compared to many states) that Jersey citizens end up paying. It is the dark cave of state finance with the taxpayers as unwilling prisoners, the tomb, the darkness, the opposite of rationality. There is a lot of government in Jersey, too much, most people feel, and its interlocking powers and numerous overlapping authorities are a rich source of corruption and blackguarding. Yet Trenton has a rich popular life of warm capable people and the stories of Janet Evanovich have brought us the characteristic feisty Jersey Girl, her heroine Stephanie Plum, a bail bond investigator, not the safest of jobs for anybody, a modern bounty hunter in thin disguise who has seen it all with her fast talk, miniscule lingerie and on-off passions with her cop boyfriend Joe Morelli. Where is the not very Platonic Beautiful and the Good in New

Jersey? Well, to be naked in the arms of Joe Morelli, that's for sure. And how do you satisfy Desire? Bounty hunting, for that is really what a bail bond investigator does. Apart from enjoying Joe's attentions, by wheeling in a bail fugitive, that's for sure, too, sex, bail bonds and rock and roll. What else does anybody need? Janet Evanovich had a long struggle to get published and then recognized as a female hard-bitten crime writer, with numerous unpublished and rejected novels in her bottom drawer, but now having sold over a million books. Here's a moral story, of a Jersey Girl making it by honest hard work and overcoming many obstacles. Benjamin Franklin might have asked her out. Or perhaps the polymath and Founding Father who loved to swim in the Thames when in London would approve of the fine City Museum in the Italianate Ellarslie Mansion, with its rollcall of Trenton ceramic and industrial artefacts. Franklin was a real American, the arch-patriot who loved to fix things, spanner in hand.

Tom Paine

Twelve short miles down the road south from Trenton is Bordentown, the town of American revolutionary ideologist, philosopher and political leader and revolutionary soldier, the English freethinker Tom Paine. Who? Where? Paine is little read nowadays except by students of the American Constitution, for as one of his few contemporary admirers Christopher Hitchens observes in his polemic *God is Not Great*, it was Paine's influence over the Founding Fathers that meant that the Constitution does not mention God at all, and only mentions religion insofar as to say it should be a private matter. I was never really sure where Christopher was on the general issue of the heritage of the Enlightenment. He believed in Reason in human affairs but was also in some senses a Kantian, a critic of those believing in its universality. Wherever, whatever is Bordentown? Many readers and probably most non-Americans may wonder. George Washington had helped Paine install himself in Bordentown in 1783 as a smallholder to thank him for his services to the revolution, feeling that his contribution had been neglected by the new Congress in Washington.

Bordentown is small and chic and leafy, spawned the earliest steam train to run in the United States and has nice Italian restaurants and bookshops. It was a Quaker foundation in 1642 and used to be called Farnsworth's Landing, after founder Thomas Farnsworth. A fellow Quaker merchant, Thomas Borden, opened up a stage coach route to Philadelphia and later another to the British military centre at Perth Amboy, near New York. Borden's other business, cooperage, also has a footnote in revolutionary history as the source of the barrels used in the famous 'mechanical keg' assault on the British ships moored in the Delaware River. Filled with gunpowder they were floated upstream and exploded between the British ships, causing panic. As the revolutionary soldiers song goes,

'Twas early day, as poets say,
Just when the sun was rising,
A soldier stood on a log of wood,
And saw a thing surprising.

Reprisals against the civilian populations are always part of guerrilla wars, and later the British colonial soldiers and their violent Hessian mercenary underlings razed Bordentown to the ground. Colonel Borden's wife observed that the British must have realized they had lost the American colonies or they would not be wantonly devastating them. But scorched earth tactics continued and the burning of New York City followed.

A rich birdlife follows the river, with egrets and cormorants and small dippers harvesting the mud on the river shores. Grey herons fish wisely in stagnant pools and enjoy the sun. In the eighteenth century in a certain sense the town was the river, and built on waterpower. In the fall and winter, sea eagles sometimes cruise the river sky, lunching on the fish. A particularly fine and well stocked old bookshop inhabits a disused Baptist chapel in the town centre. In a small leafy square with a distant view of the beautiful lower Delaware River about to flood into the Atlantic stands a statue of Tom Paine, the East Anglian radical whose ideas were as great an influence on the success of the American

independence struggle as any. His best known work *The Age of Reason* is a pithy deistic text but throbbing with anger at what he sees as the fables and myths of the Bible that Christian Churches have promoted with the 'three frauds, mystery, miracles, and prophesy'. Paine is little read nowadays. The last time I had a meal with Christopher, the Hitch was musing over mid-morning Johnnie Walker Black Label about the need to revitalize study of Paine and stop him from being a forgotten figure. For Christopher, Tom Paine was a ***prodromos***, a forerunner of his own campaigns against organized religions, and symbolized the eclipse of reason in American spiritual life by the intense emotionalism and evangelical fervour that built up after the 1812 war against the British, a war hardly anyone in Britain nowadays has heard of but which is seen in the US as a great early victory for the young state. Christopher wrote in his study of Paine: 'In a time when both rights and reason are under several kinds of open and covert attack, the life and writing of Thomas Paine will always be part of the arsenal on which we shall need to depend.'

We had had some cool years after his review of John le Carré's novel *Our Game* and what he said about the 'Larry Pettifer' character in it, but in the end Oxford radical roots were strong. We were both closely involved in the Bush/Blair foreign policy projects, I in Kosovo and Christopher in Iraq. The political contradictions could be very intense, and lose you many erstwhile friends, although how far it is really possible to trust people in the media and academia in times of war is perhaps a moot point. Perhaps it also all goes to prove, like the Princeton orange alumni jackets, the near unbreakable bonds from shared time in politics in elite institutions in youth,. The Hitchens charm and condemnations of labourist social democracy in the Kings Arms bar in Oxford echo in my ears from many years ago.

Tom Paine himself wrote on the Bible:

> When we see the studied craft of the scripture-makers, in making every part of this romantic book of school-boy's eloquence, bend to the monstrous idea of a Son of God, begotten by a ghost on the body of a virgin, there is no imposition we are not justified in suspecting them of.

Thinking back to that last lunch, it seemed his writing was closer to Paine than I had previously thought, although in *God is Not Great* he had written on a wider world compass than the world Paine knew, observing, for instance, that there is no country in the world where slavery is still practised that is not dominated by the Koran. Islam does not really connect with Paine—he knew little of it—or vice versa, only dogmatic Christianity where the profound truths of the Bible were reduced to a mechanical literal reading. So is Bordentown, with its fine Old City Hall and Queen Anne clock tower, a town of Reason now? The clock itself could be seen as embodying the ultimate spirit of Reason and rational Number, as its maker, Thomas F. Allen was the designer of standard time in the United States, and without standard time aspects of the industrial revolution would never have been possible. The town was certainly prepared to suffer for freedom; as a hive of revolutionary activity it was burnt by the British in spring 1778. Perhaps the answer is to be found in Trenton. They are in some senses the same town, and the professionals who run Trenton often live in nearby Bordentown. From the road, it seemed an uncertain destination, perhaps a little like Galicia where Philip Roth's family first hailed from, an absurd, cranky, invented Hapsburg identity, and in the late nineteenth century full of anti-Semites. No wonder Roth was so happy to be a Jewish boy in democratic New Jersey. Whatever its problems—and they are many and serious—Trenton has no doubt about what it is and why it matters. The tall neo-classical column in the middle of the city that commemorates victory in the Battle of Trenton in 1776 can seem strange, now towering grandly above the slums and poverty stricken streets with aimless black kids lolling on the wooden doorsteps of crumbling houses that look as if they were last painted in Abraham Lincoln's time.

Yet the column commemorates one of the most important battles in American history, in its way as much a landmark in history as Gettysburg in the Civil War. Trenton sits on the high southern bank of the Delaware River with its leafy deciduous woods. The American cause was at rock bottom in early 1776 and the British were rolling south. It was George Washington's army crossing the Delaware successfully as a guerrilla force of recently soldiered blacksmiths and tradesmen and farmers that led eventually to the defeat of the British troopers (many actually German mercenaries from Hanover) and the tide of the war was turned. The Trenton and then Princeton victories led directly to the establishment of the United States.

Events moved Abraham Lincoln in 1861, nearly a hundred years later, to note,

I cannot but remember the place New-Jersey holds in our early history. In the early Revolutionary struggle, few of the States among the old Thirteen had more of the battle-fields of the country within their limits than old New-Jersey. May I be pardoned if, upon this occasion, I mention that away back in my childhood, the earliest days of my being able to read, I got hold of a small book, such a one as few of the younger members have ever seen, 'Weem's Life of Washington'. I remember all the accounts there given of the battle fields and struggles for the liberties of the country, and none fixed themselves upon my imagination so deeply as the struggle here at Trenton, New-Jersey.

These words were part of a speech Lincoln gave in 1861 when as newly-elected president he attended a reception in the State House at Trenton. Few presidents bother to go to Trenton now, for any reason whatsoever. Then the battle was very usable history for Lincoln, noting the role of the guerrilla army openly and talking of 'revolutionary struggle' in a context Mao or Ho Chi Minh would immediately recognize. As the United States has achieved imperial world power, this eighteenth-century history in Jersey has become less and less prominent in American historical discourse. The Revolutionary War is, of course, taught in American schools, but often not using Lincoln's terminology in schoolbooks and occupying only a small part of a pupil's time compared to the defining moment of the Civil War and the victory of the Union. In popular culture it is the same; there have been numerous recent productions on the Civil War period in the cinema, most prominently Steven Spielberg's long, dull and hagiographic movie on Lincoln himself, a work that puzzled many audiences outside the United States. Maybe I have missed something but I cannot remember any significant recent film set in New Jersey in this key period, an interesting fact given the importance of cinema in American popular culture. The Revolutionary War in 1776 was, in its way, a victory for secessionism, for breaking away from a larger entity in the name of democracy and liberty, as in the recent British decision on membership of the European Union. The preferred dominating narrative of modern US history has always been to celebrate the Union's defeat of the army of the secessionist South and its positive long-term implications for the united development of US society and world power.

In the Cold War the United States was and still generally remains an implacable and ideological opponent of revolutionary cum liberation war. There is also the wider issue of historical consciousness in the contemporary US. The advent of world history into the curriculum in American schools is likely to further weaken memory of the War of Independence, as school pupils anywhere have only so much time to give to history—which in US schools is often a low-status, unpopular subject—and if someone is learning about the history of China or India they cannot be learning American history. States have considerable autonomy in history schoolbooks, resulting until recently in parts of the South in texts that grossly distorted the nature of slavery and the Civil War itself. Some textbooks often make prominent figures into individual superheroes who belong to a lost past, helping create the myth that America's great days are over, as illustrated in James W. Loewen's bestselling study *Lies My Teacher Told Me: Everything Your American History Textbook Got Wrong*.

Bordentown flourished most between Independence and the mid-nineteenth century. It is a small place and easy to walk around and reflect on the eighteenth-century past when many of the buildings were constructed, and when the Delaware River and Estuary were central to the main events in American history. It was at the heart of the struggle against the King of England, an imperial society, as Paine wrote in his tract for the war, *Common Sense*, which sold an astonishing 120,000 copies in America in the time the conflict was developing. Although a critic of established religion, Paine depended on some of the fervour of his English Methodist youth to convince his audience that a better future lay ahead. It is a fine walk past the large and generous houses above the Delaware through to the little square on the north-west side of Bordentown where the statue of Tom Paine stands, a short man, it seems, in strongly polemical mode with a raised finger at the world, and such a contrast as democratic public art to the massive commemorative column in the middle of Trenton. Eighteenth-century non-privileged man was a small man, and with his leather jerkin in stone and neat buckled shoes Paine in stone is such a man. It is a fine statue, and could only be cast in a free democratic country, a pure spirit in dialogue and rational debate. On the granite plinth it simply states in large carved letters: 'THOMAS PAINE (1737-1809) FATHER OF THE AMERICAN REVOLUTION'.

He argued that 'America is only a secondary object in the system of British politics':

> But where, say some, is the King of America? I'll tell you, friend, he reigns above, and doth not make havoc of mankind like the Royal Brute of Great Britain. Yet that we may not appear to be defective even in earthly honours, let a day be solemnly set apart for proclaiming the Charter; let it be brought forth placed on the Divine Law, the Word of God; let a crown be placed thereon, by which the world may know, that so far as we approve of monarchy, that in America the law is king.

He saw the war as leading to an independent society which would 'receive the fugitive and prepare in time an asylum for mankind'. Which of course was what already taking place, and had taken place ever since the arrival of the first colonists and settlers in New England over 150 years before. Yet the onlooker is bound to remember the line penned by Bob Dylan: 'As I went out one morning to breathe the air around Tom Paine'.

As early as 1859 the *Atlantic Monthly* magazine described Paine as 'only an indistinct shadow to most Americans', and the standard book on Paine by Philip S. Foner used in American colleges for many years notes that 'his death (in 1809) went almost unnoticed in the American Press'. There is no official monument to Tom Paine in the nation's capital, although in every meaningful sense he was a Founding Father of the country's independence. While quoted by Franklin D. Roosevelt in his great address to the nation after the Japanese attack on Pearl Harbour, Paine is completely absent from official discourse in the Cold War years until his bizarre revival by Ronald Reagan in his rhetoric against 'Big Government'.

In *Common Sense* Paine is explicit about the necessity of the supremacy of the struggle for the rule of law, which he counterpoised to the world of the lawless European monarchies. Law has always been of central importance in American life; as the struggles between bad men and sheriffs in any Western film show, the notion of law enforcement became inextricably linked with that of extending the frontier of civilization. Paine was later in nineteenth- and early twentieth-century historiography depicted as the 'firebrand', the 'agitator', the revolutionary inspiration rather than a serious thinker. His ideas were rarely discussed objectively. His deism has become unattractive to the Hard Men of the New Atheism such as sometime (recently retired) Oxford Professor Richard Dawkins, criticized by Hitchens for his 'cringe making ' attempt to designate non-believers as 'the brights', an ultra-elitist perspective. Paine was a man of the people and he trusted the people to come to the right decisions without the impositions of kings or bishops. The tall beach trees behind his statue move gently in the wind. Fall will not be here forever, winter will come, as it did to Paine in his turbulent life. Nobody even knows where his bones actually lie. A look down at the river from the dense plane trees on the high river banks is also a place to reflect on the fact that the War of Independence was a very small war in scale. The so-called 'Pennsylvania Navy' that helped Washington in the Battle of Trenton was only a few small River Delaware trading ships commandeered for military use by the Yankee rebels.

It is therefore a compelling irony that not that long after Paine's disappearance from Bordentown to take an active part in the French Revolution, an exiled monarch appeared on the scene and propelled the little town to a new and very different fame. Paine had loved the popular Bordentown world of his time, the hard-working egalitarian rural and trading society, and later he wrote after his return to revolutionary Europe: 'My heart and myself are three thousand miles apart; and I had rather see my horse Button, eating the grass of Bordentown than all the pomp and show of Europe.' After his narrow escape from the guillotine and other scrapes in the revolutionary turmoil in Paris, Paine returned to

Bordentown as a man might return to a loved woman, only to find that his radical views on religion brought intense local disapproval and he was chased out of Bordentown by a nativist mob in 1791, never to return.

The next famous Bordentown resident was very, very different, although his arrival was also a product of the French political upheaval. It was only twenty-five years later, after the defeat of Napoleon, that the exiled Bourbon King of Spain , Napoleon's brother, came to Bordentown and established a comic opera court-in-exile. He lived in his estate on the northern side of the town, nowadays in and around Park Street, where a fine early nineteenth-century Italianate house on the outskirts is all that remains of the original 2,000-acre estate. In its time it was known as the 'New Spain', and became a magnet for snobs and social climbers in early nineteenth-century Philadelphia society. In an odd example then of the dialectic between Trenton and Bordentown, the royal exile installed his lady love Annette Savage in Trenton and conducted a long relationship with her there. Bonaparte Park is nowadays only a small remnant of the old estate and the only truly original building left is the Gardener's Lodge on Park Street.

Technological progress impinged on Bordentown, with the first locomotive ever running in the United States arriving in pieces on a ship from Sheffield in England in 1831 and it ran on the Camden to Perth Amboy railroad. Soon the new Pennsylvania railroad was rushing past the house of early feminist educationalist Clara Barton, a local heroine who went on to become the founder of the American Red Cross. The Red Cross had always been strong in Trenton also, a detachment of volunteers helping bravely in the struggle against flooding in New Orleans after Hurricane Katrina.

Then the focus suddenly changed, the eye camera switched. I had taken a quiet spot in a café where elderly Jewish ladies were discussing their bridge club. The green tea was good, fragrant. I had found a used book about Royalist Yugoslavia that I had never heard of before, published in California in 1948. Things were looking up. Then the Drano Man appeared on the scene as I was walking back to my car. He was waving a plastic container that had Drano written on it. Here was an urban myth come alive, Fake News was walking the streets. What is Drano? It is a homely product, produced by a firm S.C. Johnson in Wisconsin, far from Jersey, and used to pour down blocked sumps and u-turns and pipes. Yet it has given rise to terrorism alerts. According to someone I knew in Windsor Township, it was just an urban myth but in fact that was not true. Drano bombs have quite a long history and warnings about them have continued to go viral on Facebook and social media until recently. With customary inventiveness kids discovered that you could put Drano, tin foil and a little water in plastic drinks bottles and then recap them and leave them lying around where people will find them. When the foil comes into contact with the Drano solution inside the plastic bottle it gives off gas as a result of the chemical reaction. Then they go pop and explode and spray high pressure caustic liquid everywhere and can do quite serious damage, both to people and property. That's what actually happens and there have been a steady stream of adolescent injuries all over the country as a result.

But what does the *mythos* say? According to the class conscious Marxist version of things, the Drano bomb was invented by an ex-Drano employee who had been fired and bore a grudge against the company. He knew the chemistry of Drano and so was able to make large bombs that he placed under street drains and manhole covers to simulate terrorist explosions. He is why you should be afraid of walking the streets of New Jersey, as again, according to the myth, this activity was all centred on the edge of Burlington County near the town of Evesham. Knowing Evesham (England) very well it was intriguing to visit but actually there is little to see, just sprawling new suburbs, small malls and no sense of a community.

Jersey reality is always somewhat different. Nothing of the Drano myth ever took place, but instead a long series of incidents long predating 9/11 and going back to the early 1990s, when kids as a prank tried to do damage to their school or something. This type of minor explosive device is easy to make, works and can blow your hand off, and the NJPD will charge you with a felony if they catch you doing it. But there are strange people everywhere. I had heard a report of a disturbed person dressing as 'the Drano bomber' and this seemed to be him, in dusty jeans, straggly curly brown hair and dark sunglasses. Maybe he just has a special relationship with the product and he showed no signs of wanting to detonate the bridge ladies or anyone else, and he proceeded down the street in the direction of the Delaware River buff and Tom Paine's statue. Drano was his fetish. The interesting thing is how the myth works, as an urban myth, in the era of 9/11. A fad with dissident kids becomes a motivated individual terrorist. It seemed to me that even in pretty virtuous Bordentown everyone is living on their nerves in Bushkratia and paranoia can easily follow. But as the terrorist doesn't actually exist, someone decides to act as if he does. It's New Jersey, people think in different ways about things. A bank of grey clouds was drifting south above the river. It was time once I had given my paper in Hellenic Studies to think of visiting Atlantic City. A mathematician I was joking with in the Triumph one day had said Bruce didn't like it and he never went there. There must be a reason for that if what he said was true

Down the road things were grinding on as usual. A woman's body had been found in a bag, dismembered and stuffed into the trunk of her Ford Mustang, her only ID a tattoo of Five Roses on her thigh. The Bloods were shooting it out with the Ñetas, but the statistics were cheerful, Trenton was down from the fourteenth worst overall crime rate in the US to the thirty-ninth, not bad. A Philly cop died after being shot in a burger bar. What did Drano matter? The Drano bomber was about the myth of violence and terrorism, but even if you are drenched in Plato it didn't seem a very necessary *mythos*. There was plenty of the real violence about all over the place.

Meanwhile Halloween was looming, and then Thanksgiving. Halloween is important in Jersey, the ghosts walk, some of them innocent and fun for children, others more sinister. The state's happily diminishing number (very small) of white supremacists have their drunken gatherings in remote places along the old 'KKK Roads', roads usually in dense forests and Pine Barrens that were used for Ku Klux Klan cross burnings and meetings in the inter-war period after the Klan had been banned.

Elsewhere, less harmfully, teenage Satanists gather to talk to ghosts in a cloud of marijuana fumes and show off their new tattoos to each other. But wholesome Thanksgiving would follow and then everybody would be good Americans and eat enormous quantities of food. Then Black Friday would come and everybody would go shopping. Or they might decide to roll down to Atlantic City and play the numbers. The numbers are always waiting for those by the ocean, in the machines with the ever-revolving Three Eyes.

8
ATLANTIC CITY: THE JERSEY DEVIL SENDS NUMBERS MAD

*Concerning Plato, Trump, Number, Desire,
Glaucon's reflections, and that fall 2007 day
the Grand Jackpot prize at Trump Plaza was
US$135,000*

Atlantic City of Expanded Desire and Opposite of the Pythagorean Ideal has tower blocks and assertive new buildings that suddenly appear on an empty horizon over the flat fields. Cows graze peacefully near a place turning over billions of dollars a year. The frontier was still very much alive when Atlantic City became what it is, in the time when the trek Wild Westwards embodied the American Dream of the time, just as later on in the mid-twentieth century the Dream was embodied in FDR's social welfare programmes and the ambition of full employment. Atlantic City exploded out of empty farmland. Yet wilderness remained, as in the remote Depression-ruled Appalachians where Bruce Springsteen's father grew up, and he moved eastwards to find work in New Jersey. As long ago as 1890 the US Census Bureau had declared the frontier time was over, with the time of ultra-individualistic trappers, railroad pioneers and homesteaders fading into history. But the end of the frontier struggle did not mean the end of internal demarcations in the country, and often the state line of law enforcement mythology is the least important. People in north Jersey call the south 'Cowtown', a place of uneducated people and long obsolete social relationships, not as backward as the Pineys but hardly in the forefront of human progress.

There is an invisible border around Atlantic City, as there are many invisible borders and frontiers that outsiders do not easily see throughout New Jersey. The north-south line is important; once a draft version of the Mason-Dixon Line would have run across New Jersey, and the culture of places in the still quite agricultural south is very different from the northern suburbs. Inside the local line Atlantic City has and has had for many years a monopoly of casino operation under the state constitution that it has profited from for decades. Casinos in north Jersey were never allowed on the same basis, and generally south Jersey has supported Atlantic City against the recurrent attempts by northern interests to change the law. Defenders of the status quo often argue that gambling is easier to control and police in a restricted zone, while critics see the law as a comfort blanket for the city fathers in Atlantic City to tolerate mismanagement, tax crises and corruption. The past is near among the skyscraper pinnacles by the shore, and the past was often violent and criminal long before the casino industry started to fight Mob control and modernize itself. As in many of his songs, like US industrial decline in 'Youngstown', a whole historic process is condensed into one Springsteen song.

In a register of the greatest rock or any popular song writing of all time, 'Atlantic City' comes very high on all tabulations. The haunting first lines say it all for most people:

> *Well they blew up the chicken man in Philly last night*
> *Now they blew up his house too*
> *Down on the boardwalk they're gettin' ready for a fight*
> *Gonna see what them racket boys can do*
> *Now there's trouble busin' in from outta state*
> *And the D.A can't get no relief*
> *Gonna be a rumble out on the promenade*
> *And the gamblin' commissioner's hangin' on by the skin of his teeth*
> *Everything dies baby that's a fact*
> *But maybe everything that dies some day comes back*
> *Put your make up on; fix your hair up pretty*
> *And meet me tonight in Atlantic City*

Pleasure with a pretty girl and desire for her is supposed to rescue the hero from the darkness and violence of Atlantic City, but it does not. That is the myth. In one sense this is the world of the musical *West Side Story*, the fights of the Jets and Sharks overtaken by love, but gone so much deeper, into mythology. This is no teenage gang aberration in an otherwise healthy society, in the myth only a problem in ethnic big cities, or the realm of homely minor criminals and cuddly wise guys of *Guys and Dolls*, but rather a society at war with itself. Who was the chicken man? Why was he blown up? Who are the racket boys going to fight? In fact, he was a man called Phil Testa. Like many Springsteen songs, there is a true story underlying the mythmaking and haunting lyrics. Lyric and reality are very close.

Who was Phil Testa? An important hood in Atlantic City for a time, he was leader of part of the Pennsylvania Mafia, born in Sicily in 1924, and dead in 1981 when he was blown up by a nail bomb. By this time he was known as the Julius Caesar of the Philadelphia Mob, and for a time boss of the Scarfo crime family. Testa was a short, unattractive man with a pockmarked face, unlike his glamorous society star son who took over his crew after his death. The family legit business was chicken farming although in reality young Testa started to make it as a professional gambler. He was also, in his way, a self-taught classicist, obsessed with the ancient history of Sicily where his family originated. He imagined himself as a Roman general: the Julius Caesar of Organized Crime.

In reality he was quite a minor figure, compared to the mighty long-tentacled *octopodi* of the Gambino and Genovese families in northern Jersey and New York City, but he has achieved immortality of a kind through this Springsteen song. And Testa has a contemporary link; he was involved through the Scarfo Mob family with casinos in Atlantic City that were being bought out by legitimate investors, and the largest of these was one Donald Trump. Testa ran labour recruiting and other rackets in Atlantic City just when it was making its transition from old fashioned strong-arm Mob control of gambling to the modern corporate business model. The song is an exquisite mixture of reality and myth.

The downstairs bar of the Chelsea Pub & Inn near the Tropicana Casino was gloomy, but the venerable, creaking establishment was open day and night, the bar never really closing, with its wooden walls laden with posters about Cadillacs and places where you can see where Billy the Kid died, a long way from the shore and Atlantic City. It predates the motels which were more or less invented for Atlantic City as the 'motor inn' and came with mass car ownership in the early 1950s. Between 1954 and 1962, no fewer than seventy-three motels were constructed in Atlantic City. Seen from here, it doesn't seem like the east's 'most fabulous seaside resort', as described by Charles. L. Scull whose family had been in the US since 1685. Atlantic City was the centre of the modern American entertainment industry before Las Vegas came on the scene but in the days of the 1920s, when the world's largest auditorium, the Convention Hall, could seat 14,000 people, and the 1930s, with sixteen million visitors to a place with a resident population of 65,000, are over. The City of the Three Spinning Eyes, Vegas, has displaced it.

The few drinkers here at eleven in the morning ranged from the sober to the mildly out of it to the comatose and totally pickled, losers or the lost with a few bills stacked in front of a bent head over the bar top wood. Here is Lost Weekend, not Marlboro country. This is another City of Numbers, but numbers only mean anything if you are sober enough to tell the difference between them. Had the numbers game been played here any time lately? I asked a regular looking black guy who was reading the horse racing page of the *Press of Atlantic City* if he knew any numbers players here. He saw it as an antiquarian question, a strange Brit rooting around on our farm.

'Numbers is dead. Tho' my Dad bet the same number for five years.'

He must have been a man of faith. These things have been thought about for a long time. Can you escape numbers? The English seventeenth-century theorist John Arbuthnot thought of playing dice as 'an epidemic distemper' and wrote approvingly in his 1692 work, *Of the Laws of Chance*, of the Byzantine emperor Justinian banning gambling in Constantinople,[*] stating that:

> The Reader may here observe the Force of Numbers, which can be successfully applied, even in those things, which one would imagine are subject to no rules. There are very few things which we know, which are not capable of being reduced to a Mathematical Reasoning...

I asked him if he knew who Phil Testa was. He looked blank and offered to buy me a drink. Collective memory at street level of alleged government triumphs against the Mob is small, as daily experience so often proves otherwise. In private discourse, scepticism also reaches to the highest levels

---

[*] In essence a semi-translation of Huygens's 1657 treatise *De Ratiociniis in Ludo Aleae*. Justinian's law is to be found in Cod.Lib.3. Tit.4.

of the US government, as in the conversation between ex-FBI Director Louis J. Freeh and President Bill Clinton recounted in the former's autobiography *My FBI* about whether recent prosecutions in New York City had actually broken the power of the long-established Five Families. Talk across the bar drifted to Bruce and the E Street Band, and how much moolah the tour was making. Faith in the *Magic* album was not needed; salvation was proceeding by works, the tour was going well, apart maybe from Madison Square Garden in New York City, as it would the following year in Britain where the *Guardian* writer Laura Barton described smuggling a small bottle of brandy hidden in her brassiere to watch Bruce and the Band making the massive Manchester Old Trafford football ground holding 60,000 'seem no bigger than the back room of a pub … he boils a whole stadium down to its very essence' with his' impeccable showmanship'. This bar and the life of the people in it seemed so far from the University.

Back in Princeton it was time for the fall bicker. Bickering is the arcane process where the fraternity dining clubs along Prospect that are the heart of the University choose their new members, a very stressful process for all concerned, like the Bullingdon Club selection rituals in Oxford. As always, traditional Princeton was moving on steadily with the advent of new residential colleges like eBay mogul Meg Whitman's having no effect whatsoever on the numbers seeking to join the old clubs. The prestigious Tower only accepted eighteen of the thirty-eight bickerees. I doubt if any member of the Tower has ever visited the Chelsea Pub. On the other hand it was a Thursday, the day when the Princeton Marxists sold the *Workers Vanguard* newspaper by Firestone Library—sometimes it does seem a college of extremes. Police violence against black people, this week in Chicago, was the theme of the front page, as it often was.

Once Atlantic City did not exist, not very long ago when the site of the Chelsea Pub & Inn, the casinos and the wider city had only been a windswept sand dune. It was easy to keep to the traditional 'live and let live' ethos of the City when there was plenty of room to keep away from potential problem people or enemies, as there certainly was in those early days. The poet Walt Whitman visited the area in 1879 and noted the 'vast salt meadows' along the coast which were only just beginning to fall within the crosshairs of developers and speculators. Agriculture was a motivation then, rather than pleasure tourism, with reclaimed land from the marshes remarkably productive. It is often forgotten nowadays how rural and backward south Jersey was then, and remained, with over 100,000 functionally illiterates in the state in 1930, mostly in the south, and many more in the century before. South Jersey work was poorly paid rural drudgery, and the only shop was a tiny mom and pop store at the crossroads and the only pleasure a game of cards or chess in the evening. The Barrens are always held up as examples of a rare backwardness and underdevelopment in the state, but in fact the entire rural south was not very different in terms of health, education or income levels until 1945. Whitman observed when he reached the tiny settlement that was Atlantic City in those days that 'worldliness' was the besetting sin of New Jerseyers. He also described the innocence of

> a flat, still sandy, still meadow region (some old hummocks with their hard sedge, in tufts, still remaining) an island, but good hard roads and plenty of them, really pleasant streets, very little show of trees, shrubbery, etc., but in lieu of them, a superb show of ocean beach—miles and miles of it, for driving walking, bathing—a real Sea Beach City indeed, with salt waves and sandy shores ad libitum.

This unspoilt landscape has gone. Now great dyke walls metres high line the shore to try to protect the city from violent Atlantic storms and hurricanes. The sea has become the enemy of the city, and perhaps it always was. Philadelphia historian A.L. English certainly saw innocence in 1884, writing that

> It is a refuge thrown up by the continent-building sea. Dame Health took a caprice and shook it out on a fold in her flounce. A railroad laid a wager to find the shortest distance from Penn's treaty-elm to the Atlantic Ocean. It dashed into the water, and a city emerged from its freight-cars as a consequence of the manoeuvre. Almost

any kind of parentage will account for Atlantic. It is beneath shoddy and above mediocrity. It is different from any other watering-hole in the world, because it is unspoilt, yet luxurious; because the air is full of iodine and chloride of sodium.

Mid-nineteenth-century writers were, of course, obsessed with fresh air, as 'bad air' was then believed to be the cause of the dreadful epidemics of cholera and yellow fever that were sweeping cities such as Newark. Frontier writer Randolph B. Marcy saw a main reason for migration west as the freshness of the prairie atmosphere.

Atlantic City now is seen as perhaps the worst and most corrupt place in a generally corrupt state, according to the stereotypes and also the experts, like New Jersey veteran investigative journalists Bob Ingle and Sandy McClure who in their book *The Soprano State: New Jersey's Culture of Corruption*, published in 2008, pilloried what they saw as a culture of sleaze and Mob infiltration of most business and public sector life centred on Atlantic City and Trenton. Little has changed over the years, in their view, since the famous meeting in 1929 at the Ambassador Hotel in the city that brought together Lucky Luciano, Al Capone and Mob financial genius Meyer Lansky in a summit on neutral ground in Atlantic City. But it did not stay that way for very long.

As the US Navy left after their takeover of the City shore and the Cape in World War I, with giant early airships no longer floating over the waves, gambling grew in the 1920s. The city had fallen under the control of a classic Tammany boss, Enoch 'Nucky' Johnson, who after 1924 ruled it with his descendants for nearly forty years with a rod of iron. The one-party state he constructed had no room for social critics or reformers, and Johnson personally interviewed every person seeking a public-sector job to make sure they would fit in to his 'Boss' patronage system. Law enforcement was socially marginalized, if it took place at all. A central role for the police was to see that the brothels ran smoothly and profitably. The election of pliant people in office to support the Johnson machine was achieved through 'street money', a generous supply of dollars and drink for party activists to get people to vote the right way. The arrival of Prohibition made Atlantic City in its modern form, where illegal drinking halls, whorehouses and shebeens flourished, after long previous years when the city had already practised breaking the pre-Prohibition law by serving drinks on a Sunday. Corruption just became commonplace, and all employees had to contribute from their wages to Republican Party funds to keep their jobs. Liberals, particularly in Europe, often express surprise at the warm welcome a mainstream businessman like Donald Trump received when he began to make his major contemporary investments in the City's casinos after 1995 but few realize that for over a hundred years, criminal control of the city in different guises had been the norm.[†]

In terms of the moral atmosphere—always something important when thinking of the history of the Jersey Shore—Nucky Johnson inherited an ideal situation, with the breakdown of the last vestiges of the infamous 'Blue Laws' regulating shore behaviour. Only a few years before, Hector MacQuarrie, a British Army officer based in the US on war work, had a weekend off in Atlantic City in 1917, noting it was 'a long thin town stretching along the shore', and also noticing the intense preoccupation of the city authorities with a puritanical dress code for the beach and shore. He saw the strange long bathing skirts that were prescribed for ladies at the time, and heard that his landlady had seen 'policemen measuring the length of a girl's swimming skirt'. Men were similarly restricted, although Atlantic City was not as austere as more northern Jersey shore resorts where all swimming gear was supposed to be black and display of the bare male torso was forbidden.

Walking was perhaps more important than swimming for purposes of display. It is closely linked to the emancipation of women as the nineteenth century wore on, and to the arrival of mass market female fashion. The characteristically Jersey shore invention of the boardwalk was important in Atlantic City, where it was very long and where thousands of people could display themselves and their apparel without any dress

---

† For more detail, see Nelson Johnson's fine study *Boardwalk Empire: The Birth, High Times and Corruption of Atlantic City*, 2011.

code issues applying. The boardwalk is not really about the beach or the sea at all; in most senses it is about the arrival of democratic modern fashion, women's new freedoms in society and the confidence of women to display themselves, even if enclosed securely in awkward wasp waited formal gowns and tight whalebone corsets, and possibly then to meet men they did not already know. It is also a place where women can wear shoes with high heels that do not immediately sink into the sand dunes and cause embarrassing upsets. The evening stroll became known as the flirtation walk. The boardwalk was a usable female space, as opposed to the still largely male domain of sea swimming, and shore recreation is still the biggest industry in New Jersey today.

From the earliest days, periods of progress in Atlantic City have often been punctuated by disaster. In the period after the early colonists established themselves, the coastal inlets became infested with small-scale privateer boats, the so-called 'Barnegat Pirates', criminals who made a living from plundering shipwrecks. They had rich pickings in some years, right into the following century as in 1847-48 when sixty-four vessels were wrecked on the shore in Atlantic County. The wreckers and pirates could become rich very quickly. The booming whaling industry of the seventeenth and early eighteenth centuries collapsed into disaster, to be replaced by the destruction (like the whales) of the fine cedar forest along the shore south of what is now Atlantic City, and its replacement by swamps and useless small trees. Cattle ranching began in the area after about 1835, but never rivalled game hunting of the huge coastal flocks of ducks and geese and fishing as a food supply. Black snakes, garter snakes, adders and hop toads proliferated on the sand dunes.

The city was really re-founded in its modern form as a health resort, a refuge from the burgeoning and unhealthy new cities of the eastern seaboard, and above all grimy Philadelphia, with the first ever railway train running from Camden in July 1854. Wilderness was close; one nineteenth-century traveller said how he disliked the 'City' and saw only a desolate swampland with sand dunes, ponds, cedars and brambles'. Human constructions on the land have often been the target of the sea, with the first pier built in 1881 only lasting a year before it was swept away, or later as on 6 March 1962, when a vicious combination of very strong easterly Atlantic gales and high spring tides dumped millions of gallons of water into the city in twenty-foot waves, smashing down wooden houses and washing away sea islands.

Economic disaster also beckoned as long as the Mob controlled the casinos. Apart from the violence and tax evasion they brought, their business model also has a critical fault in the development of modern casino capitalism—simply lack of capital. The casino modernization and arrival of electronics in gambling proved to be extremely expensive for the owners and a new type of casino was evolving that was much larger than the old Nevada models and associated with comfortable hotel accommodation, greater variety of games and shopping malls to fritter away winning on clothes or jewellery. The enormous sums of money could only be found with the banks, which were unwilling to get involved with known Mafia figures such as Testa and the Bruno clan in Philadelphia. Also closely linked to these calculations were property speculation issues. In 2006 casino profits had risen on the basis of real estate plays as much as casino profits, and the Las Vegas market had soared very high, with Atlantic City drawn up with it. The Colony Capital organization offered US$1.4 billion to buy the Tropicana Casino in a bid to create the world's third largest casino company. No Mob figure could ever find capital to take part in transactions of this size, but others could.

Much of the fortune of President Donald Trump has been made from seeing this early on and, as a respected New York property developer, by buying big into the Atlantic City world before prices soared to astronomic heights. Where did this money actually come from? In reality, Trump and other NYC investors did not have it in their back pockets any more than the Mafia did, but unlike the latter they could borrow and Trump worked with Wall Street financiers like 'Junk Bond King' Michael Milken who, in the words of gambling historian David Johnston, 'raised money the mob never could'. It was not risk free, and after the death of key Trump honcho, the Mormon gambling odds mastermind Steve Hyde in a helicopter crash, the financial house of cards folded and Trump faced bankruptcy proceedings.

He only survived as a casino owner through the good offices of the New Jersey Casino Control Commission. They could see a way to use Trump to lever the Mob out of Atlantic City in a new climate. Yet Donald Trump kept his nerve, and his debtors had to wait months for any payment on the Taj Mahal Casino Resort construction work, but even with debts equal, according to one estimate, to thirty-five times his assets, he fought to live another day and eventually run for the US presidency in a remarkable one-man campaign. Two different historical times existed in these transactions, Mob temporality, tied largely to the present, and the temporality of the new owners from corporate America, who could think long and borrow long to achieve their objectives.

It is an interesting journey down from Trenton and there is much to see on the way if the traveller avoids the fast but monotonous Atlantic City Expressway. Turning away south from the Expressway onto Route 54 South, the road runs through farmland towards little Buena, and skirts the heartland of Italian south Jersey, the Vineland agricultural area, with its excellent wines on sale by the roadside. Over a million gallons of wine a year are produced in this area of south Jersey. In the 1930s Buena was a tiny settlement of hardly more than 100 people on a crossroads that started as an old stage coach stop and stables called The Midway but has now grown considerably, and nearby is the main shrine to Padre Pio, a religious figure who is very popular in south Jersey. The people here pride themselves on a different culture from the world of the Italian-Americans in the northern industrial suburbs and in particular focus on being hard-working, honest, rural, devoutly Roman Catholic farmers free of criminal or dubious associations.

In reality, the community has had its share of dramas like any other. Away north at Centerville, Monmouth County, a respectable Italian farmer Raffaele 'Ralph' Eovino escaped execution for murdering his wife Amelia whom he caught *in flagrante* with her lover Tony Ruggerrio in 1922, and in many of the serious Italian-American crimes in the state records there is a common thread of crimes of passion, but nobody talks about them much, especially when 'the unwritten law' is in action, eclipsing US common law and in this case excusing a husband murdering an errant wife.

Personal piety is important here. The dignified concrete Padre Pio shrine is a contemporary creation completed in 2002. As in Italy itself, veneration of Padre Pio appeals to southerners, so near Bari one of his main statues stands powered exclusively by solar panels, the world's first fully ecological saint's shrine. Here in the Landisville part of Buena rests the glove of Padre Pio as the shrine relic and there are three statues, of Padre Pio himself, the Blessed Mother of Christ and the Sacred Heart of Jesus on the monument, standing on ten acres of land. It is a quiet place for spiritual contemplation, but not somewhere to learn a great deal about Padre Pio himself, and the shrine seems oblivious to the discrediting of many of Pio's claims to sainthood. It is also not immune from the travails of the wider world, after physical attacks on the shrine and above all the recent discovery of an Islamic extremist, Sharif Mobley living in the area and his subsequent demise. The ancestors of the Vinland people came from southern Italian communities which were often primitive and remote and where people lived all the time under fear of attack by the evil eye, evil spirits and rural demons. Belief in magic was almost universal, within living memory in some places. The shrine sends a message of divine protection from the Old Country, the Boot, in an uncertain New World.

It is in marked contrast to Atlantic City, the world of virtuous and sensible work on the land, where money is made through good crops and honest regulated trade, without magic, without hitting it big on the slots or the tables. Critics of the shrine, many themselves Catholic, see it as glorifying a man who for many years had a questionable credibility and whose stigmata claims have been questioned by experts. His adherents point to the fact that many of the doubters within the Church are or were either northern Italian bishops with a suspicion of what they see as credulous southerners, or urban sophisticates in northern New Jersey who reflect the secularist atmosphere of New York City.

The Casino as the Cave: The Tyranny of Images

There is an invisible frontier around each major casino, where approaching gamblers are seen by hidden closed circuit television cameras and every move they make is scrutinized long before they enter the building. Inside they have as much privacy as a goldfish in a small bowl. Casinos are known to make a good deal of money but until the economics and mathematics of gambling became a college subject of study in the last generation few knew how much. In general this study growth coincided with the phenomena set out by casino authority David Johnston in his lengthy book *Temples of Chance*. The numbers are astonishing, so much so that it has been claimed that at one recent point the Holiday Inn group owned and ran about 1,600 Holiday Inn hotels in America but twenty-eight cents of every dollar of company profits were made in its single Atlantic City casino. The murder of Phil Testa set out in the Boss's song is also a history of an event which on the surface could never happen again, a Mob war for casino control in Atlantic City. The Springsteen view of casino gambling is realistic, particularly on the mathematics. In a thirty odd year-old song, 'Roll of the Dice', he sets out a doomed vision:

> *Well I've been a losin' gambler*
> *Just throwin' snake eyes*
> *Love ain't got me downhearted*
> *I know up around the corner lies*
> *My fool's paradise*
> *In just another roll of the dice*

This song closed the set at the May 2003 *The Rising* tour concert at Boardwalk Hall in Atlantic City by Bruce and the Band, perhaps a brave decision in a post-9/11 set of otherwise uncontroversial classics played in a city where he does not often perform. Since the early 1990s casino gambling in the US has boomed everywhere, and without gambling revenue the city would be quickly bankrupt and could take much of Jersey's finances with it. In essence, this is what has happened with the gambling crisis and decline after 2014. Once there were only casinos in Las Vegas and Atlantic City but now thirty-three or more states (at last count) have them. The pressure to legalize gambling has been irresistible given government tax and revenue shortages. How do the maths work? Most of the equations are beyond non-mathematicians' comprehension, but as this book would not be complete without a gaming equation it can be expressed thus, according to casino economics theorist Robert C. Hannum,

$$\frac{HA = EV}{Bet \times 100\%}$$

where the House Advantage (HA) is the negative of the expected value of the bet (EV) expressed as a percentage of the amount bet. What does this mean on the tables and in the gambling halls? Typical house pricing gives a house advantage on roulette of maybe 5 per cent, on three-card poker maybe 3 per cent, blackjack 2 per cent, but on slot machines often between 5 and 10 per cent, which are thus hugely profitable for the casino. According to some estimates, revenue from slots, the favoured gamble of the working class and the less educated, has risen from about 40 per cent of the casinos' take in 1978, when they were under Mob control or influence, to about 70 per cent now, maybe more. Visitors to Atlantic City are sometimes struck by the open nostalgia shown for the gangsters by people there, but in fact the Mob often gave the slot punters significantly better odds of winning than the public corporations and billionaire owners do now. As Nicholas Pileggi wrote as long ago as 1995 in *Casino*:

> A casino is a mathematical palace set up to separate punters from their money. Every bet made in a casino has been calibrated within a fraction of its life to maximize profits while still giving the player the illusion that 'they have a chance'.

Slots have been around a long time, invented in the nineteenth century as 'the random number generator', and people love them. The great thing about playing slots is, as professional gambler and gambling theorist Frank Scoblete has pointed out, that it establishes a realm of apparent absolute freedom for the player: 'No busybody is going to tell you what

to do, or that you did it wrong, as such busybodies will at blackjack and other table games. At slots you play the machine you want, the way you want, and at your own pace, too.'

For the tens of millions of ordinary punters in America and the world generally who work in very authoritarian environments, where conformity to laid down rules is essential, there is little or no scope for personal initiative and the boss rules all your time, this apparent freedom with slots is psychologically very enticing. It is also way a way to bet small and win big, very occasionally. The spinning wheels the player sees are nowadays only there for show, the machine is computer controlled and the Random Number Generator runs whether anyone is playing or not. For the occasional lucky player on a machine with a 'progressive' jackpot, taking away an awful lot of money is possible. But Mr Trump and the other casino owners also know this and employ very serious mathematicians and programmers on huge salaries to give the house a big 'edge' on these machines. Hence the sentiments in the Springsteen song, or for that matter endless Methodist and other anti-gambling sermons from nineteenth-century pulpits. Recently some mathematicians have argued that the increasing sophistication of computers, artificial intelligence and computer programming will tip the odds back in the punter's favour but there is no sign of that taking place at the present time.

Gambling in this part of the state has always had strong opponents. Entire settlements came into being in south Jersey and elsewhere in the state in the late nineteenth century on the specific basis of Utopian social theories, almost all of which focussed on hard manual work and vehement opposition to gambling. An accessible example is the Jewish Utopian village of Woodbine about half an hour's drive south-west of Atlantic City. Established by the philanthropic Baron de Hirsch's trustees, the fund purchased 5,300 acres of undeveloped land. The baron was an idealistic German financier who wanted to establish model agricultural communities for oppressed European Jewry throughout the world, including Central and Latin America. His agricultural school, established in 1897 in Woodbine, produced world renowned scientists and doctors. One was Nobel Prize winner Dr Selman Waksman, the discoverer of streptomycin. With education, the commune gradually collapsed in the years up to World War II and now a visit to the little settlement with its very wide and open main street echoes the urban planning ideals of the founders. It is well worthwhile going to see the fine little museum of the old days, the very good antique and used bookstores and a garage with huge paintings of bald eagles on an American flag, but there is little left of the old community. Although many Jewish people still live in the general vicinity, nobody I met could speak Yiddish. The Whitesborough community was a similar social experiment, led by a philanthropist from Carolina, but also declined and died, as did the string of Utopian socialist or semi-socialist communities elsewhere in the state like the Fourierist North American Phalanx at Colts Neck, established in 1843, and the Jewish Alliance Colony, established in 1882 in Pittsgrove Township, Salem County. But the hard truth is that many casinos are still there and turning over billions of dollars a year while the Utopian rural settlements have long disappeared.

9
RETURN TO THE SHORE: CAPE MAY

*Concerning Cape May, where the sea dominates
the land, and where the state of New Jersey fades
into the Delaware estuary*

One William Wood wrote this ditty in 1634:

> The dainty Indian maize
> Was eat with clam-shells out of wooden trays,
> The luscious lobster, with the crab-fish raw,
> The brinnish oyster, mussel, periwiggie
> And tortoise sought by Indian squaw,
> Which to the flatts dance many a winter's jiggie

Cape May has the sea and the sea is the one sure source of beauty in New Jersey where on land finding it is an often uncertain quest. Atlantic City was a city full of, and determined by, numbers but it was impossible to tell which of them were true or false. This is not a new dilemma. As Socrates observed in Plato's dialogue *Hippias Minor*, it is hard to be sure who is honest about numbers and who is not:

Socrates
Is the liar, then, a liar about other things but not about number—he wouldn't lie about numbers?

Hippias
But yes, by Zeus, about numbers, too.

Socrates
So we should also maintain this, Hippias, that there is such a person as a liar about calculation and number?

Hippias
Yes.

Socrates
Who would this person be?*

---

* *Hippias Minor*, 367b. Hippias was a prominent Sophist philosopher.

Plato is often much better at asking questions than answering them. The ocean at Cape May was beyond numeration and calculation, numbers meant nothing in trying to think of it or describe it, and the salt water and the fishes and sea creatures within it are always in flux. A shark must move to live. The ancient philosopher sees our human nature as dualistic, as the land and the sea are dualistic. Modern American power is, though, exercised primarily through the US Navy, and many would argue that the welfare of many citizens living on the land has, through no fault of the US Navy, been somewhat neglected. American ships must move ceaselessly over the oceans for the power of the US to survive. Cape May is about the ride to the sea, the last place in New Jersey, the frontier, the border and invisible boundary of the River Delaware. The quest for justice through the election of particular politicians in Trenton or Washington thus seems unimportant. Perhaps the promised land, the American Dream, is unattainable. A long time ago there was a Springsteen song, 'Racing in the Street', and it is a far away, distant bridge in spirit to some of the songs in the 2007 *Magic* album.

> For all the shut down strangers and hot-rod angels
> Rumbling through this promised land
> Tonight my baby and me we're going to ride to the sea,
> And wash these sins off our hands

Or from the ancient tragedian Euripides:

> The sea washes away the ills of man.

Up shore north along the Parkway to Atlantic City there didn't seem any shortage of sins. Away from the madness of the numbers and the players at Atlantic City, Cape May was waiting forty miles down the coast and perched exposed on the last tip of the Delaware Estuary. That has always been its job; to offer a short visit to Paradise, even if just for the annual summer vacation. The state line can be crossed by sea. An excellent modern ferry runs across the Delaware Estuary, broad and oceanic and a rough ride journey on a windy winter day but idyllic in the summer, to dull

Lewes in Delaware and then there is an even duller drive across prim rural Delaware smelling vaguely of chicken farms down towards Baltimore and Washington DC. It is worth it to save the driving time on the highway and to see the views of the wide empty estuary that the colonists on their wooden ships must have seen.

The Delaware Bay is a sacred place in the colonization of America, for on 28 August 1609 the navigator Henry Hudson sailed his ship straight into it, but found the navigation difficult because of the shoals. Cape May has seen a little more recent history. In the mid-eighteenth century Methodist founding father George Whitefield of the Great Awakening preached nearby on one of his seven evangelical journeys in America. The town was blockaded by the Royal Navy gunboats of Commodore Beresford for a time in the war of 1812. Then it hit lucky and it built big, with Cape May as as the first planned American seaside resort, and extraordinary it was. The rich, particularly cotton merchants and slave owners, flocked there to escape the torrid heat and humidity of the South. The old Mount Vernon Hotel was thought to be the biggest hotel in the world when it opened in 1852, a monster construction with 2,100 rooms, a shooting range, a gasworks, pinball alleys and, above all, hot and cold running water in every room. The Great September Gale of 1821 had devastated the area, a wandering but not spent hurricane coming up the coast from the Caribbean, blowing down stone chimneys and taking the roofs off houses. Salt water was blown fourteen miles inland, killing trees and crops, and tidal water on the marshes was twelve feet deep. Afterwards Cape May was rebuilt on a massive scale. But life was short for many of these edifices. The original Stockton Hotel, almost as large as the Mount Vernon, was a miraculous survivor of the Great Fire of 1878 but by 1910 was considered past it, and torn down in days.

The Jersey side of the river estuary is lined with a row of small lighthouses, warnings to the unwary. On the beaches facing east, the shore here has a very regular, innocent and pristine beauty; a handful of sand feels gritty and tangible, easy to squeeze into new shapes, plastic, past and present in a state of the union, Jersey. At its best Bruce Springsteen's music has a classic simplicity and directness, an emotional authenticity which for the non-

initiated can seem off-putting. Both conceal endless contradictions. Many of the best songs are about the dialectic of innocence and experience, like William Blake's poems, where the lyrics have a deceptive simplicity and may tell a simple story, but with endless reverberations that go to the heart of the deepest dilemmas of American life and identity. The Cape May beach also speaks mathematics in its way as the sand runs in vast oblong and square patterns on the dunes, with cubist rock angles lying across it in some places, small glacial erratics that have found their way down to the sand or been dumped there to try to hold the beach together in winter's brutal storms.

The sea to the east seems to run to infinity, empty except for a small, intrepid sailing boat or a distant cargo ship. Beyond the sea-horizon is Europe, the Old World, then Asia, then the Pacific that meets the other sea off Cape Horn. The blue horizon is the perfect prime number, ever dividing and then multiplying as the sea moves, in stasis and in flux. The wildlife on and in the sea is a bridge to human time, for the birds and the whales and the dolphins and the fish, like us, must live and die. Yet they can endlessly repeat themselves, like an infinitely developed equation that can be taken back to its symbolic origins and then ceaselessly redeveloped in different ways. The sea is infinite, the land is finite and divided into different national states, the shore is where men meet and recalculate, just as the casino bosses and the gambling commissioner meet in buildings near the shore and consider what the odds should be on the roulette wheel or blackjack table and recalculate them again and again. The blue collar factory worker from Philly or Trenton escapes from the routines and fixed programmes of work to meet unpredictability on the shore, the randomness of numbers, hoping for control, Hegel's patterns of numbers over the flux in the spin of the wheel of fortune, transference.

The Cape May shore is also a kingdom of the birds. The vast flocks of migrants, oyster catchers, geese and snipe, are much tamer than in Europe and allow the curious visitor to join their world for a while and sit on the sand with them. It is the most perfectly preserved Victorian-era seaside resort in the United States, and set in salt-shore and sand dune aspic since that time, in its early days at the time of the French Revolution a mecca for the Southern rich and their black slave servants. There is a small slaves' section of the cemetery in the Goshen district of the city with modest, lonely tombstones. A blackjack dealer in the city had recommended a trip to the Emlen Physick Estate in Washington Street, the strangely named star turn of Cape May called after an obscure Philly magnate of the time, and an awesome Victorian gem of a museum house, he said. It was strange that people always described Cape May as Victorian, after the nation had fought so hard and for so long to eject British monarchical rule. On the other hand, no nineteenth-century citizen would have understood 'awesome' that way at all, but rather as a Biblical term. In the Edwardian period the town remained very fashionable, and had its own lyricists. The songs were not very good, as 'Cape May Spray' spells out, written by Charles Tomlin in 1913:

So glad I live in the land of peaches
Down near the Cape May beaches
Look away! Look away! Look away! Jersey Land:
New Jersey Land was where I was born

Early on one frosty morning
Look away! Look away! Look away! Jersey Land:
Then I'm glad I am in Jersey,
Hooray! Hooray!
To Jersey Land I'll take my stand
To live and die in Jersey
Away. Away.

Atlantic City had once had similarly glorious nineteenth-century Gothic hotels and houses, but they had been destroyed in gales or by development and fires. The surviving 650 or so in Cape May are Victorian-era fantasy mansions on the Cape—for that is what they are and always were—and are one of the hidden gems of the New Jersey Shore. And as Cape May has the largest fishing fleet along the shore and trades in shellfish with Canada, it is also a very good place to eat. The resort is heavily marketed at holiday times and offers a Victorian Dickensian Christmas with all the trimmings, an irony given that Charles Dickens's first visit to the United States in 1842 was most unhappy and he took away a strong dislike of America on his return to England. It took until 1867 before he could be persuaded to return. Late afternoon glasses of sherry are popular with visitors, many of whom are the far side of eighty years old, and there are wonderful gas lights illuminating some central streets. Sherlock Holmes might walk around the corner and bump into you. Cape May is safe, there is minor crime but not much; the Grand Jury Indictments in the local paper are small beer compared to some places, a few small drug busts, a burglary, an assault, a strange story involving child pornography, with all the accused listed, as the paper says, 'innocent until proven guilty beyond reasonable doubt'.

Cape May was designated a National Historic Landmark in 1976, a fortunate and far sighted decision that saved the town from the excesses of the developers who have wrecked (literally) important Springsteen song landmarks around Asbury Park and elsewhere. Named after one Captain Jacob May, who explored the Delaware Bay in 1623, the Cape was his memorial and has so remained. A little later, in 1630, two Dutch settlers called Peter Heyser and Giles Caster bought a parcel of land at Cape May for the Dutch West Indies Company. Local Native Americans were at war at the time, a tribal chieftain of the Kechemeches was fighting the Susquehannock confederation along the Delaware Valley, with about 2,000 warriors involved, and their disunity inland gave the European settlers an easy ride, for a time, although the first colony at Cape Henlopen, near present-day Lewes and established in 1631, had been destroyed in a massacre by Native Americans in 1632. To the north on the shore the land was deserted except for a few Lenape, the smoke from their fires in the wigwams drifting across the breaking waves. Ancient tools from their culture have been found in old oyster shell mounds at Hills Creek near Toms River.

The colonists must have come as a threat from the sea in the eyes of the Indians as much as the rogue Great White Shark of legend in the Great Jersey Shark Attacks of 1916, the basis of the Jaws story. Now, as then, trouble was coming from an unexpected direction. Instead of a man-eating Great White Shark of an unprecedented size arriving uninvited, the alien menace of the banking crisis of an unprecedented size was going to arrive uninvited, and eat jobs and people's houses. It is the great American story, alien menace cracking open the American Dream, terror breaking innocence, as after 9/11. From the pirate Bluebeard, who was supposed to have haunted the inlets north of Hill's Creek, to the shark in *Jaws*, which was directly descended from the great whale in *Moby Dick*. Now the menace was on land and not coming from the sea.

When I first started in the United States, I did not know what a Garage Sale was; now they were everywhere as the mortgage foreclosures accelerated and people tried to raise a few dollars from auctioning their spare possessions before moving on. There was a sense of unease in the East Coast American air. The days were beginning to shorten quickly, and the fall evenings when it was still possible to sit outside and smoke in Quarry Street were turning to damp chill. A visiting English colleague was enjoying her menthols as she sat and read about the Emperor Constantine but she was wearing her anorak. The squirrels were carefully collecting small nuts and stashing them somewhere unseen. Their economics were clearly better than ours—the primitive accumulation the Keynesians despise works if you live wearing a grey fur coat among the Princeton shrubberies and thorn bushes.

The *Magic* tour was somewhere in a city far away to the west, and it felt distant from the songs and the Band, although going to the Pittsburgh concert was looming. The atmosphere was changing and there was no doubt a major financial crisis was coming, although at this stage it was impossible to forecast what form it would take. Son and daughter had also visited and brought news of rumours of a probable bank failure in the City of London and the troubles of a mortgage bank called Northern Rock about which we then knew virtually nothing. The pound was at what seemed to me like ridiculous heights worth nearly two dollars and they spent a good deal of time shopping.

The old certainties were going, the world was on thin ice. We went down to the stadium and watched the Princeton girls obliterate the Columbia girls at lacrosse. It was a nice sunny afternoon under the glare of the huge metal tiger staring threateningly down from the stadium entrance. The Princeton girls seemed at least a size bigger than those from Columbia. The Tiger female who steamed down the wing at high speed near us whirling the ball in her stick net seemed absolutely terrifying, a shock of fine red hair trailing in her slipstream.

'City girls. Columbia. You can tell. Smaller.'

For a second you could see the broad acres of the estates of the Old South across the stadium grass. Europeans are often ignorant of many things about the United States and the continuing existence and political clout of the old landed elite from the South and West is one of them. They had no need to gamble or listen to rock music although many of them did so. Cape May and Atlantic City were developed as the playgrounds of the new rising middle class in an industrial society and to give the workers somewhere to relax away from their often unhealthy neighbourhoods in (mostly) Camden and Philadelphia. Cape May stayed genteel, but Atlantic City soon became blue collar. Travel to the shore was towards the safe and reassuring east, towards Europe from where many of them had recently emigrated, and then you returned home, equally safely on the railroad car.

Travel in the opposite direction was very different, and when Atlantic City boomed in the late 1860s onwards, travel to the West was illuminated by volumes like Randolph B. Marcy's famous *The Prairie Traveler*, published in 1859. This book became the Bible for the westward-bound pioneers. Marcy was an ex-US Army officer and his book gives a riveting picture of the hardships and dangers that were immediately encountered by the travellers once they had left Jersey and crossed the Appalachians and the Ohio River, that 'dark and bloody stream', as one recent historian called it in his depiction of the conquest of the valley for the United States.

This period was important in forming the stereotypical image of New Jersey and its people that has dogged the state for decades. Those who came to Jersey from Italy or wherever and stayed and prospered have not shared the frontier experience, so a man like Tony Soprano is proud not merely of being born and bred a Jersey boy but also of rarely needing to leave the state or New York to live a full life, as he sees it. He is happy with who he is, in contrast to the transformative prospects of the trek to the West, with railroad pamphlets being officially distributed throughout the state in 1860, promising immense wealth, land and the implied social status of the free Jeffersonian independent farmer. As Jonathan Raban observes, commenting on the spurious material produced by the US government to attract settlers to Badlands in far-west Montana in 1909 a generation later, the emigrant might go to the US but also would always leave part of his or her old identity behind. In their Jersey identity Tony and his family are continually translating themselves back and forth between being Italians and Americans in an unresolved dialectic, even though it is clear that their ancestors left the Boot a long time ago. Plato felt dialectic should only be practised by mature people, but American democracy has released this capacity to people far outside the elite and they live out its dilemmas every day. The law, embodied in Tony's FBI adversaries, is purely American and brooks no compromise with old legal codes imported from elsewhere, particularly if they seem to leave room for criminality.

Faced with the might of the US government machine, different people reacted in different ways. Italians, in particular, as the most numerous immigrant group in New Jersey and central in forming the popular image of the state, faced particular pressures. Like many temporary or permanent inhabitants in the state, I was soon struck by how many Italian-Americans I met seemed to be called 'Lombardi' or similarly northern Italian names, while when talking to them it was equally obvious that their family roots lay in southern Italy or Sicily. The explanation was simple, in that during and after Prohibition and the connected vast mythologization of Italian-American mobsters in life, in books and above all in films, mainstream Americans just started to automatically associate coming from Sicily with gangsterdom, and if you put a Sicilian name on the job application form, you didn't get the job. So you modified your name.

West of the Cape the road curves in and out of the forest towards the shore and meets the estuary and then after a few minutes the white tower of the Cape May lighthouse is sticking into the air, very white and proud of itself as one of the most important lighthouses in the United States. It seems the end of the road, in every sense, a banner for the large Cape May fishing fleet, a watchtower with the US Coast Guard training school nearby, and down the river is little Bivalve, surely one of the strangest place names in a state of often strange names. It echoes back to the time of the tons of clams and oysters that used to be harvested here, until the Delaware became too polluted to eat them. Driving to the end of the Bivalve road, it seems like a place time forgot, a scattering of nice white houses and clumps of trees and woodland, its name maybe thought up by a man or woman sitting in an office in Trenton at some point. The fish are still there and very good, even if the shellfish are not. The sailfish come by and are good sport for serious and expert anglers, while the foodies go for striped bass, a cautious fish which only really bites at night, and better still, the weakfish, the American version of the European sea trout, the same size and prize eating.

Buddy groups of men form up and take the boat out at night; the only thing missing in the boat is Hemingway on sea fishing, its joys and disappointments, Utopia on the waves. The beam of the lighthouse is very powerful and flashes every fifteen seconds to reach twenty-four miles out to sea. After it was built in 1859 the number of shipwrecks dropped dramatically and the wreckers' profession declined with it. Further out at that distance, the sea is the realm of the great creatures, the orca, the killer whale, the many more peaceful whales and dolphins and the sharks. Whale watching trips are popular with summer visitors. Cape May did not suffer the legendary attacks of 1916 like Spring Lake and Asbury Park but the Delaware Estuary is shark sea nonetheless, with modern oceanographic science revealing that some miles offshore and causing no trouble to bathers is a nursery area of growing sharks of several species. Dying and dead whales are a favourite food since sharks need rich fatty blubber if they can find it, and only at this juncture do Great Whites normally appear, far from human vacation crowds.

It is the most maritime part of the state, where the dominance of the ocean over human perceptions is as complete as it could be. In the far south of New Jersey everyone is a willing visitor come to sit on the beach or walk among the sand dunes. It was once very different in the far north-west corner of the state, where in the remote Ramapo Mountains, a range of high forested hills near Mahwah on the border with New York State lives a community descended from the most reluctant of often unwilling immigrants to the United States. In the years of the American Revolutionary War in the eighteenth century, over 3,000 women from England and the Caribbean were shanghaied and transported to the US, most of them prostitutes from the port brothels of Plymouth, London, Portsmouth and other naval towns and from Jamaica. They were trafficked for the use of the English soldiers in and around New York and the Hessian mercenaries who served under their command. When the war was over they were released but chased out of New York City, arriving half-starved in the Ramapo Mountains. There they found a surviving tribe of the Lenape (the name Mahwah is *Mawewi*, meeting place in the Lenape language), and soon began relationships with them and with abandoned Hessian mercenaries and criminals, escaped slaves and a few Native Americans from Carolina. Their mixed race descendants lived on in the forests in extreme poverty and backwardness and became known as the Jackson Whites. Nowadays they are recognized by the state as a Native

American group, although not by the Federal government in Washington. What has this to do with Cape May now, let alone Atlantic City? The key opponent of the ambition of the people there to achieve recognized Native American status has been none other than Donald Trump.

The trek to the reunion on the shore had been a willing journey and now a trek to Pennsylvania beckoned, an unwilling pilgrimage in essence. Bruce Springsteen had been to Mahwah after Ford closed the big car factory there in 1982, and wrote one of the most memorable songs of his early 1980s period afterwards, 'Johnny 99':

> *Well they closed down the auto plant in Mahwah late that month*
> *Ralph went out lookin' for a job but he couldn't find none*
> *He came home too drunk from mixin' Tanqueray and wine*
> *He got a gun, shot a night clerk, now they call 'im Johnny 99*

If Trump had failed in his 1993 lawsuit, the Ramapo tribe would not only have their identity as a minority respected but could have set up a reservation, and no doubt a casino would have soon followed, as on most reservations nowadays. The Trump gambling empire based on Atlantic City would have suffered badly from direct competition near New York City. As always in Jersey history, the past is much nearer the present than many citizens think. Certainly the rules of Thrasymachus, Plato's strong wise guy, were operating in those remote woodlands for people of whose ancestors hardly any wanted to be in the United States in the first place, particularly the women. The young people, nowadays out of work with their tattoos and Goth outfits, go into the same woods to do what they see as *Magic* as a refuge from the power of the numberocracy, those who exclude them. In the multidimensional world of the *Magic* album a meaning of most of the songs is to be found in belief, and in refuge from the failure of the government.

10
THE SCHLEP TO PITTSBURGH

Concerning a nightmare drive on the Penn Turnpike, the Appalachian crossing, and sundry matters, before reaching Melloncity

'Schlep: pronounced SHLEP, to rhyme with "hep", and SHLEPPER, to rhyme with "pepper". From the German: *schleppen*: "to drag" e.g. "Don't shlep all those packages". "At the rate you are schlepping along, we will never finish."

   Leo Rosten, *The Joys of Yiddish*

Cape May and Atlantic City seemed distant now, if still real. The reunion on the shore in September seems a faraway dream when the geese were still flocking around the Plasma Physics laboratory and the leaves brushed bright green on the surface of the Raritan Canal. It is a grey dull morning in New Jersey. It is 13 November 2007, the 317th day of the year. The sea at Cape May was a very long way away now on this important date. Tomorrow is exactly 1442 years since the death of the Emperor Justinian in AD 565. This was an auspicious date as he was the first ruler in world history known to have attempted to ban gambling in a legal code and, if it existed in his time, also no doubt the numbers game. Where would Joe Moriarty have ended up in a previous life in Byzantine Constantinople? How would a numbers runner in the streets of the *polis* conduct themselves, and what percentage would they have got on bets on the Blues versus the Greens in the Hippodrome? Scholars can inform. Numbers mobsters would probably have ended with their decapitated head on a spike above the town gates, except it was not a town but a capital of a universal empire, like America. Universal states find illegal gambling hard to handle.

   American life is full of ironies. After the run in with the rightists from the Keystone State and their friends in the security world in September it was now November 2007 and I was driving to that state in order to get a chance to see Bruce and the Band perform the entire *Magic* album live. There was no alternative. What song might be the most appropriate to listen to while driving to the Steel City? Did it matter? The dark financial clouds were casting a shadow over every state, the financial numbers were falling out of bed. Despite what the administration in Washington DC might have hoped, the US had the same problems everywhere, on the far side of the Delaware River as much as the Jersey side. This was also the view of a new arrival in the cigar lounge that week, Will, a Princeton mathematics major who was a thin, quiet young man with cheap clothes and a straggly beard who came from a very poor background in rural Texas with numerous brothers and sisters and belonged to a fundamentalist church. He was obviously outstandingly intelligent and attempted sometimes to explain his work to the assembled company, like how to develop an equation in a cool, stylish way. This usually resulted in one of the richer brethren buying him his cigar. Cigars and writing equations were his life. He had little interest in most of the United States, and seemed to see Texas as a separate world, and for all most people in our cigar store knew of it, it probably was. He was a tribute to the University's skill in finding people of real talent from poor and obscure backgrounds.

In a certain sense, at least in the view of the founding fathers of the Constitution who were drenched in the ancient classics, each US state was a separate *polis*, a city state in many senses, and each state had its own temporality and defined space. Yet a powerful US state, above all expanding early nineteenth-century New York, could, like ancient Athens, soon extend its power into neighbouring states, as in many ways Philadelphia had done with the creation of Atlantic City in the later nineteenth century. It was back to the philosophy of the shore in antiquity. The philosopher Thales of Miletus in ancient Ionia had mulled over the idea that the Ionians should set up a common government in a central position, with the different Ionian cities recognizing its authority, a principle George Washington also followed in his choice of the city on the Potomac.* American cosmology had become universal with globalization, or at least had attempted to, but all around in 2007 the Iraq War was causing many thinking people to question what was actually being achieved. At the time people were mainly and understandably concerned with the US military death toll. Almost every week the local paper recorded another

---

* For the ancient models, see Richard Seaford, *Cosmology and the Polis: The Social Construction of Space and Time in the Tragedies of Aeschylus*, Cambridge, 2012.

loss, a Jersey boy or girl who would never come home from Iraq to see those white clapboards again, but the wider question of the end of Iraq as a functional state was also important.

There were also other (minor) local distractions. A friend of a Princeton friend who knew someone high up in the NJPD had said that the case was breaking soon at Cheeks and that as I was getting interested in law enforcement issues while at Princeton it might interest me to see how things developed. I had said no, but in practice it was impossible not to hear about and follow what was happening. Cheeks turned out to be a downmarket Bada Bing-type juice joint some way away north at Pemberton Township. Juice bars are so named because in New Jersey it is illegal to run a strip club which serves alcohol, or in the time honoured words often repeated in court hearings, 'with breasts there's no wine or beer'. There had already been a spectacularly over-the-top raid of Cheeks with about five different law enforcement agencies busting what the paper called 'seven scantily clad prostitution suspects', hapless young women who turned out to come from Brazil. Apparently the reason for the hyper reaction was the fact that the bar was often frequented by servicemen from the nearby Fort Dix military base in the Pine Barrens, and as Fort Dix was security sensitive and held a group of alleged Al-Qaida suspects of Balkan origin the girls were thought to pose a security threat. Paranoia was the name of the game in NJ at that time in some official quarters. The women were in reality victims, not criminals.

So what song? It was hard to say as the *Magic* album is not built around one song like say the *Born to Run* album thirty years before, with a single meaning. Playing 'Born to Run' focuses a Boss arena show, and the song has been played no fewer than 1,484 times in concerts in those years, the easily available statistic and a tribute to the obsessions of some fans with as much enumeration as anyone in Washington DC. 'Badlands' comes next, with 1,193 performances, and 'Thunder Road' third with 1,168. They are all, of course, classics not just any classics, but defining classics is the process of trying to save the rock and roll tradition from the tide of bad music that has threatened to overwhelm it both in the US and elsewhere. It is as if Bruce and the E Street Band stand motionless like classical sculptures looking across a public park where a vast tsunami tide of plastic trash is blowing towards them. Was Pittsburgh in the world of trash music? Or does rock and roll survive there?

Pittsburgh looked a long way away on the map, a schlep down to Philly on Route 95 and then a sharp right turn over the Delaware River and onto what looked like the interminable grey snake length of the Pennsylvania Turnpike. Like anybody thinking of Pittsburgh I had the famous wartime journey of BBC radio journalist Alistair Cooke of *Letter from America* in mind. His description of the industrial landscape he saw in 1942 with the mines and steel mills reviving under pressure of World War II rearmament needs is unique:

> By day, one who loves the American landscape has the feeling of riding over its cut-over grave, and by night he may not even enjoy the deception of darkness, for all around him the hoarse glare of converters and furnaces, and the blue lights squinting out from the blackened panes of factory windows, will jeer at his antiquarian regrets. There is hardly a modern industry that is not pounding day by night or day through this frenzied area. Bituminous coal lies under it, and through it into West Virginia and through Pennsylvania. Steel factories and tinplate. Glass factories at Toledo. Ordnance and TNT and shell loading plants. Every small supply trade that can use the basic diet of the mines and the mills... I was struck by the music, for whether it was good or bad it too seemed to allow them no surcease from the pulse of the rhythms they worked to. In Pittsburgh jazz seemed more apt than other places. I remembered William Empson's definition of jazz: the hypnotised abandonment of self to the exact rhythms of machinery.

So Pittsburgh was a jazz city then, but would it be a rock city now? It was 14 November 2007, sixty-four years after Cook had written and when many of those industries were in ruins. The *Magic* album was being gradually assimilated by the public, and reviews were appearing. Bruce was interviewed for that week's *Rolling Stone* magazine, the nearest thing the rock scene has to a Book of Revelation (and Sacred Words and Prophetic Sayings), which was drawing together various prominent individuals to pronounce on Where We Are Going, the future of the United States. The prophetic tradition was no longer confined to the early hellfire preachers of the Jersey Shore but now included economists like Princeton *luminous* Paul Krugman, actor Tom Hanks, liberal establishment politician Al Gore and recent ex-President William Jefferson Clinton himself. The Springsteen take on things was acute and realistic, saying that in the last election there had been no candidate capable of throwing the Bush 'bums' out:

> As you get older you become pessimistic about the movement of government and the way government moves. To think that the country could veer this far rightward and that no one has addressed poverty since Lyndon Johnson... don't believe you can create a great society, a real American civilization, with an enormous percentage of the people left out... So I'm a bit sceptical and pessimistic... But at the same time I run into so many people that are working so hard to push the country towards that place that I feel very optimistic.

It was good to read that while contemplating having to travel to somewhere I was sure I would not like and where I did not want to go, for a variety of reasons. More material was emerging about the activities of Richard Mellon Scaife and his media smear machine that worked successfully against President Clinton to secure his impeachment in 1998-99. The obscurantist billionaire had not given up on activity aimed at spearing liberals and he was said to loathe modern Princeton and all who dwelt within it. He was alleged to see New Jersey as little more than an animated and overcrowded compost heap. The heir to the Mellon banking and industrial billions had already given over US$500 million to finance ultra-conservative causes. He was said to be still devoted to his first alma mater at Yale although he had been sent down after a drunken brawl where he had broken somebody's leg. Then he did eventually get a degree from the University of Pittsburgh and remained fanatically and alcoholically devoted to ultra-right politics in the city and nearby for the rest of his life. Given the Mellon billions, Pittsburgh was bound to be, in a certain sense, Scaife City. His 2007 'reconciliation' with Bill Clinton was widely discussed in my Princeton orbit that fall and seemed a problem for all concerned. The Clintons seemed to me and many others short on principles over this, but by this time the nomination was slipping away from Hillary towards Obama anyway.

Apart from the issues back in September, in my own work orbit studying modern Balkan history, Pittsburgh had been the centre of support among the Yugoslav-American Diaspora during World War II for the Nazi puppet Ustaše regime in Croatia, to such an extent that the FBI set up a secret unit in the city to follow what was happening and report directly to the state and to FDR in the White House. Some of the mildly tiresome aspects of Old Princeton revolved around Old Money families from the Pennsylvania industrial aristocracy. A generation back, historic enquiry does not have to be conducted by professors to soon see that there was, at some stages of the war, quiet support for Hitler from those in America with recent German roots—as well as the Croats—along with the usual dash of anti-British feeling from many Irish-Americans who took their lead from the neutralist line of John F. Kennedy's ambassador father. Pittsburgh was a very Irish immigrant city, with people who had spent, as one author points out, the first half of the nineteenth century digging canals and the second half working down the mines. Pittsburgh also had its fair share of pro-Nazis given the German family roots of many of the most prominent industrialists and politicians. Scots like Andrew Carnegie or an Ulster-descended family like the Mellons were not typical. It was a nasty, bitter cocktail. As Alistair Cooke shows so graphically, rearmament saved millions of Pennsylvania families from the dire poverty of the 1930s, but when war came, many of them were either still pro-Hitler, or isolationist, or at best not too sure of the right side to support.

It was a quiet, foggy November day all along the East Coast, and the lighthouse beams shone through the mist in the fading daylight. Hooters boomed out over the still sea and the beach was utterly deserted. New Jersey was still, very still, the still navel of the United States, the *omphalos* with hardly a branch moving, and seemed about to disappear into impenetrable fog. The very high towers of the US Coast Guard microwave towers recorded the exact position of shipping and could warn of possible collision risks. World trade was floating by on the Atlantic waves. In the deserted Pine Barrens north of Stone Harbor dew dripped off the trees into the sodden marshland below. Groundhogs, squirrels, skunks and racoons were laying in stores for the bitter months and hunkering down in warm, dry places. Wild turkeys huddled under people's wooden house steps like refugees.

Thanksgiving was approaching, the shopping splurge day of Black Friday, the desolate atmosphere of the strange, visionary landscape back from the shore vying with relentless brightly lit consumption in the malls. China was still booming, goods were cheap in Wayne's Willowbrook Mall, the Feds seemed to have nailed Tony Soprano and globalization was motoring successfully onwards. The Petraeus 'surge' was supposed to be winning in Iraq, a fast New World Order car was driving into the sunset. That was the Bush administration script, and in its internal logic it was not so different from the intellectual world of the Clinton administration that had preceded it.

In the Pocono Mountains on the Jersey-Pennsylvania border hunters were cleaning their guns, and the odd black bear began to move down away from the coyotes and disorder of the mountains to the rich food supplies in and around suburban gardens. The ducks may have landed in Tony's swimming pool in North Caldwell and disturbed his unconscious mind again, but the pool would be covered with dead leaves. The pole dancers were moving repetitively day and night at Satin Dolls, breasts and bottoms quivering in the lights, while Jennifer Melfi was recovering from her brutal rape experience. Jennifer and Tony were both dead, metaphorically, for the series was over and Tony was also twice dead as the result of taking his final hit, yet they were alive in everybody's heads as any chat in a sports bar or McDonald's would bear out. How could you represent this extraordinary society, let alone say something worthwhile, sometimes brilliantly apt, in a rock song lasting two or three minutes? *The Sopranos* had taken hours of television in its epic story of modern New Jersey.

Yet the Boss and a few others had achieved that, so perhaps the best way to understand what he has achieved is to follow critic David Masciotra in downplaying the representational in a song: forget seeing the song as a mirror of America. There was no doubt that the *Magic* album had caught the depth of feeling against the war, the sense that Jeffrey B. Symynkywicz describes when he says *Magic* is about 'living in a time when anything that is true can seem like a lie', or as the line in the song in the album goes, 'trust none of what you hear, and less of what you'll see... This is what will be...' Or as a Bush administration adviser is alleged to have said at a Washington press conference the month before in an abusive exchange with a journalist, 'We make our own reality; you guys report it. We make it.' The Iraq War is the tragedy in the album that prevents the American nation from finding its way back home and in the process renewing its progressive and democratic identity.

Many Americans were not listening to this message. Then there was a sense that the E Street Band's audience was changing. There was a good deal of new feminist scholarship on Bruce and the Band around, a happy debate starting with where they were with gender issues and a long way away from the original early 1990s diatribes from feminist materialists like Paula Moss who thought Bruce and the Band glorified untamed masculinity and the unequal power relations between the sexes. She thought, in Denise Green's view, that Bruce depicted women as either slutty sex objects or pure, unreal, ethereal beings, and the E Street Band were immature males obsessed with expressing their sexuality through cars and motorcycles. It was a complex field and hard to follow the literature and it was equally hard to know whether the singer and his band were aware of it at all. Most people who become involved with Springsteen's music find it very empowering and confidence-building, whoever they are, male or female, and it is foolish for some female scholars to deny the sexual edge in rock and roll, as Ruth Padel and others have conclusively shown. Men do not make young women tear down their pants and fling them at the stage when their idols are playing. They decide to do it themselves. It is all there in songs like 'Thunder Road' where a young man persuading a girl to ride away with him to a better life has nothing to do with gender manipulation but is the heart of the American Dream in music.

Sometimes there was a reminder of darker issues, linked in some ways to the Soprano-like events over at Cheeks club. The papers were full of the so-called Five Islamists who were awaiting trial for allegedly plotting an attack on the Fort Dix military base in central Jersey. They were being held there in solitary and in very tough conditions in a special unit in the high security unit of the prison and were complaining about lack of access to their lawyers and to law books. In the hearing, US District Judge Robert Kugler had told them, 'It's not a hotel, it's a gaol.' The terrible attack on the United States at Ground Zero was over six years ago, but 9/11 still seemed very near. I followed it all closely in the newspapers as at least three of the defendants came from the town of Debar in western Macedonia, which had an ethnic Albanian majority. Unlike anyone else in Princeton, I had been in Debar several times and knew it well from Kosovo wartime days. The little town, an ancient Roman sulphur spa, was lost in a remote area in the mountains near the border with Albania, and in fact should have been put inside Albania by the Boundary Commissioners after World War I. It had a fine late Ottoman Conquest period mosque nearby and a beleaguered small bus station where I had wasted many hours many times waiting for a bus to Struga or Skopje. There was a sulphur water *banya* where tubby middle-aged ladies sat half naked in the water and sang folk songs to each other. It did not seem particularly Islamic then, let alone a nursery for jihadists, but people can change.

The road signs were up, the great sweep west over the Delaware Memorial Bridge and then onto the Pennsylvania Turnpike. The tyres would not be touching the tarmac of New Jersey much longer but the tarmac of Pennsylvania. Out of the car window was a sign to the West but the sound of the news on the car radio pointed east; an American reporter based in London was doing a story about Northern Rock, and whether it might have to be nationalized. Prime Minister Gordon Brown had met US Treasury Secretary Hank Paulson to discuss 'the growing turmoil'. I knew nothing about Mr Paulson except that he seemed on TV a very serious and capable man, an architect of the American opening to China and, apparently, a devout Christian Scientist. The Northern Rock chairman had resigned a few weeks before and Paul Krugman down in Princeton had said it was a time to worry. There was a distinct change in the atmosphere; a sense of political unease was developing. Time and perceptions of time were changing; the official world of the educated in NJ and in Washington DC was running still on New World Order time that had begun when the Cold War had ended in 1990 and a new temporality of progress and optimism had been socially constructed by the elite, while the time of the financial crisis was rapid, impoverishing so many people and outside the parameters of the expected. As he had just got his Nobel Prize in economics people listened to Krugman, and he was also a very good journalist and used his column in *The New York Times* well whether anyone agreed with everything or anything he wrote. The space of this great crisis was small, the banking halls of Wall Street compared to the great dustbowls of Oklahoma in the 1930s. The radio report bore that out: for once academic economists and journalists on the same wavelength.[†]

Crossing the state line seemed unimportant with these unfolding world dramas. The foreclosure tide was said to be running as high in the Keystone State as in Jersey. As it turned out, the Northern Rock crash was the herald of the wider collapse of banks that was to come, like the Biblical forerunner. Where were/are Christian Scientists with prophesy, as with many other American-born religions? I didn't know

---

[†] With hindsight, the decline in the Clintons' fortunes began around this time, although it was hard to be sure at the time.

the math, or the theology. Hank Paulson was the good moral face of Washington at a time when those kind of people were in very short supply, a selfless public servant who helped save the economy at that time and was given signally little direct credit for it in George W. Bush's memoirs. Looking out of the car there was the sign to little Moorestown, NJ, in reality now a Philly suburb but recent winner of a competition to find the best small town to live in the United States. It was still living in the world of Prohibition, a bone dry town that had carried on its 1915 ban on all liquor sales long after Prohibition had ended in 1933 right to the present day. It was a Quaker foundation, inevitably. There was apparently controversy over whether the total booze ban should be maintained among the residents, if only in small licensed restaurants.

Then the gloom and smoke of spread-out and beleaguered Camden appeared, in reality the New Jersey part of Philadelphia where I had cautiously ventured a little while before in order to see Walt Whitman's little grey house in Mickle Street. The poet of *Leaves of Grass* had moved there in 1884 as he wished to live near the Delaware River, and then Camden was booming on the back of US Navy shipbuilding and later became the company town of the RCA Victor Talking Machine Company. Whitman always seemed to me to be America's answer to Lord Alfred Tennyson, a very gifted man who wrote much too much and was too close to the conventional wisdom of his time. But he was a humane, generous man and it beggars belief to think what he might make of twenty-first-century Camden. Now it is a wasteland, described by Chris Hedges in *The Nation* as 'the physical refuse of post-industrial America', where most of its mayors seemed to get arrested and gaoled for corruption and with a drug trade fuelled gang, homicide and street crime rate that in some years was the worst in the entire country. That summer all the schools and police were taken over centrally and operated by the state to prevent their collapse. It felt tragic; once 30,000 people had worked in the Camden shipyards on the Delaware River which had a heroic role in the victory over fascism in World War II, turning out Liberty ships for the Allies in record-breaking time so that we in Britain could

eat. At night the streets are a wilderness of constant violence with looting of any worthwhile property, a bitter testimony to the effects of the Bush administration's cuts in police numbers and funding. The Republican case was that the long years of neglect of the American industrial base by the Clinton administration had set the scene for the current social and economic crisis there. It was also difficult for the solid and successful Big Pharma companies in Jersey like Johnson and Johnson, Bristol-Myers Squibb and Merck, which had carried on working hard for America and rarely received much positive—or any—publicity for their efforts, to have a basket case like Camden in their midst.

Camden has, like most places in Jersey, had some odd claims to fame in the past. Apart from being the last home of Walt Whitman, it was the scene of the discovery in 1858 of the first more or less complete skeleton of a dinosaur, which turned up in a marl pit in nearby Haddonfield: *Hadrosaurus foulkii.* The bones were named after William Parker Foulke, a local gentleman and amateur scientist. He found in the deep grey slime of the marl pit the bones of a creature far larger than an elephant but with the structure of a mixed lizard and bird, all this happening on the eve of the Civil War. It was at the beginning of study of prehistory in the United States, and the public gradually realized that in the very distant past not just this part of what is now New Jersey but all of the US was ruled by these huge reptilian creatures. The whole issue disturbed some Biblical fundamentalists as there was no mention of *Hadrosaurus* in the Good Book. Yet passing by Camden that November day it seemed somehow symbolic that the skeleton had been discovered in Jersey. Temporalities intersect in the state: the time of the impossibly remote past when America was ruled by dinosaurs, the time of the intense contradictory present in the Bushkratia.

As soon as the old Lincoln entered Pennsylvania the landscape changed, away from the heavy factories surrounding Philadelphia and into a different world of agriculture, with cows and sheep in the fields and many little houses that looked like close copies of Irish cabins from the old days. There was a toll to pay on the 276 and then a long gentle loop to the south with Norristown coming up where the road divides and the Eastern Expressway begins with its rough potholed lanes and great rigs loaded to the gunwales kicking up blinding spray.

The weather was closing in and turning very wet and foggy. The three-month quest was approaching its end, my ambition to see Bruce Springsteen perform in the country of his birth. The journey with number was almost over, going from a zero on an Atlantic shore to a person at a rock concert, a human being; I would complete my circle as the Greeks say. The ticket had a number on it, so was no longer showing zero. Back in September on the shore at the beginning of the tour, the Asbury Park cheats and scalpers could roast people black (that's what they say in Texas) but now they seemed unimportant with a real concert ticket in my wallet. StubHub had worked and a nice modest ticket had arrived with a nice note from a man in Tennessee who said he had been stymied in his hopes of using it. Still, Pittsburgh was a famous old city and there must be better people there than the September shore crowd of Scaife's henchmen, or whoever else they were. Vast wealth had been dug out of the ground in and around Pittsburgh and names like Frick, the inventor of modern coke manufacture, Carnegie the steel king and William Scheide had been very generous benefactors to the good causes of Princeton. The Frick Collection of Old Masters standing in Manhattan speaks volumes, as do the songs of the Penn working class about his rapacious greed and violent union-busting activities when he was making his pile.

The Penn Turnpike does not give itself high billing, and there is just one sign: 'PENN TURNPIKE'. The little farm on the far side looking west had healthy sheep, programmed eating machines. Perhaps there had once been Welsh immigrant farmers here, moved down from the original strongholds of Welsh immigration up around Utica and Syracuse in northern New York State, hundreds of miles away north. Utica College's library has the biggest archive of Welsh language newspapers anywhere in the United States. A farmhouse in the distance had a thin pillar of smoke winding up into the air; this was getting nearer to the world of 'Home on the Range' and Jeffersonian democracy. Perhaps there was something about the poor relationship between the two states here. Jersey never really had homesteading in the same way as states further to the west, but a heritage of large landed estates left over from colonial times and numerous yeoman farmers, descended directly very often from early colonists. Pennsylvania has hovered between the two, in one sense a place of easy settlement, in another a place of pioneers with a touch of the real West in the lands towards the Ohio River and what was for many years unknown wilderness and Native American country. Pittsburgh itself had been the land of the Seneca people, one of the six nations of the Iroquois. The junction of the two rivers, the Allegheny and the Monongahela, had made this a strategic point in military and commercial matters as they meet to form the Ohio River, so goods manufactured in Pittsburgh could be shipped directly via the Mississippi to the Gulf of Mexico. Yet the pastoral images were misleading. The state was not just primarily industrial but also a place dominated by the concept of struggle, the struggle for production in industries like iron and coke, and the struggle for justice in a world where men worked long hours in blistering heat in the furnaces for two dollars a day. Rebels were incarcerated in Western Penitentiary, opened in 1826 with cells only about six feet by eight feet and a large iron ring in the centre where the convict was chained 'to expiate his offences'.

It is hard to think of the past when driving on the Penn Turnpike, the present is overwhelming. But the historian in the United States constantly finds the past in daily life, however much the overseeing Federal government authorities may wish everyone to live in the present with an optimistic view of the future. The Turnpike is a rough and only two-track road for most of the way, long overdue then for modernization with gritty place names like Ellwood City, Beaver Falls and Enon Valley passing on the signs as the car wheel is held tight and the metal absorbs the thud as hundreds of gallons of water are thrown up by a passing rig. Death may be near, sitting up on the embankment among the fir trees watching members of the heavy metal procession roll by carrying American trade in steel containers. Death often visits this road and makes a hit; on the 76 West there was a crunched and half burnt out SUV abandoned with yellow tape round it and warning sign a way back. The road was built in the New Deal public works frenzy in the 1930s before modern traffic volumes had come on the scene and when bridging the Appalachians was a pioneering achievement. Then it was a great innovative road, but now it is a symbol of the deteriorating infrastructure of the United States in recent years. Then there is the first Pro-Life billboard. Then they begin to appear very regularly, grand invocations to protect the Unborn Child and reject the Abortion Lobby. Appalachian Pennsylvania is increasingly Christian right territory, in a way New Jersey is not although Jersey is one of the states with the highest percentages of Roman Catholic citizens and some of the most important Catholic educational institutions in the country

Soon Amish country comes along, it is Lancaster County. The weather is so bad that there is little sign of life in most of the small farms, and it is all not far from the Pennsylvania anthracite coalfield, now in decline but once the black diamond mineral that fuelled the coke for the steelworks. Near the edge of the road is a picturesque farmhouse and behind it enormous ramshackle old farm buildings that at first look like an agricultural museum. Outside is an old reaping machine or maybe a baling machine that seems to be half constructed of rusty wheels and a solemn-looking brown horse. He clearly pulls that machine for a living. It is a different landscape, more domestic, calmer and with few modern cars. There are billboard advertisements for Amish products. This is Swiss Mennonite agriculture as it was in 1760, the land of pioneers who were later labelled the Pennsylvania Dutch, frozen in their parallel temporality from Washington DC. It is a bad day in November 2007 and the Amish are indoors. There is a good deal of picturesque farm life but hardly a human being to be seen, and patchwork quilt production will be high today. The Amish are rarely idle.

The highway pushes on relentlessly towards Harrisburg and the crossing of the mighty Susquehanna River. Virtually nobody in Europe had heard of Harrisburg before the Three Mile Island nuclear emergency. The film around the killing of investigative reporter Karen Silkwood is all that many remember now. The road levers and winds its way round the city above the river, reminding me of Cincinnati in its fine situation above the Ohio River. Then it rears like a horse towards the crest of the first hill range below the Tuscarora State Forest with the vast US Army Depot at Letterkenny to the south of the road, another Appalachian fortress.

There is a long dark valley at Willow Hill, poor Appalachian country with some houses as little one-storey cabins with a single central door and with someone trying to get an old car to start in the sluicing rain. Worn denim overalls are more or less a uniform round here. Rural poverty like this is hardly ever seen in Jersey, where there are the urban poor instead. This is the Appalachian world Bruce Springsteen's father came from and left to move down to the relative prosperity of New Jersey to find a job. Only welfare payments prevent social collapse in these communities where the old trades like tanning and distilling (at least legal) have long disappeared and nothing much has replaced them. The big road is indifferent; a billboard advertises an adult store, sticking out of the forest with a girl in a negligee hanging out on it against the background of the dark trees. Then there is the summit and a neat public rest area.

The Appalachian crossing has been done in an hour or so, but for over a hundred years it seemed to be a major barrier to the westward spread of the United States. Vast wealth beckons, for as soon as the mountains finish the bituminous coalfield starts, a relic of a huge inland sea millions of years ago. It is enormous, some 15 billion tons of coal have been mined in Pennsylvania since 1760, and about 31,000 people died in the mines between 1870 and 1996, the cost of a small war every year. Youngstown, Ohio, is just over the border, home of the old munitions industry, and there was no way of knowing whether the Boss and the Band would include 'Youngstown', his hymn to deindustrialization in his concert set in Pittsburgh the next day.

Still the wet forests are sweeping by the car window and then urban life on the margins, someone sleeping and living in an old car by a very polluted little river, and a shack belonging to a really poor person with a broken sewer pipe spewing grey water into a stream. It might be the outskirts of some impoverished Turkish or Middle Eastern city. In fact, it is the edge of the Pittsburgh metropolitan area, where poor people from the mountains are still trying to get into the city and get going economically. I endured the Turnpike as far as Monroeville, where my Marriott bed was waiting. The road had been a watery wilderness. It is easy to forget what a harsh winter climate many parts of the United States have, and a phrase from a Washington Jewish friend came to mind. He said he could never understand why his grandparents who had arrived in the US to get away from Polish anti-Semitism and pogroms had stayed in Maine where they landed, unless it was to have severe weather and the billions of birch trees they had been used to at home near Lvov. But it was an Appalachian monsoon today. Maybe a rig would not catch fire if it crashed, the rain would see to that. In a flood of water of Biblical dimensions there is a great cleaning of the mountains in progress; the Lord has ordained that they should be washed. Even Pittsburgh would go through His wash, and as the rain fell a little less down a dark forested ravine the city was undeniably approaching.

The Turnpike is now closing down, running out of steam like an old train, puffing to a slow halt as the city surrounds the car. The road will dive down through a ravine, Pittsburgh is a city of ravines and for a moment there is a glimpse back at some parts of Bulgaria, then a plethora of German-origin place names on the signs followed by a symphony of Scottish ones. Monroeville where I plan to sleep is moving nearer. Nobody in Witherspoon Street had ever heard of it, the town is not on the Princeton mental map, and one mile to the end of the road the sign says. There are little humpy hills, and it seems that Pittsburgh is built on humps separated by ravines. Soon there will be an escape from the Turnpike, the room where there is the chance to bunk down like a hobo bunks down in a shed in a Woody Guthrie song. Or in one of Mr Cash's great songs, now ironic on the car radio:

I heard the train a-coming
It's coming round the bend
I shot a man in Reno, just to see him die
I heard that train a coming, I hung my head and die

How would Mr Cash and Mr Springsteen talk if they met? Did they ever meet? Cash was always open about the link between his art and breaking the law, in a way perhaps Springsteen has not been. Cash is framed in memory by the 1968 Folsom Prison concert as much as a vase of cornflowers is framed in a Van Gogh oil painting. Or June Carter Cash walking in on an E Street Band performance, jamming with the Band, what a dream that would have been.

Monroeville is actually the toll booth town, somewhat glorified, and rows of tolls collect dollars from drivers while the Marriott is neat and inevitable and virtuous and is not far from the road's edge. Is there any even half decent song about driving the Penn Turnpike on a bad winter day? Entering Pittsburgh seemed like a door opening to the underworld through swinging grey gulches that immediately recalled the Welsh valleys but on a much larger scale. They dip from the Penn plateau like hard grooves on a plank with a confused pattern of old and new houses, some in good shape, others falling apart. The expressway cuts through it all like a knife. It is an uncompromising place with the modest skyscrapers of the financial district and the strongly reviving city centre and on one of them is a very large neon sign that reads 'Mellon'. The streets run down in deep, intersecting patterns and a homely Victorian church steeple is a welcome pointed relief from the cubist angles of the triangles and squares. In his dotage one of the early Mellon patriarchs had observed that the Reformation was a good thing, as it had replaced meaningless ritual with rational Christianity. But in the severe and gloomy wet streets it seemed in Pittsburgh to have meant the tyranny of geometry. Pittsburgh is a real Euclidian town; every important city in the United States has its own peculiar links with mathematics, but Pittsburgh means rigid triangulation.

Due to its uneven topography, Pittsburgh has 712 sets of steps, with 44,645 individual treads, a great many steps. Ninety-five million tons of steel were made here in World War II, steel for freedom from Nazism. That was good. Another number is not so good. In 1950, around 680,000 people lived in and near Pittsburgh. After steel had more or less collapsed, by 2000, only maybe 330,000 people lived here

The Doors of the Dome Open: Yet Another Cave?

The Mellon Arena is a pantheon like circular structure in the middle of town, the symbol of the new Pittsburgh. The roof can slide open so it is a marvel of modern engineering. In the distance there are worthy civic buildings, most still pretty grimy, a distant redbrick church steeple might be in Sheffield or Manchester. It is a city copying dreams of Pugin from long distance. The Mellon dome is a circle, inevitably, and the circle has a long history. It was much easier for primitive tribal people to understand than the square or the triangle; warriors formed a circle and danced sacred dances to celebrate victories over neighbouring tribes. It is relaxed outside without any of the frenetic energy of the shore and with a large and well organized parking lot outside and a few security men pulling on cigarettes in the distance. This is not a beach shrine for cult members as the Asbury Park hall was, but a community venue open to the public but without the sense of public celebration of the music there had been in New Jersey.

Later the next day the concert began. My ticket worked. It had been alive with meaning, then it was handed over and I walked into the Mellon Arena. The ticket had died now; it was dead, without meaning. It was a floor ticket and standing on the floor with a crowd of strangers the wide circle of the dome dominated as much as that walk into the Pantheon in Rome so many years ago, the circle opening to the darkening evening sky. Perhaps Pennsylvania was Rome, New Jersey Greece. I had come up lucky and was going to be able to hear the music and as Socrates said, according to Plato, good fortune is the greatest of good things.

11
MAGIC (AGAIN)

Concerning Robert Christgau's observation that 'arenas are for Michael Jackson and Bruce Springsteen', concert day plus one, and a few reflections

In the morning light the sun was trying to break through in and around the 'Burgh. Jim Morrison of The Doors said that 'when the Music's over, turn out the lights'. That morning the sunlight may not have been turned on. The road to philosophical knowledge is littered with hazards and roadblocks, as the road to achieving this ticket and getting to Pittsburgh and this concert in the Mellon Arena had been. Sun, *helios*, beauty and wisdom seemed somewhat distant. Jim Morrison, the Lizard King, the most beautiful young man of all the acid rock generation, had also in moments of lucidity understood what a rock band does better than many other people, writing: 'Music liberates my imagination when I sing, that's a dramatic act, not just acting as in a theatre, but a social act.'

In Pittsburgh certain things were possible, in neo-Platonic terms: the escaped prisoner from the cave had returned. On the journey to Pittsburgh there was the voice of Reason, Philosophy, or that was the theory. And now there would be the difficult return, where the chained were waiting. How would they react? Would they be scared or worried and afraid of knowing philosophical truths, and dislike philosophy and philosophers? They kill, put away, slot those who try to set them free.

New Jersey had been a place to expand the consciousness and intellect. In Princeton, with its fizz and wealth, at one level the antithesis of what the rest of the state is like in some eyes, the novelist F. Scott Fitzgerald had written, 'Princeton inevitably gives the thoughtful man a social sense.'

Perhaps this is true but nowadays it is better applied to the state as a whole, as Jersey is a place where people have to try to get on with each other, however difficult it may often be. It is crowded, and people keep bumping into each other, and the fantasy of a new America of pious Christian households simply does not hold water here. It is a state with a fair glue of ethnic tribalism (not only the Italians and Jews), and it is not the American Dream to dream of a monocultural community of mostly white believers. These problems are not new. The Puritan settlers set up a theocratic dictatorship in New Ark, but it did not last very long. The Bush administration did not change anything much in New Jersey nor, it appears, has the Obama successor, apart from better medical care for some people.

In coming to Pittsburgh to see Bruce and the E Street Band perform was I as much trapped by empiricism as anyone? After all, I was seeking knowledge through direct perception as much as someone who turns on the television to watch them perform. What philosophical reasoning about their music could emerge from just being a fan and watching a concert? Fans' heads are not actually tied but it is also a fact that when the star and his band are on stage we look nowhere else, and fans might as well be physically controlled by Springsteen, they surrender their freedom to him. They do not achieve the position in things when they realize he may not lead them automatically towards the Sun, Wisdom and Understanding.

At least small mammals don't have this kind of thing to worry about. A squirrel shed grey fur and raced into a hole under my motel room window. On the highway busy commuting Pittsburgh was going to work, a steady hum and swoosh of cars and trucks mostly heading into the city. There was a patch of green by the car park that Marriott provided to us guests and the usual rows of shrubs, tough grasses colonizing the space underneath them. A solitary blackbird, with its longer American tail feathers. Maybe it hadn't seen the squirrel, maybe it had, maybe it didn't care.

What had happened the night before? I had seen, at last, an entire Bruce Springsteen and the E Street Band concert, seen his vibrant and vivid image on the stage, a small man, and then his huge face on the screen projection. It was hard to relax with the music. I had felt uneasy at the barely suppressed dislike, even aggression, of some of the Irish-Americans around me on the area floor, once they sussed I was English.

'We all wear the green here, you know that?'

A burly middle-aged woman was less than welcoming. Someone needed to tell them the war in Ulster was over, and the republicans had signed up to peace, of a kind. Maybe rock critics and authors can help understand what this means? For Theodore Gracyk, a very learned professor of philosophy as well as author of books on rock and roll, it is all about identity, it's 'I Wanna be Me', so I have found the social construction of gender identity on the Mellon Dome floor, I am more a man from having attended the event, and maybe classicist Ruth Padel is thinking the same way when she writes: 'Music is a brilliant agent of ideology. It has a unique power to make things seem natural, seem "just the way things are".' The implantation of Irish musicians and musical rhetoric into the set-list was a help to an affirmation of a particular view of the modern American identity, exclusivist and hostile to the British colonial roots of the United States. So is Springsteen in the end a conservative, reinforcing a view, a vision of American identity that is lost somewhere in a better past, as much as the favourite Walmart clothes range of 'Faded Glory'? And yet, there was something disturbing. The identity of the music and the singer and band did not seem to be what I had experienced. The feel and tempo of some songs seemed to be different. The set was *Magic* but with classics like 'She's the One' scattered in between, old cut gems among the new diamond, different from what I had expected; the chords even did not seem to be the same... Perhaps I had failed to be a good initiate, and was not in the right frame of mind to see and hear the Band? Ruth Padel in her study *I'm a Man* quotes this text, without explanation, and then explains what it actually is:

> If a man comes for initiation into a mystic recess of overwhelming beauty and size, sees many mystic sights and hears mystic sounds in the darkness with suddenly changing lights and many other things happening, and sits down, and people dance around him, how could he experience nothing in his soul?

This is actually not Ruth Padel, but the recollection of an Eleusinian mystery novice she quotes, written in first-century AD Rome, yet most of the points apply to what happens to a rock fan in a concert hall nowadays. A democratic artist like Springsteen understands this and holds open rehearsals such as the reunion on the Shore of 26 September. But it does not really work. The performance where the ordinary punter stands a chance of obtaining a ticket takes place in a closed, controlled space; it is an arena and as the rock critic Robert Christgau has written, Bruce is in his element here. The Boss is at home there, it is his passion, as the critic writes, 'for maintaining contact with his fans that has made the difference to them, and to him'.

The question is bound to come as to whether Springsteen is in the mainstream of American rock culture at all, or at least whether he has been since the long distant years when songs like 'Born to Run' and 'Two Hearts' emerged. If it is correct, to see the songs and the music as part of the millennial tradition in New Jersey life, reaching back into a lost and distant part of the state that most people know little about, then concerts like the Pittsburgh event are marginal. It only gained meaning through the distinct Irish flavour of the music, the insertion of extra musicians into the band for the 'Irish' gloss, and so on. The linear and essentially positivist history of rock with its sanctification of Elvis and the continuing narrative through to the Beatles and even the Rolling Stones has become a tyranny. So does the only valid history reside in a particular song as performed at a particular time in front of a particular audience? Is rock without history? Springsteen's songs grip the imagination and refuse to leave it and the owner of the imagination alone... but they do not do so because they are part of an approved rock history narrative. Finding musical roots is a complex, continuous process, as the Boss himself showed by turning his back on the vast electrical power and energy of the *Magic* album and towards the folk and acoustic embrace of the icons of the immediate past like Leadbelly and Pete Seeger in the *Seeger Sessions* recordings.

Music is beyond words. Here are Mr Springsteen's Words. Did Plato allow the cave dwellers to use words? Or only look at the images displayed in front of them?

In the world of the Mellon Arena, *Magic* rang out. It was performed slightly faster than it sounded on the CD, and the fans were with it but only to a fairly modest degree. They were overwhelmingly fairly well set and prosperous Irish-American professionals, they had little or no identity issues, they were pleased and successful Americans. There were no black faces anywhere as far as it was possible to see. I was neither, although at that time at an immensely prestigious American university and owner of a US Social Security number, a work visa and other American essentials, as much as a baby needs a nappy. I shopped occasionally at Walmart. The band was focussed and enjoying themselves. Nils Lofgren spun on the spot in a wonderful riff, a marionette dedicated to his guitar, bringing to mind Eric Clapton but then also Clapton's reply when asked what it was like to be the best rock guitarist in the world: 'Ask Prince.'

Rock music, as Theodore Gracyk has pointed out, is only rhythm and noise—Mick Jagger's 'It's Only Rock and Roll (But I Like It)'—but it did not seem that this was what was happening that night. Gracyk explains that to be 'drawn in' to rock music is to endorse the activity, the processes, of its production, as Patti Smith describes herself being 'drawn in' to the world of Little Richard and what became for her the birth of rock and roll. This did not seem to be happening here very much. Little or nothing new was being born at all, except explorations of Irish heroic immigration. The musicianship of Bruce and the Band was extraordinary but it was very much to a grateful, captive audience, away from the early uncertainties and adrenaline. The music had no more or no less impact than listening in the car driving along the Turnpike. The Boss and the Band were for the punters mirrors of their own success, as they saw it. Dionysus seemed to have paused at Delaware Water Gap. Maybe he lost his car keys on the way over from Jersey.

'Magic' was the new song, one of them, profound, prophetic, a glimpse back at Orpheus, the artist as master musician, the man who has slipped his shackles and escaped the prison in the cave. But it is a hard world he escapes into, very hard, sometimes violent, in some ways primitive, even murderous, New Jersey straight without bells or whistles, where the freedom sought is spectral, drifting like a ghost among the trees. Escaping the cave into the sun does not bring reason and philosophy but dead bodies, the debris in America as Springsteen and many others see it that was caused by the Iraq War. In attending the concert here I felt I was becoming complicit in something I was not sure I understood, the freedom and beauty of the shore very far away. Scott Fitzgerald and Zelda often felt the need from all sorts of places and locales to wind back to Princeton but then ended up on the shore, drinking themselves into oblivion and to early deaths. They found Irish-American identity more problematic than many of those in Pittsburgh. Within a few years of this event in the city this Mellon Arena, 'the Igloo', was itself torn down and the central symbol of the revival of Pittsburgh was no more. The reality of this concert has faded into a dream of the past.

I got a coin in my palm
I can make it disappear
I got a card up my sleeve
Name it and I'll pull it
out your ear
I got a rabbit in my hat
If you want to come and see
This is what will be
This is what will be

I got shackles on my wrist
Soon I'll slip 'em and be gone
Chain me in a box in your river
And I'll rise singin' this song
Trust none of what you hear
And less of what you see
This is what will be
this is what will be

I got a shiny saw blade
All I need's a volunteer
I'll cut you in half
While you're smiling ear to ear
And the freedom that you sought's
Driftin' like a ghost amongst the trees
This is what will be, this is what will be

Now there's a fire down below
But it's comin' up here
So leave everything you know
And carry only what you fear
On the road the sun is sinkin' low
There's bodies hangin' in the trees
This is what will be, this is what will be

These are the lyrics from the song 'Magic'. The following year, in November 2008, George Bush ceased to be president of the United States and Barack Obama won the election to be his successor. Bush was, however, the winner (easily) of the competition in **Rolling Stone** magazine to decide who was the worst ever president of the US. So the history of this time of the **Magic** launch and tour was unusual. The poll was adjudicated by senior Princeton modern historian and also international authority on Bob Dylan, Sean Wilentz. A friend at the Woodrow Wilson School predicted the election result very accurately: Obama did a few points better than Kerry in 2004 but not as well as Gore did on the popular vote in 2000, when the latter was probably swindled out of victory in Florida. But it was enough for Obama mania to begin for a while. What had all this to do with the perfect society, the American Dream? Not very much, from the world Oxford's Walter Pater described where

> In the imagination of Pythagoras is the dream of the Perfect City, with all those peculiar ethical sympathies which the Platonic Republic enforces already well defined—the perfect mystical body of the Dorian soul, built, as Plato requires, to the strains of music.

The music could look after itself. In Jersey in 2008 voting day was quiet, the result a foregone conclusion, even the limited number of Princeton faculty admirers of the Republican candidate John McCain thought he was probably too old, and as always in the first week in November billions of dead leaves were waiting to be vacuumed up into trucks, mostly plane tree leaves all unmoved and unstirred by any great wind of change. The most a dead leaf can hope for is about four years, botanists write, and so there is not a lot to look forward to then, for a leaf. It is Halloween, that most American time of year in America, with the gloom of Thanksgiving to follow (for resident aliens) and leaves just die. The leaf pile is just the waiting room for the crematorium around All Souls time. The gorgeous, wild and scary dressing of the house in Mercer Street was there as usual, every Halloween a beautiful bride-to-be poised on the roof and wrapped naked in threads of a vast white spider's web yards wide, about to fall in love with a lethal looking skeleton tied to the front doorpost. Even in the City of Numbers the Gothic side of the New Jersey imagination and subconscious is around. A zombie walks (well-dressed, of course), a predator like MS-13, along Nassau Street. He could turn the children's hamster in the house into a predator. New Jersey is full of predators. But it's okay, someone responsible has tied him to a doorpost. As the song goes, 'he fought the Law and the Law won'.

Princeton was wall to wall for Obama, more or less, something like 80 per cent of the staff and faculty went his way. Princeton wanted to punish the Republicans and they did and the University was feeling even more than usually pleased with itself. And the soup in Olive May was always lentil, sheep's yoghourt returned to the shelves and civilization seemed to be returning to the US. Only a few were thinking that the stock market had peaked a few weeks before then or that the banking crash was looming.

Those are almost the last words of this book. Or maybe they are not .The defining twentieth-century New Jersey poet William Carlos Williams has the last words, from his poem *Paterson*: 'This is the blast/ the eternal close/the spiral/the final somersault/the end.'

Williams and those like him are the best answer to Plato: the American state likes and respects its artists, like Mr Williams, Mr Gandolfini and Mr Springsteen. They don't have to leave town. The cave is there but you don't have to stay in it. On the shore the sea runs in and out with the tides, and they are rising every year. In Pythagoras's truths of number, the essential laws of time and space, a two-foot overall tide rise would flood about 1 per cent of the state, a less likely four foot rise would cover about 4 per cent of New Jersey in deep water. Returning for the last time to the numbers magic, in 1950 about 3,300,000 people lived along the shore, and now it is 5,250,000, so with global warming many homes will disappear into the ocean. The state ecosystem is home to about twenty-five endangered species, and that does not include the Soprano family now the series has ended. The tourist industry is worth about US$16 billion a year to the shore communities, but the increases in sea level caused by melting ice at the poles will cause constant beach erosion, episodic inundations of the swamplands and all that means. Celebrate the state while you have it, the border between the land and the sea.

TRUMP
TAJ MAHAL
TRUMP
TRUMP
RESORTS
SHOWBOAT
Hard Rock CAFE
Hard Rock CAFE
PLAY JUNE 1
TO MEET THE C
SOPR
JUNE 2

EPILOGUE:
FROM ONCE
AND FUTURE
DONALDGRAD

Concerning ten years of time past, the changes in
Atlantic City, the arrival of Donald Trump

4 November 2017

Donald Trump has been and gone from Atlantic City, his monument of the old casino at Trump Plaza sitting like a derelict drunk, squatting closed and cordoned off in the middle of the city behind the famous boardwalk and the Atlantic sea defences. It finally closed in September 2014 as gambling declined as an attraction and in the aftermath of a bitter labour dispute. You might try to meet him in Atlantic City but you would not get very far. Yet ten years ago, in 2007, Trump was only a rich New Yorker property man who had saved his wealth by the skin of his teeth after the Atlantic City casino development nearly broke him. And now he is president of the United States, the leader of the most powerful democracy in the world. There are some reversals of fortune the ancients would have recognized here. Some people think that Americans mostly live in sub-cultures under the dominant main conformity, people into coin collecting mostly relating to other coin collectors, people who follow trotting racing with other trotting fans, the people who love casinos with other fellow gamblers.

Whatever happens to the Plaza, it will not be cheap; it cost US$42 million to raze the 2,100-room Riviera in Las Vegas last year. Raze, tear down, implode, many will watch, and over 100,000 people watched the Riviera go. A vast dust cloud will blow across the waves. The fall mist swirls in off the sea and over the pretty golf course near the Plaza and away down at the Stockton Seaview Hotel. The damp from the spray saturates the hotel and the crumbling Taj concrete. The dignified pretty Stockton hotel has lasted better. Built by a 1920s Philly magnate, the Seaview—unlike the casinos—is an elegant old pile and the light over the sea and the golf course shimmers pale blue and is very beautiful. The president must see golf as very beautiful too, for golf courses bearing the Trump name cross three continents, often by the sea, often windy, an echo of his mother's Scottish birth in the Hebrides where the wind never stops blowing and hardly a tree will grow. The president is a man of the Atlantic east coast. The winds down from Labrador in winter must have cut his winter clothes as a boy in Queens, New York City. Gales must chill Trump Tower on Fifth Avenue.

The Scottish link is strong in the world of golf equipment. The little buggies that ferry the older players round the course are called Troons, and loud plaid breeches and hairy thick tweed skirts are common. American golf is a very serious game, the men who play it and women who play it take themselves seriously. The American women's championship is played on one of the Stockton courses, and although this is Jersey, it is the Other Jersey that hardly ever appears in the crime series or in Martin Scorsese's movies set in north Jersey or New York. The golfers are Republicans (mostly), comfortably off, socially conservative and predominantly white. Things are a little old fashioned but people are very nice, with echoes of a simpler past; a monument is up inside the Stockton to that previous White House golf fanatic, President Dwight Eisenhower, who played on the Stockton courses, and in his time in the White House the numbers swinging a club in the United States doubled. That was when Bruce Springsteen was a little boy. Now in his Indian summer he is on Broadway, solo, bearing witness for music and against the Donald, but with the glory days of 2007 and the *Magic* album tour a distant memory. He says he always sought to tell the story of the American people through his songs. One is titled 'Glory Days', but his Broadway sets are mostly the well-known classics. The Glory Days of the pre-banking crash economy are also a distant golden dream for most people, hence the killer appeal of the new president's slogan To Make America Great Again. A passing couple of schoolteachers say they voted for him as the Clinton-Obama years destroyed the work ethic amongst the children. They see @POTUS as a high achiever based on hard work and dedication to the job on hand, and someone who says what needs to be said.

Why is the golf course so important to the people who run America now? At one level it could be said to be very good exercise (it is) that suits older people, and promotes (mostly) male socialization. But it is not really about this, at a deeper level. The golf course is tamed and manicured landscape, up to the beautifully level greens that look as if they have been cut with nail scissors one blade of grass at a time. It is humanized nature where the player can relax in a controlled environment, where trees may be planted for the sake of a better hole aspect, or a lake dug to offer a mild hazard in play. There is no threat in the golf ambience, all is right with man and nature in a harmonious relationship, in much the same way as the cricket pitch appeals to the English, or croquet suits an Oxford College lawn. It is a game that fits with the conservative sensibility and also the individualistic ethos, it is a game of individual prowess and not a team contest. It may have been invented in its modern form in Scotland but it perfectly suits Middle America, and in Jersey the little hills offer just enough variation in the landscape or the humps of the sand dunes by the sea make the course interesting. Golf also implies a certain degree of economic achievement. It takes time to play a round of golf, especially on a big American links, and again like cricket, it implies leisure. It is also moral and predictable, fitting for a nation with a strong evangelical bias in its subconscious. If you play a bad shot you will land in the rough or in the lake or a sand bunker. It is your fault for making an error in your sport (life) and you will have to go and do penance and dig yourself out of the mess that you are in. A steady shot up the fairway is the exact antithesis of the gambler's ethos.

Atlantic City is trying to wean itself off gambling although how far it will be able to do so remains to be seen. Legislators have not signed off casinos in northern Jersey, as was predicted in the year of *Magic* in 2007, and even if business is not all it might be, Americans are still gamblers and the numbers can still try to rule against the gamblers' revolt against the odds. The coaches from Philly and towns no one has ever heard of still disgorge for a fun weekend at the Resorts Casino Hotel and other remaining casinos. A deeply learned but semi-incomprehensible article in *The Press of Atlantic City* by renowned gambling theorist John Grochowski calculates the odds against the house if nickel machines are played in a casino by an expert player. After complex mathematics odds are calculated to two decimal points. Away from the green baize tables and the ever seeing eyes of the security cameras the city grinds on. The mayor rails against those said to be buying homeless people's votes in the coming gubernatorial election. Much of what he says, no doubt true, could have been put in the paper during the high on the hog party days of corruption and the bloodsucking political machines of the 'Boardwalk empires' of the 1920s. But the Trump Plaza complex is scheduled to fall, to be 'imploded' as the media put it, even more expressive than the normal but jagged Americanism of 'tearing a building down'. Maybe here in AC people implode structures, the tearing down left to the sea and the ocean gales. The site on the foreshore would certainly be worth a great deal of money to a developer, and is now owned by billionaire activist investor and Princeton alumnus Carl Icahn. Contrary to the often sleazy image there have been some attractive new developments in Atlantic City in the last years, and some outer suburbs like boatie Brigantine are close to nationally important nature reserves and line up equally expensive boats, chic cafés and classic sports cars in monied harmony.

Politics is always in the background. Hillary Clinton won New Jersey by thirteen percentage points in November 2016, but that was 5 per cent less than Obama received in 2012. The state is in general a Democratic sea, but with Republican islands, some like Lakewood in Ocean County north of Atlantic City largely based on ethnic factors where its large Orthodox Jewish community is solidly Republican. Well-to-do middle-class Italian-Americans from across south Jersey often vote for Republicans, with their concerns about spiralling property taxes under so many Democratic regimes in Trenton. Areas with high minority populations stayed with the Democrats, although this did not prevent Donald Trump polling significantly better than Mitt Romney did in 2012.

A visiting golf professional in the golf shop speculated that he didn't know whether Romney really wanted to be president at all, and maybe he threw down the cards he was dealt against Obama. Nobody could harbour those doubts about The Donald. The view from the golf course matters now. Golf is a democratic game and also gender neutral, there have been women players for a very long time. According to legend the term 'birdie' was invented here at the Atlantic City Country Club out of a then Jerseyism, 'that was a bird of a shot'. Another golfing island of both Republicanism and Trump support is pretty Bedminster with its astronomically expensive golf club where it is said members can pay extra to be buried in their coffins on the course and so, in a certain sense, never leave the eighteenth hole. Retiring Republican Governor Chris Christie is said to be a frequent visitor to presidential conclaves at the club but has yet to receive the top administration job his brave and early stand against opioid abuse might have led many to expect. Maybe his line on climate change, which certainly swung many coastal votes to Obama in 2012, is still held against him by the fundamentalists on that issue in Washington nowadays. The golf course is for them an ideal American landscape with nature controlled and set pathways where players can achieve what they want to achieve, nature tamed and civilized, an understandable ideal in a vast country where in many places nature is still seriously wild and dangerous in the raw and with a sometimes brutal and hostile climate, from the glacial cold of the Rockies in the winter to tornados in the West and hurricane and flood disasters in the South

Climate change is never far away. With sea levels said to rise, in a few hundred years' time the Stockton course might be deep in water. In the air less will change, or perhaps there is change coming here also. The monarch butterfly migration is one of the highlights of the Jersey shore year, with until recently the last day of October the yardstick used by experts watching the long, heroic and dangerous journey every year of the lovely stained glass-veined butterflies from the northern US states to their winter residence in Mexico. They are, in their way, as much snowbirds as the inhabitant of North Dakota with his winter apartment in Florida. Some Americans migrate, monarchs migrate. Last year in early November thousands of monarchs were found resting in a tree near Cape May Point and the timing of their mass migration seems to come later and later. As on many other subjects to do with climate change, experts disagree: the increase in numbers may simply be due to that year's mild fall weather. The butterflies do not escape the numbers; a count of those going through is published weekly, also to two decimal points. Whatever the details, the good news is that this is

the best year for them for seven years and they are happily tucking into gardeners' marigolds and red cannas, a roadside meal for them and fast food on a journey where the overused Awesome word really does seem appropriate. Maybe not all will reach Mexico but they all will have tried. They have an American dream, if not the American Dream, and they follow it in a heroic way, regardless of how hard the way may be and how difficult the journey.

The city certainly has a difficult journey back to something like normality. It was taken over by the Jersey state government in 2016 as bankruptcy and debt default loomed, with the classic bankruptcy signal of inability to pay people's wages. Brian, an Irish-American garage operator mused, on the future: 'Gambling on that scale destroyed our identity. We have to get it back.' In ancient philosophy that would mean the city would need to find new and virtuous men to rule. That may not be easy. In a climate of huge tax increases and reducing living standards, running Atlantic City is not a job for everybody. The Soprano culture may be too dug in for easy modification. There is more and more competition in gaming with Pennsylvania set to allow mini-casinos in some set locations like airports.

The sun sank slowly and the last light began to fade. Winter is coming, and the shore will be left to the birds. It will seem to be outside Time, but onshore the clocks are going back by one hour to mark the equinox, the unstoppable logic of time marches on, as unstoppable as the logic facing the gambler that in the end the House will win and hopes of sudden wealth will car crash and disappear. Yet the American Dream depends on hope, and as Plato-junkie Shelley wrote a long time ago, hope creates from its own wreck the thing it contemplates. The Platonic dream of the Ideal Republic lives on with every pull of a slots handle. Meet You in Atlantic City, the song says, come to New Jersey, explore, travel around. Be alive in a unique way, as Bruce Springsteen and the E Street Band inspire you to be in their music (whatever the system throws at you).

FURTHER READING

There is a substantial journalistic and scholarly literature on Bruce Springsteen and the E Street Band, stretching over forty years. The recent publication of his autobiography *Born to Run* will stimulate further work. New Jersey as a state has always been studied in its own right and as part of the wider history of the United States. For social background on the North Jersey suburbs Philip Roth's novels and *The Sopranos* TV series on HBO DVD are indispensable, as are Martin Scorsese films for the Italian-American and underworld scene, particularly *Mean Streets, Goodfellas* and *Taxi Driver*, and his rock and roll documentaries. Richard Ford's novels set on the Jersey Shore are a favourite of the Boss himself.

Princeton and the University have been described in many books. The novels of F. Scott Fitzgerald, particularly *This Side of Paradise* and *The Great Gatsby*, are set in the seminal 1920s period and have cast a spell over the University ever since. John Dos Passos' *USA* trilogy also has a Princeton and NJ dimension. Walt Whitman wrote a good deal about the New Jersey of his time, as did Modernist poet William Carlos Williams. There are many books about President Woodrow Wilson, some of which illuminate his time in leading NJ government positions, and then as Provost of Princeton University. Janet Evanovich's stories give a good picture of popular and lowlife Trenton. There is a vast literature on gambling, the Mafia, loan sharking, racketeering and correctional and judicial systems. There are many local historical societies which sponsor research and publish various materials, for instance the Verona Historical Society www.myveronanj.com . New Jersey churches and synagogues often have well-kept records which can be of assistance to those engaged in tracing genealogies.

Eric Alterman, *It Ain't No Sin to Be Glad You're Alive*, New York, 1999

George Anastasia, *The Last Gangster*, New York, 2004

Shirley Ayres, *Asbury Park*, Charleston NC, 2005

James Axtell, *The Making of Princeton University*, Princeton NJ, 2006

Henry Charlton Beck, *Forgotten Towns of Southern New Jersey*, New Brunswick NJ, 1936

Jim Beviglia, *Counting Down Bruce Springsteen*, Plymouth MA, 2014

Joseph Brandes, *Immigrants to Freedom*, Philadelphia PA, 1971

Jeff Burger, *Springsteen on Springsteen: Interviews, Speeches, Encounters*, London, 2013

Joanna Burger, *A Naturalist along the New Jersey Shore*, New Brunswick NJ, 1996

H. Borton Butcher, *The Battle of Trenton*, Princeton NJ, 1934

William. S. Burroughs, *The Last Words of Dutch Schultz*, London, 1970

George W. Bush, *Decision Points*, New York and London, 2010

Michael Capuzzo, *Close to Shore*, New York, 2001

Peter Ames Carlin, *Bruce*, London, 2012

Daniel Cavicchi, *Tramps Like Us*, New York, 1999

Robert Christgau, *Grown Up All Wrong*, Cambridge MA, 1998

Clarence Clemons and Don Reo, *Big Man*, London, 2011

Robert Coles, *Bruce Springsteen's America*, New York, 2003

Alistair Cooke, *American Journey*, London, 2007

Charles R. Cross, *Backstreets Springsteen*, New York, 1992

Jim Cullen, *Born in the USA*, New York, 1997

John T. Cunningham, *New Jersey: America's Main Road*, New York, 1966

Michael D'Antonio, *Never Enough: Donald Trump and the Pursuit of Success*, New York, 2015

Florence N. David, *Games, Gods and Gambling*, London, 1962

Daniel L. Deardorff, *Bruce Springsteen: American Poet and Prophet*, Lanham MD, 2014

John Dos Passos, *USA*, London, 1992

Marcus Du Sautoy, *The Number Mysteries*, London, 2011

A.L. English, *History of Atlantic City*, Philadelphia PA, 1884

Janet Evanovich, *One for the Money*, London, 1995

Federal Writers Project, *Stories of New Jersey*, New York, 1938

Federal Writers Project, *New Jersey*, New York, 1939

Louis J. Freeh, *My FBI*, New York, 2005

David Fischer/Joey, *Joey the Hitman: The Autobiography of a Mafia Killer*, New York, 2002

Jennifer Gillan et al (eds), *Italian American Writers on New Jersey*, New Brunswick NJ, 2002

Angus Gillespie and Michael Rockland, *Looking for America on the New Jersey Turnpike*, New Brunswick NJ, 1989

Theodore Gracyk, *I Wanna Be Me: Rock Music and the Politics of Identity*, Philadelphia PA, 2001

Theodore Gracyk, *Rhythm and Noise: An Aesthetics of Rock*, London, 1996

Gary Graff (ed.), *The Ties that Bind: Bruce Springsteen A to E to Z*, Canton MI, 2005

Clinton Heylin, *E Street Shuffle: The Glory Days of Bruce Springsteen and the E Street Band*, London, 2012

Christopher Hitchens, *Thomas Paine's Rights of Man*, London, 2009

Christopher Hitchens, *Arguably*, New York and London, 2011

Godfrey Hodgson, *The World Turned Right Side Up: A History of the Conservative Ascendancy in America*, Boston MA, 1996

Carl A. Huffman, *A History of Pythagoreanism*, Cambridge, 2014

Patrick Humphries, *The Complete Guide to the Music of Bruce Springsteen*, London, 1996

Iamblichus, *On the Pythagorean Life*, Gillian Clark (ed.), Liverpool, 2011

Michael Immerso, *Newark's Little Italy*, Newark NJ, 1997

Bob Ingle and Sandy McClure, *The Soprano State*, New York, 2008

Mark di Ionno, *New Jersey's Coastal Heritage*, New Brunswick NJ, 1997

Rhodri Jeffreys-Jones, *The FBI*, New Haven CT, 2007

Philip Jenkins, *Mystics and Messiahs: Cults and New Religions in American History*, New York, 2000

Nelson Johnson, *Boardwalk Empire*, Medford NJ, 2002

David Johnston, *Temples of Chance: How America Inc. Bought out Murder Inc. To Win Control of the Casino Business*, New York, 1992

Ryan Jones, *Trading Games: Playing by the Numbers to Make Millions*, New York, 1999

George Joynson, *Murders in Monmouth: Capital Crimes from the Jersey Shore's Past*, Charleston NC, 2005

James. R. Karmel, *Gambling and the American Dream*, London, 2008

John. P. King, *Stories from Highlands, New Jersey*, Charleston NC, 2012

Cat Klerks, *Lucky Luciano: The Father of Organized Crime*, Canmore, Canada, 2008

Irving S. Kull (ed.), *New Jersey: A History*, 4 vols, New York, 1930

Francis Bazley Lee, *New Jersey as a Colony and a State*, 5 vols, New York, 1902

Maxine N. Lurie and Marc Mappen, *Encyclopedia of New Jersey*, New Brunswick NJ, 2004

Maxine. N. Lurie and Peter O. Wacker, *Mapping New Jersey: An Evolving Landscape*, New Brunswick NJ, 2009

Marc Mappen, *There's More to New Jersey Than the Sopranos*, New Brunswick NJ, 2013

Greil Marcus, *Dead Elvis: A Chronicle of Cultural Obsession*, New York, 1991

Greil Marcus, *Mystery Train: Images of America in Rock 'n' Roll Music*, London, 2005

Greil Marcus, *The History of Rock 'n' Roll in Ten Songs*, New Haven CT, 2014

Dave Marsh, *Bruce Springsteen in the 1980s*, London, 1987

Dave Marsh, *Bruce Springsteen: Two Hearts: The Definitive Biography*, 1972-2003, New York, 2004

Dave Marsh, *Bruce Springsteen on Tour 1968-2005*, London, 2006

Brett Martin, *The Sopranos: The Complete Book*, New York, 2006

David Masciotra, *Working on a Dream: The Progressive Political Vision of Bruce Springsteen*, New York and London, 2010

Richard P. McCormick, *New Jersey from Colony to State 1609-1789*, New Brunswick NJ, 1984

Art Montague, *Crime Boss Killings: The Castellammarese War*, Alberta, 2003

Art Montague, *Meyer Lansky*, Alberta, 2005

Helen Morales, *Pilgrimage to Dollywood*, Chicago IL, 2014

Iris Murdoch, *The Fire and the Sun: Why Plato Banished the Artists*, Oxford, 1992

Julian U. Niemcewicz, *Under Their Vine and Fig Tree: Travels through America in 1797-1799*, Rahway NJ, 1965

Meredith Ochs, *The Bruce Springsteen Vault: An Illustrated Biography*, London, 2015

John R. O'Donnell and James Rutherford. *Trumped!: The Inside Story of the Real Donald Trump - His Cunning Rise and Spectacular Fall*, New York, 1991

Ruth Padel, *I'm a Man: Sex, Gods and Rock 'n' Roll*, London, 2000

Michael Parenti, *Waiting for Yesterday*, New York, 2013

Walter Pater, *Plato and Platonism*, London, 1909

Tim Perry and Ed Glinert, *Fodor's Rock and Roll Traveler USA*, New York, 1996

Helen-Chantal Pike, *Asbury Park's Glory Days*, Asbury Park, 2005

Plato, *Early Socratic Dialogues*

Plato, *The Republic*

Plato, *The Laws*

Don and Pat Pocher, *Cape May*, Dover NH, 1998

Barbara Pyle et al, *Bruce Springsteen and the E Street Band 1975*, New York, 2015

Jurgen Renn, *Albert Einstein: Chief Engineer of the Universe*, Weinheim, 2005

Andrew Robinson, *Einstein: A Hundred Years of Relativity*, Princeton NJ, 2015

Michael Rosen, *On Voluntary Servitude*, Cambridge, 1996

Robert K. Rudolph, *The Boys from New Jersey*, New York, 1992

Robert Santelli, *Greetings from E Street*, San Francisco CA, 2006

Robert Santelli, *Guide to the New Jersey Shore*, Guildford CT, 2006

June Skinner Sawyers (ed.) *Racing in the Street: The Bruce Springsteen Reader*, London, 2004

Greg B. Smith, *Made Men*, New York, 2003

Barbara Solem-Stull, *Ghost Towns in the New Jersey Pine Barrens*, Medford NJ, 2006

Bruce Springsteen, *Born to Run*, New York, 2016

Miriam V. Studley, *Historic New Jersey through Visitors' Eyes*, Princeton NJ, 1964

Jeffrey B. Symynkywicz, *The Gospel according to Bruce Springsteen*, Louisville KY, 2008

Craig Unger, *The Fall of the House of Bush*, London and New York, 2007

Roslyn Weiss, *Socrates Dissatisfied*, Oxford, 1998

Barbara Westergaard, *New Jersey: A Guide to the State*, New Brunswick NJ, 1998

Robert J. Wiersema, *Walk like a Man: Coming of Age with the Music of Bruce Springsteen*, Vancouver BC, 2011

William Carlos Williams, *Paterson*, New York, 1992

Harold F. Wilson, *The Story of the Jersey Shore*, Princeton NJ, 1964

E.M. Woodward, *Bonaparte's Park and the Murats*, Trenton NJ, 1879

Daniel Woolf, *4th July Asbury Park*, New York, 2005

Journals, Magazines, Internet

Rolling Stone, Uncut, New Musical Express, The Star-Ledger, Princeton Packet, The Trentonian, Vanity Fair, Asbury Park Press, The New York Times, Weird NJ, Mother Jones, The Monmouth Journal, The Cigar Aficionado, The Wall Street Journal, Jersey Journeys, Tri-City News, US 1, Forbes, Cape May Herald, The Nation, The Press of Atlantic City, The Daily Princetonian

There are numerous Internet sites and chat rooms concerned with Bruce Springsteen and the E Street Band, such as www.brucespringsteen.net. For streamed radio www.siriusxm.com, E Street Radio and others.

ACKNOWLEDGEMENTS

Thinking about the past needs books and libraries and I would like to express my thanks to the New Jersey Historical Society in Newark, the Bodleian, Vere Harmsworth, All Souls College and Oxford Union libraries in Oxford, the Firestone Library and the Hellenic Studies programme at Princeton, the New Jersey State Library in Trenton, and the Library of Congress in Washington DC. My fellow Balkan historian Miranda Vickers first laid down the each way racing bet that led to her fine book on the histories of the islands in the River Thames and (eventually) this book. Both were born in a dark winter evening in London, when we were inside a pub in Strand-on-the-Green by the Thames. It was a while ago. We both felt we needed a brief change from writing modern Balkan history after the turmoil and conflicts of the 1990s and wartime period in the region (although in fact we have carried on writing it through all that period). Averil Cameron has been a source of patient generous encouragement and wise advice. Everybody who writes about any aspect of rock music owes a debt to Ruth Padel, who in her seminal book *I'm a Man* has created a new vocabulary incorporating insights from classical literature and anthropology to analyze the power of rock and roll to move us in performance. Peter Brown at Princeton provided the final impetus one night over gin and tonic to convince me I should write something about New Jersey beyond Princeton, and the relationship between popular music, the state and the University.

Correspondence with Denise D. Green in Illinois University at Urbana, study of the Penn State University 2005 Springsteen conference papers and discussions with Dije Perolli, Tom Urquhart, Joe and Elke Gordon, Scott Carlson, Denny Lane and Naoko Aoki have also been very helpful, as have my publishers James Ferguson at Signal Books, Oxford, and Michel Moushabeck at Interlink in Massachusetts. There is an extensive scholarly literature developing on many aspects of Springsteen's life and work, and also on *The Sopranos* television series. As I have indicated in the final Further Reading section, there are also many books about Bruce Springsteen and the E Street Band, New Jersey history and culture and rock music in New Jersey which range from the very good to the helpful to the spectacularly awful. I am sure there will be many more.

I have used pseudonyms to protect the identity of some individuals, mainly those currently active in the law enforcement, gambling, criminal or government worlds.

This book is dedicated to my late friend of nearly forty years, Christopher Hitchens, who had little interest in rock music but called me a polymath in his memoirs. Whatever the truth in that, he taught us all more about Bush's America than anyone else, and ended up after our long journey from our rebellious Oxford undergraduate days of the '68 generation becoming a loyal and effective American citizen. There are many ways of following the American Dream and in his life Christopher found a way that worked well for him. I hope he would have approved of this book but sadly he passed away before it was completed.

Long Branch, NJ-Oxford, UK 2018

Credits

p. i: RaksyBH / Shutterstock.com; p. viii: Michael G. Mill / Shutterstock.com; p. xvi: Andrew F. Kazmierski / Shutterstock.com; p. xviii: Glynnis Jones / Shutterstock.com; p. 7: James Pettifer; p. 8: Joe Benning / Shutterstock.com; p. 13: Tomwsulcer / Wikimedia Commons; p. 16: Andrew F. Kazmierski / Shutterstock.com; p. 58: courtesy James Pettifer; p. 60: T photography / Shutterstock.com; p. 65: Apc106 / Wikimedia Commons; p. 74: LEE SNIDER PHOTO IMAGES / Shutterstock.com; p. 81: Library of Congress, Washington DC; p. 88: James Pettifer; p. 136: Helen89 / Shutterstock.com; p. 162: James Pettifer; p. 176: Famartin / Wikimedia Commons; p. 191: Andrew F. Kazmierski / Shutterstock.com; p. 202: Stephen Bonk / Shutterstock.com; p.

The author and publishers would like to thank Jon Landau Management and Grubman Shire Meiselas & Sacks, P.C. for granting permission to reproduce the following:

INDEX